MICROECONOMIC MODELS

MICROECONOMIC MODELS

K. C. KOGIKU
University of California, Riverside

HARPER & ROW, PUBLISHERS
New York, Evanston, San Francisco, London

CONTENTS

PREFACE

This volume presents contemporary microeconomic models constituting the theory of resource allocation and the price system. Marginalist models are presented in Part I, followed by linear and set-theoretic models in Parts II and III, respectively. The volume presents not only partial equilibrium analysis so predominant in traditional theory, but also general equilibrium theory handled more systematically by relatively newer models.

One of the most important objectives of microeconomics has been to examine optimality of allocation in the market economy. In this book positive theory is presented first, and is followed wherever feasible by normative analysis. Principles of welfare economics are covered in all three parts.

The theory of resource allocation and the price system are presented in this volume in terms of concise formal models. This field is essentially a logical and quantitative discipline. It is therefore inevitable that a compact treatment calls for the use of some mathematics.

In Part I the mathematics needed includes calculus and determinants. Additional topics can be handled if the theory of nonlinear programming is employed. In Part II the mathematics required is the theory of linear programming. Part III calls for some point set topology. Essential concepts in these areas are reviewed in the mathematical reviews in the Appendix. The volume minimizes the level of mathematics needed. Concepts new to average economists, such as quasi-concavity, are not introduced unless they offer clarification of the theory.

Needless to say, maturity in mathematical thinking is important, and this can only come from constant use of mathematics in economic model-building and manipulation. The powerfulness of the mathematical approach in social sciences, especially in economics, has been amply proven. The role of the theoretical economist is to observe economic reality and apply the scientific methods. Mathematical methods are essential in applying the scientific methods to understand the phenomena arising from social interaction of economic units.

The models in this book are built upon a foundation of work by generations of economists who have contributed to the development of economic theory. To them I owe my greatest debt.

K.C.K.

INTRODUCTION

MICROECONOMICS

Contemporary economic theory views resource allocation and the price system roughly as follows: Individual economic units such as consumers and producers strive for optimum allocation of their limited resources among alternative uses. Given the institutional setup of the economy, this optimizing behavior of individual economic units produces a corresponding system of prices for goods. In fact quantities and prices of these goods are determined interdependently.

To amplify the preceding paragraph, any theory of an economic system is built upon the theory of behavior of its components, such as the consumer and the firm. Contemporary theory assumes the common behavior principle controlling these economic units to be economic rationality, that is, the desire to attain their objectives to the utmost given limited resources. For example, the consumer allocates expenditures out of his limited income among various goods so as to maximize his satisfaction, while the firm hires various factors of production to produce goods under technological constraints so as to maximize its profits. Such efforts of individual economic units interact within the institutional setup of the economy and produce a set of magnitudes for the quantities and prices of goods and services produced, exchanged, and consumed. The study of such resource allocation processes and the price system is called *microeconomics*.

It is the purpose of this volume to present contemporary economic models describing various aspects of this process of resource allocation and the price system in the market economy.

A PREVIEW OF THE MODELS OF RESOURCE ALLOCATION AND THE PRICE SYSTEM

The contemporary theory can be divided into two parts: *partial equilibrium* and *general equilibrium* analysis. The former applies to any analysis based on *ceteris paribus* assumptions. For example, analysis of the behavior of the consumer faced with a set of prices of products and factors and a fixed income, the behavior of the firm faced with a set of prices of products and factors and given technology, the determination of the price and quantity for one commodity assuming no changes in the markets for other commodities—All these belong to partial equilibrium analysis.

In general equilibrium analysis, one considers the simultaneous determination of the prices and quantities of all goods, produced and exchanged in an entire economy. It uses the results of partial equilibrium analysis as the building blocks. One may consider a competitive economy to reach equilibrium in all markets as follows: All consumers and producers take an initial set of prices as given. Each consumer's initial endowments of products and factors, and any profits distributed from the firms, determine his income. Given the prices and therefore his income, each consumer will determine how much of each product to demand and how much of each factor to supply. Given the prices, each firm will determine how much of each product to produce and how much of each factor to demand (and any profits are distributed to the consumers who own the firm). The behavior of all the consumers and all the firms will determine the total demand and supply for each product and factor. In some markets there may be an excess of demand over supply, and in others an excess of supply over demand. This will lead to a new set of prices, and this process will be continued to reduce the excess demand and supply. In this sense the market mechanism can be considered a huge computer determining resource allocation in an economy made up of decentralized decision-making units. The working of the dynamic mechanism for reaching an equilibrium in all markets is beyond a simple description, but the above should give some idea about how modern theory explains resource allocation and the function of the price system. Of course, more sophisticated models are needed to take into account the characteristics of the real world and actual processes.

This kind of analysis is in contrast to *macroeconomics* whose chief concern is with various aggregate magnitudes of the entire economy such as national income, general price level, total employment, and aggregate capital stock.

MODELS AND THEIR FUNCTIONS

An *economic model* here is a representation of an economic subject (such as an economic entity, economic process, economic system). Its primary function is to explain the behavior of *economic variables*, such as the price, production, and consumption of a good. The model can also be used for prediction and control.

A *microeconomic model* is primarily concerned with explaining the behavior of economic variables relating to individual *economic units*, such as the consumer and the producer.

An economic model can use words and graphs. But in modern economics, formal models describe economic entities, processes, and systems by mathematical concepts, such as equations, inequalities, and sets.

Each model concentrates upon a certain aspect of an economic subject. This volume presents a number of models, each concentrating on different aspects of the economic reality. In each economic model certain variables are *endogenous*, that is, they are to be explained by the model. Other variables in the model are *exogenous*, that is, they are not to be explained by the model in question, but are assumed given from outside the model.

MICROECONOMICS AND MATHEMATICS

Attempts to analyze optimizing behavior of individual economic units have inevitably called for mathematics, following the road physical sciences traveled earlier. The maximization principle as one of the unifying principles of economic theory has been recognized for many years. Cournot was one of the first to systematically present economics as maximization or minimization problems.[1] Samuelson has asserted that the two pillars of economic theory are equilibrium based on maximization or minimization of some magnitude by individual consumers and producers, and stability of the resulting market equilibrium.[2]

Mathematical tools used in analyzing these models have continued to expand. Classical calculus dominated the scene at the beginning. Theories of mathematical programming and more fundamental notions of mathematics such as sets have been introduced. These additional mathematical techniques have helped in analyzing aspects of the economy that were never analyzed satisfactorily before. The present volume examines some of these models that increasingly approximate the real world.

---

[1] Assuming the demand and cost functions given, Cournot (1838) constructed a model determining the price and quantity demanded. He set up an equation giving the condition for maximizing the producer's profit. This represents the simplest (partial) *static equilibrium* theory. He also considered how the equilibrium values would change as a result of changes in the tax and transport costs. This is *comparative statics*.

[2] Samuelson (1947).

It will be convenient to do so beginning with models using more familiar mathematical techniques and working up to those using more recently introduced mathematical techniques.

MARGINALIST MODELS

Differential calculus was the first mathematical technique to be used extensively in microeconomic models. Models based on this approach have been used widely since the marginal-utility revolution in the analysis of consumption, production, and economic equilibrium. They assume smooth indifference curves and production functions, and concentrate on marginal changes or derivatives of such functions. Hence these models may be called *marginalist models*. An alternative is to call them neoclassical models. But this term is avoided to prevent association with any specific models or economists in the past.

Marginalist models use general and simple assumptions. Because of these characteristics, they have been widely used in economic analysis to analyze real situations and justify certain economic policy recommendations. The generality and simplicity, however, spell their weaknesses. Marginalist models tend to stop with the enumeration of implicit optimality conditions. It is very often more desirable to be able to specify various explicit conditions on consumption and production, in order to provide some specific decisions.

LINEAR MODELS

Mathematical programming and linear algebra have provided such tools. These techniques are used in linear programming models of the firm and input-output models of a region or economy. In these models the ratios between input and output are assumed constant. Relations involving inputs and outputs are expressed as linear equations and linear inequalities. Application of these techniques can usually provide more specific answers to economic problems, whether in business management or in national or regional economic policy-making.

SET-THEORETIC MODELS

The third group of mathematical techniques have been provided by set-theory-oriented concepts and theorems, which have been used in generalized models encompassing the marginalist and linear models as special cases. Such techniques have been found essential for a more rigorous formulation and examination of the general equilibrium of all markets.

PART 1
MARGINALIST MICROECONOMIC MODELS

Marginalist microeconomic models occupy a predominant place in the current body of microeconomics. The distinguishing characteristic of this class of microeconomic models, as compared with the more recent linear and set-theoretic models, is the predominance of marginal concepts, such as the marginal rate of substitution in the consumption theory, and marginal productivity in the production theory.

First it should be pointed out that the degree of versatility of an economic model is often limited by that of the mathematical tool used. By marginalist microeconomic models in Part I are meant those which depend mainly on the *classical calculus approach*. Although there have been marginalist microeconomic models that used more advanced techniques (such as *nonlinear programming*) and therefore can subsume special situations (such as boundary optima and inequality constraints), the main mathematical techniques of Part I are those of classical calculus.

The marginalist microeconomic models are classifiable into the following six component submodels (each of which is taken up in turn, in the next six chapters).

1. consumer's optimum
2. firm's optimum
3. competitive market equilibrium
4. general competitive equilibrium
5. imperfect competition
6. intertemporal competitive equilibrium

Thus models examining how the consumer and the producer behave are presented first, followed by models studying the interaction of the consumer and producer behavior in one market determining price and quantity of the good traded. This will be followed by models examining the simultaneous determination of the prices and quantities in all markets, accompanied by models examining the efficiency of resource allocation by the price system in a market economy. Finally, an intertemporal interpretation is presented.

CLASSIFICATION OF GOODS

In these marginalist models goods will be classified into two groups: products and factors. *Products* are demanded by the consumer for purposes of consumption; they include services as well as physical commodities. *Factors* are demanded by the producer for use in the production of commodities; they include labor, land (natural resources), and capital goods such as machinery and equipment.[1] *Intermediate goods* are those currently produced and used in the production of other products, such as steel ingots. In this Part for simplicity, products are assumed to be produced directly from factors.

THE MAKEUP OF THE ECONOMY

The economy is regarded to be made up of two sectors: the consuming sector and the producing sector. The *consumer* is the smallest unit of consumption. He provides factors of production for the firms in exchange for factor payments. The factor payments, and any profits received from the firms, make up his income. He allocates his income among different products. The *firm* is the smallest unit of production. It purchases various factors of production and combines them to produce various products which are sold to the consuming sector. Further, there is a market for each product and factor where interactions between demand and supply take place. The models consider product and factor markets, and equilibrium in these markets.

---

[1] For durable goods, it is important to distinguish services which are a flow, from assets which are a stock, and the price of services (rent and rental) from the price of stocks themselves.

ASSUMPTIONS

In order to avoid complications that can be handled more efficiently by other types of microeconomic models using more advanced mathematical concepts, models in this part assume that

• Each consumer consumes some of each of the products, and supplies some of each of the factors, while each firm uses some of each of the factors and supplies some of each of the products, *unless stated explicitly otherwise.*
• All products and factors are perfectly divisible, so that infinitesimally small adjustments can be made in the quantities of products and factors. Similarly infinitesimal adjustments can be made in prices. Thus quantities and prices can be represented by real numbers.
• All relevant functions are twice-differentiable,[2] so that there exist, for example, smooth marginal (ordinal) utility functions and smooth marginal productivity functions to yield unique (tangency) solutions.

The two-product, two-factor cases are considered primarily in order to simplify the exposition. These models can easily be expanded to the general case of more than two products and factors.

CONCERNING THE DESIGNATION OF SECTIONS, EQUATIONS, AND FIGURES

Section 1.2 refers to the second section of the first chapter.
MR1 refers to the first mathematical review in the Appendix.
Equation (3) refers to the third equation within the same section.
Equation 1.1.3 or (1.1.3) refers to the third equation of Section 1.1.
Equation (MR1.5) refers to the fifth equation of the first mathematical review.
Figure 1.2.4 refers to the fourth figure of Section 1.2.

---

[2] A widely used definition runs as follows: A function $y = f(x)$ is said to be *twice-differentiable* when there exist f' and f''. This definition does not preclude the existence of higher-order derivatives. A twice-differentiable function has a derivative function that has no kinks or jumps. It is smooth and continuous.

1
MODELS OF THE CONSUMER'S OPTIMUM

1.1 INTRODUCTION

The models of this chapter examine the consumer's optimizing behavior, thereby deriving the demand functions for products and the supply functions for factors of production. The central topic will be the consumer's resource allocation behavior in the face of scarcity represented by the given amounts of his resources. The models will show how the consumer with certain tastes will shift his demands among different commodities when their relative prices change; they will also show how the consumer changes his demand for a commodity when one of the product prices or his income changes. The analysis of this chapter will be integrated into the later analysis of resource allocation and the price system in a market economy.

In this chapter it is assumed that

• The consumer takes the product and factor prices as given.
• The consumer's income is given by his initial endowments of factors of production, and he spends his entire fixed income on products.

Prices are assumed given here, but the general equilibrium models in Chapter 4 will show that they are determined simultaneously in all the markets. The consumer is assumed to make quantity adjustments taking prices as signals representing the conditions of demand and supply in various markets. The theory of the consumer's optimum outlined here may be regarded as the core of the neoclassical theory of consumer behavior.

1.2 THE UTILITY FUNCTION

The original utility theory of demand developed in the 1870s was followed by a controversy concerning the measurability and interpersonal comparability of "utility." Economists like Pareto dispensed with such a concept by using indifference curves. Following these precursors, modern economists have replaced the traditional cardinal utility theory with the preference theory of demand, or ordinal utility theory. On the basis of this approach, the marginalist microeconomic models have analyzed the behavior of the consumer.

The utility function considered in this section represents an ordinal index as compared with the traditional cardinal utility that assumes the measurability or interpersonal comparability. More specifically, a utility function of a consumer is simply a function from the commodity space to the real line which preserves the ordering of the indifference curves in the commodity space. This point will be analyzed in greater detail in Part III.[1]

PREFERENCE MAP

Assume that there exist only two commodities. A pair (or more generally, a collection) of quantities of the two commodities is called a *commodity bundle*. It can be represented in the *commodity plane* (or more generally, the commodity space) by the typical point x, which has the coordinates x_1 and x_2. A commodity bundle consisting of x_1' units of commodity 1 and x_2' units of commodity 2 can be represented by a point x' whose coordinates are x_1' and x_2' in the commodity plane as shown in Figure 1.2.1. Another commodity bundle x'' can be similarly represented.

Consider each consumer to be rational and consistent and able to rank-order various commodity bundles according to his pattern of tastes. Take a consumer faced with two commodity bundles x' and x''. When he considers x' at least as desired as x'', write

$$x' \, R \, x'' \tag{1}$$

and call it a *preference relation*. Suppose x' and x'' represent the same commodity bundle. Then the consumer will find one commodity bundle at least as desirable as the other, that is $x \, R \, x$. This property of the preference relation is called *reflexivity*. Further, if $x'' \, R \, x'$, and $x''' \, R \, x''$, then $x''' \, R \, x'$. This property of the preference relation is called *transitivity*.

---

[1] For details see Debreu (1959), Chap. 4; Debreu (1964).

Figure 1.2.1

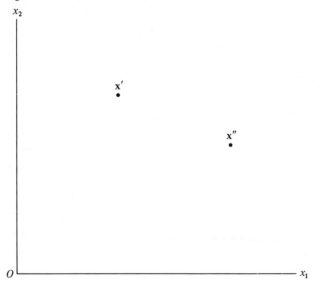

Figure 1.2.2

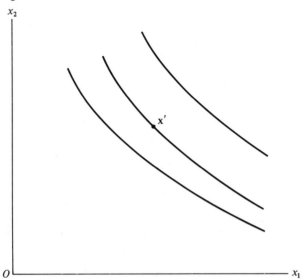

When the preference relation

$$\mathbf{x}'' \, R \, \mathbf{x}' \qquad (2)$$

as well as (1) is true, then $\mathbf{x}'$ is just as desirable as $\mathbf{x}''$. In this case, write

$$\mathbf{x}' \, I \, \mathbf{x}'' \qquad (3)$$

and call it the *indifference relation*. It is possible that the quantities in $\mathbf{x}'$ are different from those in $\mathbf{x}''$, and yet the consumer considers $\mathbf{x}'$ just as desirable as $\mathbf{x}''$.

Imagine in the commodity plane a curve made up of all points that are just as desired as a point $\mathbf{x}'$, as shown in Figure 1.2.2. Call such a curve through $\mathbf{x}'$ an *indifference curve* or more generally, *indifference surface*. There are an infinite number of such curves. The collection of all indifference curves is called the *preference map. Two indifference curves cannot intersect.*

THE UTILITY FUNCTION

The consumer's preferences among commodity bundles can also be represented by an index showing the degree of his satisfaction associated with each commodity bundle. Such an index—called the utility index function, or simply, the *utility function*—assigns a real number, say $U(\mathbf{x})$, for each point $\mathbf{x}$ of the commodity plane so that, for commodity bundles $\mathbf{x}'$ and $\mathbf{x}''$, whenever $\mathbf{x}' \, R \, \mathbf{x}''$,

$$U(\mathbf{x}') \geq U(\mathbf{x}'') \qquad (4)$$

That is, the utility function need only preserve the ranking by the consumer's preferences. In this sense the utility function is *ordinal*; the utility function here is defined by the preference relation on the commodity plane.

Therefore the utility function is not unique; if U is a utility function, and f is a strictly monotone-increasing function, then the function

$$V(\mathbf{x}) = f(U(\mathbf{x})) \qquad f' > 0 \qquad (5)$$

is also a utility function. Therefore, the utility function is said to be unique only up to monotone one-to-one transformation. On an indifference curve the utility function of course assumes a constant value.

Because of the assumptions concerning the perfect divisibility of commodities and the twice-differentiability of all functions, there exist

$$U_1 \quad U_2 \quad U_{11} \quad U_{12} \quad U_{21} \quad U_{22} \qquad (6)$$

The first two partial derivatives may be called the consumer's marginal ordinal utility, or simply the *marginal utility*, of commodities 1 and 2, respectively. It is assumed that the marginal utility is always positive. In other words, each good is always desirable, and the consumer is never satiated. That is, for any commodity bundle $\mathbf{x}'$ there exists a commodity bundle $\mathbf{x}''$ such that

$$U(\mathbf{x}'') > U(\mathbf{x}')$$

Hence the consumer will spend his entire income in order to maximize his utility. We should also note that the magnitude of marginal utility changes when the utility function undergoes a transformation, and because of the differentiability assumption,

$$U_{12} = U_{21}$$

STRICT QUASI-CONCAVITY OF THE UTILITY FUNCTION

The models of consumer behavior here assume strict quasi-concavity of the utility function.[2] From MR5 the bordered Hessian of the utility function is positive.

$$\begin{vmatrix} U_{11} & U_{12} & U_1 \\ U_{21} & U_{22} & U_2 \\ U_1 & U_2 & 0 \end{vmatrix} > 0 \tag{7}$$

The strict quasi-concavity means that the indifference curve (or more generally, surface) is strictly convex to the origin, or alternatively the marginal rate of substitution is diminishing. Consider the indifference curve representing the utility index level U^0:

$$U(x_1, x_2) = U^0 \tag{8}$$

Along the indifference curve,

$$U_1 \, dx_1 + U_2 \, dx_2 = 0 \tag{9}$$

Hence the negative of the slope of the tangent of the curve is

$$s \equiv -\frac{dx_2}{dx_1} = \frac{U_1}{U_2} \tag{10}$$

which has been called the *marginal rate of substitution*. It represents the rate at which x_2 is decreased as x_1 is increased along the indifference curve.

This rate is invariant with respect to the choice of the utility index. For if

$$V = F(U(x_1, x_2))$$

then

$$V_1 = F'U_1 \qquad V_2 = F'U_2$$

---

[2] On quasi-concavity and concavity, see MR5.

Figure 1.2.3

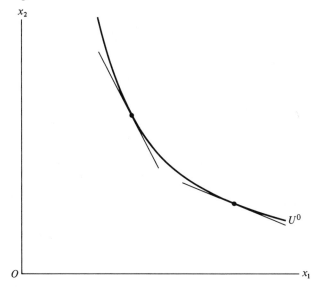

The marginal rate of substitution with the new utility index V_1/V_2 gives the same magnitude as (10).

The inequality (7) can be verified by the sign of ds/dx_1. From (10),

$$ds = \frac{U_2\, dU_1 - U_1\, dU_2}{U_2^2}$$

$$= \frac{U_2(U_{11}\, dx_1 + U_{12}\, dx_2) - U_1(U_{21}\, dx_1 + U_{22}\, dx_2)}{U_2^2}$$

Hence, using (10),

$$\frac{ds}{dx_1} = \frac{U_1^2\, U_{22} + U_2^2\, U_{11} - 2U_1 U_2 U_{12}}{U_2^3} \tag{11}$$

The diminishing marginal rate of substitution means that the numerator of (11) is negative, that is, (7) is true.[3]

$$-U_1^2\, U_{22} - U_2^2\, U_{11} + 2U_1 U_2 U_{12} > 0 \tag{12}$$

This inequality is invariant with respect to the choice of the utility index. If a new utility index is chosen such that

$$V = F(U(x_1, x_2))$$

---

[3] On the quasi-concavity assumption, there are various justifications advanced, such as Hicks (1946), pp. 23–24; Koopmans (1957), p. 28; Gorman (1957a, b).

then

$$V_1 = F'U_1 \qquad V_2 = F'U_2 \qquad V_{11} = F''U_1^2 + F'U_{11}$$
$$V_{22} = F''U_2^2 + F'U_{22} \qquad V_{12} = F''U_1U_2 + F'U_{12}$$

(13)

The expression

$$-V_1^2 V_{22} - V_2^2 V_{11} + 2V_1 V_2 V_{12} > 0$$

gives the original inequality (12) when (13) is substituted.

STRICT CONCAVITY

A stronger assumption is strict concavity, which implies not only diminishing marginal rate of substitution but also diminishing marginal utility. Then the Hessian of the utility function

$$\begin{bmatrix} U_{11} & U_{12} \\ U_{21} & U_{22} \end{bmatrix}$$

(14)

is negative definite, and

$$U_{11} < 0 \qquad U_{22} < 0 \qquad U_{11}U_{22} - U_{12}^2 > 0$$

(15)

the first two inequalities meaning diminishing marginal utility for each commodity. From (13) it is clear that the last inequality is not invariant with respect to the choice of the utility function.

The cardinalist utility theory such as Jevons' assumed the law of diminishing marginal utility, and the independence of utility defined by

$$U_{12} = 0$$

thereby assuring the diminishing marginal rate of substitution, (7) or (12). The last equality (also $U_{12} > 0$ defining complementarity and $U_{12} < 0$ defining competitiveness) is not invariant under monotone transformation either.

Strict quasi-concavity does not imply strict concavity, while the latter implies the former. It is possible to have the diminishing marginal rate of substitution *and* increasing marginal utility for at least one of the goods.[4]

---

[4] For example, consider

$$U = -(a - x_1)^3 + x_2^3 \qquad 0 < x_1 < a \qquad 0 < x_2 \qquad U > 0$$

for which

$$U_1 = 3(a - x_1)^2 > 0 \qquad U_2 = 3x_2^2 > 0$$
$$U_{11} = -6(a - x_1) < 0 \qquad U_{22} = 6x_2 > 0 \qquad U_{12} = 0$$

and the left-hand side of (12) is

$$54x_2(a - x_1)[-(a - x_1)^3 + x_2^3] = 54x_2(a - x_1)U > 0$$

Since the utility function is invariant under monotone-increasing transformation, and since under certain regularity conditions a quasi-concave function can be transformed into a concave function by a strictly increasing monotone-transformation,[5] the utility function can often simply be taken as concave.[6]

1.3 THE CONSUMER'S OPTIMUM

The consumer is purchasing optimum amounts of several commodities if he is maximizing his utility out of his limited income. According to this chapter's assumptions (p. 8) the commodity prices p_1 and p_2 and the consumer income M are given, and the entire income is spent. Mathematically, therefore, the consumer's problem is to maximize

$$U(x_1, x_2) \tag{1}$$

subject to

$$p_1 x_1 + p_2 x_2 = M \tag{2}$$

Equation (2) has been called the *budget equation*, which can be graphed as a straight budget line (or more generally a budget plane or hyperplane) through the preference map, as in Figure 1.3.1. Its slope is $-p_1/p_2$.

Figure 1.3.1

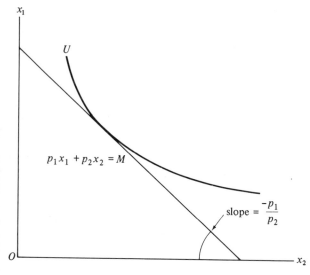

x_1

U

$p_1 x_1 + p_2 x_2 = M$

slope $= \dfrac{-p_1}{p_2}$

O

x_2

[5] *Cf.* Fenchell (1953), pp. 127–137.
[6] On the indifference curve, see Hicks (1939) chap. 1. On the utility function, see Samuelson (1947), pp. 90–96; Hicks (1946), math. app., sec. 5; Debreu (1959), chap. 4.

This mathematical problem can be solved by the method of the Lagrange multiplier. To obtain the first-order necessary condition,[7] write the Lagrangean function

$$L = U(x_1, x_2) + \lambda(M - p_1 x_1 - p_2 x_2) \tag{3}$$

differentiate it with respect to the independent variables x_1, x_2, and λ, and set the partial derivatives equal to zero, obtaining

$$U_1 = \lambda p_1 \tag{4}$$

$$U_2 = \lambda p_2 \tag{5}$$

$$M = p_1 x_1 + p_2 x_2 \tag{6}$$

The three equations can be solved for the three unknowns x_1, x_2, and λ in terms of p_1, p_2, and M provided the condition of the implicit-function theorem[8] is satisfied.

EQUILIBRIUM CONDITION

Equations (4) and (5) can be combined and written

$$\frac{U_1}{U_2} = \frac{p_1}{p_2} \tag{7}$$

From (1.2.10) and (7), *in equilibrium the marginal rate of substitution equals the price ratio.* In Figure 1.3.1 this is equivalent to the tangency of the budget line to the highest possible indifference curve.

Let $\bar{\lambda}$ be the solution value of λ for (4)–(6). Equations (4) and (5) can also be combined to give

$$\frac{U_1}{p_1} = \frac{U_2}{p_2} = \bar{\lambda} \tag{8}$$

Therefore, the condition for the consumer's optimum is that the *ratio of a commodity's marginal utility to its price is equal for all commodities.* This theorem has been called the *Second Law of Gossen,* or the *law of equi-marginal utility.* In

---

[7] The reader should be reminded that these first-order conditions hold when the maximum is interior, that is, x_1, x_2 and $\lambda \neq 0$, as assumed in the first assumption for this part, on p. 8, and in the preceding paragraph. See (21) for the boundary optimum solution.

[8] See MR 6. The condition is satisfied since the Jacobian of the system (4)–(6)

$$\begin{vmatrix} U_{11} & U_{12} & -p_1 \\ U_{21} & U_{22} & -p_2 \\ -p_1 & -p_2 & 0 \end{vmatrix}$$

must be positive by (17) below.

view of (MR5.48) the solution value $\bar{\lambda}$ of the Lagrange multiplier is the rate of change of the consumer's utility with respect to his income. Therefore, it can be called the *marginal utility of income*.

DEMAND FUNCTIONS

From equations (4)–(6) one can derive the consumer's demand for each commodity as a function of prices and income,

$$x_1 = f^1(p_1, p_2, M) \qquad (9)$$
$$x_2 = f^2(p_1, p_2, M) \qquad (10)$$

and the Lagrange multiplier also as a function of prices and income:

$$\lambda = f^3(p_1, p_2, M) \qquad (11)$$

It is simple to show that (9) and (10) do not change, but that (11) changes, when the utility function (1) undergoes a monotone-increasing transformation. Let the new utility function be

$$V(U(x_1, x_2))$$

then the Lagrangean expression is

$$L = V(U(x_1, x_2)) + \lambda(M - p_1 x_1 - p_2 x_2)$$

The first-order condition is

$$V'U_1 = \lambda p_1 \qquad (11a)$$
$$V'U_2 = \lambda p_2 \qquad (11b)$$
$$M = p_1 x_1 + p_2 x_2 \qquad (11c)$$

The first two equations imply

$$\frac{U_1}{U_2} = \frac{p_1}{p_2}$$

Hence equations (11a)–(11c) can be reduced to equations (7) and (6), just as equations (4)–(6) can be reduced to (7) and (6). Since the values of x_1 and x_2 are determined by the common equations, they are the same. However, the Lagrange multiplier λ now is V' times the original value U_1/p_1.[9]

Equations (7) and (6), which determine the demand functions (9) and (10), can be written

$$\frac{U_1}{U_2} = \frac{\dfrac{p_1}{M}}{\dfrac{p_2}{M}} \qquad (7')$$

[9] For the general case of n commodities, see Samuelson (1947), pp. 104, 133–135.

and

$$\frac{p_1}{M} x_1 + \frac{p_2}{M} x_2 = 1 \tag{6'}$$

Hence x_1 and x_2 are determined by p_1/M and p_2/M, and therefore do not change when p_1, p_2, and M change by the same percentage. Thus *the demand function is homogeneous of degree zero in the product prices and income.*

ELASTICITY OF DEMAND

In (9), suppose p_2 and M remain constant but p_1 changes. The *own-price elasticity of demand* for x_1, denoted by η_{11}, is defined

$$\eta_{11} = \frac{\partial x_1}{\partial p_1} \frac{p_1}{x_1} = \frac{\partial \ln x_1}{\partial \ln p_1} = \frac{\dfrac{dx_1}{x_1}}{\dfrac{dp_1}{p_1}} \qquad p_2, M = \text{constant} \tag{12}$$

As will be shown in Section 1.4, $\partial x_1/\partial p_1$ is negative; hence this elasticity is negative. It measures the consumer's responsiveness to price change. For finite changes Δp_1 and Δx_1, the elasticity (called the *arc elasticity*) can be considered as the ratio between proportionate changes $(\Delta x_1/x_1)/(\Delta p_1/p_1)$.

For example, consider a straight line demand relation that falls downward to the right:

$$x_1 = a - bp \qquad a > 0 \quad b > 0 \tag{13}$$

$$\eta_{11} = \frac{dx_1}{dp_1} \frac{p_1}{x_1} = -b \frac{p_1}{x_1} \tag{14}$$

When p_1 falls, x_1 rises; therefore p_1/x_1 falls. Thus the elasticity decreases in absolute value as p_1 decreases in this particular case.

In (9), assume p_1 and M remain constant, but p_2 changes. The *cross (price) elasticity of demand* with respect to the price of good 2, denoted by η_{12}, is defined by

$$\eta_{12} = \frac{\partial x_1}{\partial p_2} \frac{p_2}{x_1} \tag{15}$$

The two goods are called *gross substitutes* if (15) is positive, and *gross complements* if (15) is negative.

If in (7) p_1 and p_2 are to remain constant, but M is to change, then the *income elasticity of demand* is defined as

$$\frac{\partial x_1}{\partial M} \frac{M}{x_1} \tag{16}$$

This elasticity is a measure of the consumer's responsiveness to income change.

THE SECOND-ORDER CONDITION

The second-order condition for maximum of (1) subject to (2) is from (MR5.31),

$$\begin{vmatrix} U_{11} & U_{12} & -p_1 \\ U_{21} & U_{22} & -p_2 \\ -p_1 & -p_2 & 0 \end{vmatrix} > 0 \tag{17}$$

Note $U_{12} = U_{21}$. From MR5, U is quasi-concave. Alternatively, expanding the determinant results in

$$2U_{12}\, p_1\, p_2 - U_{22}\, p_1^2 - U_{11}\, p_2^2 > 0 \tag{18}$$

From (7)

$$p_1 = \frac{U_1}{U_2} \cdot p_2 \tag{19}$$

Substituting (19) into (18) and rearranging gives

$$U_{11}\, U_2^2 + U_{22}\, U_1^2 - 2U_{12}\, U_1\, U_2 < 0 \tag{20}$$

Using equation (1.2.11), this implies that *in equilibrium the marginal rate of substitution is diminishing*, and *the indifference curve is convex to the origin.*[10]

WHEN A GOOD IS NOT CONSUMED

The preceding model assumed that the consumer ends up consuming a positive quantity of each good. Taking into account the possibility that a good is not consumed, the problem must be cast in nonlinear programming terms,[11] and equations (4)–(5) must be replaced by

$$\frac{\partial L}{\partial x_i} = U_i - \lambda p_i \leqq 0 \qquad \text{for } x_i = 0$$

and

$$= 0 \qquad \text{for } x_i > 0 \tag{21}$$

This is the case of boundary optimum or *corner optimum.*

---

[10] On the theory of the consumer's optimum, see Hicks (1939), math. app.; and Samuelson (1947), chap. 5.

[11] See MR9.

Such a situation may be seen in Figure 1.3.2 where the consumer's optimum is reached with $x_2 = 0$. In this case

$$x_1 > 0 \qquad \frac{\partial L}{\partial x_1} = 0 \qquad \text{that is, } U_1 = \lambda p_1$$

$$x_2 = 0 \qquad \frac{\partial L}{\partial x_2} \leq 0 \qquad \text{that is, } U_2 \leq \lambda p_2$$

Therefore

$$\frac{U_1}{U_2} \geq \frac{p_1}{p_2}$$

The price ratio does not exceed the marginal rate of substitution as can also be seen in Figure 1.3.2.

Figure 1.3.2

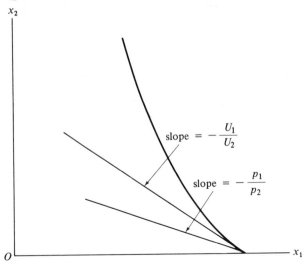

1.4 PROPERTIES OF THE DEMAND FUNCTION

This section derives additional results concerning consumer behavior. These results are invariant with respect to the choice of the utility index. The derivations in this section will analyze the case of three goods.

THE SLUTSKY EQUATION

The consumptions x_1, x_2, and x_3 are determined once the prices p_1, p_2, and p_3 and income M are given. The curve showing how the consumer changes, say

x_1 when the price p_1 or another price (p_2 or p_3) changes but M is held constant, is called the *price consumption curve*; an own-price consumption curve is shown in Figure 1.4.1. The curve showing how the consumer changes x_1 when M changes but all prices remain constant is called the *income consumption curve* (or *Engel curve*), and is shown in Figure 1.4.2.

Figure 1.4.1

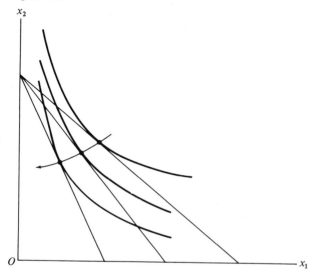

Figure 1.4.2

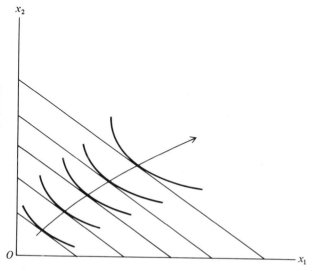

These relationships can be obtained from the analogue of (1.3.4–6) for three commodities. Let the utility function be

$$U = U(x_1, x_2, x_3) \qquad U_1, U_2, U_3 > 0 \tag{1}$$

Maximize U subject to the budget constraint,

$$M = p_1 x_1 + p_2 x_2 + p_3 x_3 \tag{2}$$

The Lagrangean expression is

$$L = U(x_1, x_2, x_3) + \lambda(M - p_1 x_1 - p_2 x_2 - p_3 x_3) \tag{3}$$

The first-order condition is

$$U_1 - p_1 \lambda = 0 \tag{4}$$

$$U_2 - p_2 \lambda = 0 \tag{5}$$

$$U_3 - p_3 \lambda = 0 \tag{6}$$

$$M - p_1 x_1 - p_2 x_2 - p_3 x_3 = 0 \tag{7}$$

Solving the four equations in four unknowns (x_1, x_2, x_3, and λ) gives the demand functions:

$$x_1 = f^1(p_1, p_2, p_3, M) \tag{8}$$

$$x_2 = f^2(p_1, p_2, p_3, M) \tag{9}$$

$$x_3 = f^3(p_1, p_2, p_3, M) \tag{10}$$

determining the allocation of the consumer's income among three goods. The marginal utility of income function is also obtained

$$\lambda = f^4(p_1, p_2, p_3, M) \tag{11}$$

Taking differentials of the first-order condition (4)–(7) above,

$$\begin{bmatrix} U_{11} & U_{12} & U_{13} & -p_1 \\ U_{21} & U_{22} & U_{23} & -p_2 \\ U_{31} & U_{32} & U_{33} & -p_3 \\ -p_1 & -p_2 & -p_3 & 0 \end{bmatrix} \begin{bmatrix} dx_1 \\ dx_2 \\ dx_3 \\ d\lambda \end{bmatrix} = \begin{bmatrix} \lambda dp_1 \\ \lambda dp_2 \\ \lambda dp_3 \\ x_1 dp_1 + x_2 dp_2 + x_3 dp_3 - dM \end{bmatrix} \tag{12}$$

let Δ be the determinant of the coefficient matrix, and Δ_{ij} be the cofactor of the (i, j) element of the matrix. Then, by Cramer's rule,

$$dx_1 = \frac{\lambda\, dp_1\, \Delta_{11} + \lambda\, dp_2\, \Delta_{21} + \lambda\, dp_3\, \Delta_{31} + (x_1\, dp_1 + x_2\, dp_2 + x_3\, dp_3 - dM)\, \Delta_{41}}{\Delta} \tag{13}$$

Forming the partial derivatives

$$\frac{\partial x_1}{\partial p_1} = \frac{\lambda \, \Delta_{11}}{\Delta} + \frac{x_1 \, \Delta_{41}}{\Delta} \tag{14}$$

$$\frac{\partial x_1}{\partial p_2} = \frac{\lambda \, \Delta_{21}}{\Delta} + \frac{x_2 \, \Delta_{41}}{\Delta} \tag{15}$$

$$\frac{\partial x_1}{\partial p_3} = \frac{\lambda \, \Delta_{31}}{\Delta} + \frac{x_3 \, \Delta_{41}}{\Delta} \tag{16}$$

$$\frac{\partial x_1}{\partial M} = \frac{-\Delta_{41}}{\Delta} \tag{17}$$

Equations (14)–(16) give the effects of price changes, and equation (17) gives the effect of an income change. Using (17) in (14)–(16),

$$\frac{\partial x_1}{\partial p_1} = \frac{\lambda \, \Delta_{11}}{\Delta} - x_1 \frac{\partial x_1}{\partial M} \tag{18}$$

$$\frac{\partial x_1}{\partial p_2} = \frac{\lambda \, \Delta_{21}}{\Delta} - x_2 \frac{\partial x_1}{\partial M} \tag{19}$$

$$\frac{\partial x_1}{\partial p_3} = \frac{\lambda \, \Delta_{31}}{\Delta} - x_3 \frac{\partial x_1}{\partial M} \tag{20}$$

The second term on the right-hand side of (18)–(20) is called the *income term*, since it contains $\partial x_1 / \partial M$.

The income effect can be eliminated by a compensating income change. Suppose an increase dp_2 in p_2 is accompanied by a simultaneous compensating increase in income dM such that

$$dM = x_2 \, dp_2 \tag{21}$$

while p_1 and p_3 remain constant. Then the demand x_1 for commodity 1 is a function of p_2 and M, and therefore from (8),

$$dx_1 = \frac{\partial x_1}{\partial p_2} dp_2 + \frac{\partial x_1}{\partial M} dM \tag{22}$$

Substituting (21) in (22),

$$dx_1 = \frac{\partial x_1}{\partial p_2} dp_2 + \frac{\partial x_1}{\partial M} x_2 \, dp_2$$

Hence the change in demand with a compensating income change, dx_1 / dp_2, is

$$\frac{dx_1}{dp_2} = \frac{\partial x_1}{\partial p_2} + \frac{\partial x_1}{\partial M} x_2 \tag{23}$$

Substituting expression (19) for $\partial x_1/\partial p_2$ in (23),

$$\frac{dx_1}{dp_2} = \lambda \cdot \frac{\Delta_{21}}{\Delta} \tag{24}$$

Equation (24) shows that the first term on the right-hand side of (19) represents the compensated variation in demand where the change in real income due to the price change is eliminated. It is called the *substitution term*. The sign of the term depends on that of Δ_{ij}/Δ. To be exact it should be called the *cross-substitution* term for goods i and j.

Because $U_{ij} = U_{ji}$ the coefficient matrix of (12) is symmetric, and $\Delta_{12} = \Delta_{21}$. Hence *the substitution terms are symmetric*, that is

$$\frac{dx_1}{dp_2} = \frac{dx_2}{dp_1}$$

This property reduces the number of independent cross-substitution terms (dx_i/dp_j, $i \neq j$) by one half.

The subsitution term (24) represents the rate of change of x_1 with respect to p_2 with a compensating change in income. If this term is positive, a compensated rise in p_2 will result in an increase in x_1. If the substitution term with respect to its own price is negative, as will be shown later, this means that x_1 rises while x_2 falls with a compensated rise in p_2. Thus these two goods are defined as *net substitutes*. Similarly, if (24) is negative, the goods are called *net complements*.[12]

Equation (24) gives the rate of change in x_1 with respect to p_2, when p_2 and M were changed as specified while holding p_1 and p_3 constant. This compensated variation dx_1/dp_2 can be shown to be that which holds the level of the utility index constant as follows: Let p_1, p_3, and x_3 be constant in the budget equation

$$p_1 x_1 + p_2 x_2 + p_3 x_3 = M$$

By taking the total differential of both sides,

$$p_1\,dx_1 + p_2\,dx_2 + x_2\,dp_2 = dM$$

Since dM was set equal to $x_2\,dp_2$,

$$p_1\,dx_1 + p_2\,dx_2 = 0$$

Thus

$$-\frac{dx_2}{dx_1} = \frac{p_1}{p_2}$$

[12] In the two-commodity case, the term cannot be negative. See footnote 16 of this section.

But in equilibrium, by (1.3.20),

$$\frac{p_1}{p_2} = \frac{U_1}{U_2}$$

Hence

$$-\frac{dx_2}{dx_1} = \frac{U_1}{U_2}$$

That is

$$U_1\, dx_1 + U_2\, dx_2 = 0$$

Therefore

$$dU = U_1\, dx_1 + U_2\, dx_2 = 0$$

That is, U is constant.

Therefore (24) can be rewritten

$$\frac{dx_1}{dp_2} = \frac{\partial x_1}{\partial p_2}\bigg|_{U=\text{constant}} \tag{25}$$

and (19) as

$$\frac{\partial x_1}{\partial p_2} = \frac{\partial x_1}{\partial p_2}\bigg|_{U=\text{constant}} - x_2 \cdot \frac{\partial x_1}{\partial M} \tag{26}$$

This equation is known as the *Slutsky equation*.

If $\partial x_1/\partial M < 0$, that is, a rise in income results in a fall in demand, then the good is said to be an *inferior good*.

Suppose good 1 is not an inferior good (that is, $\partial x_1/\partial M \geq 0$) and it is a net complement for good 2 (that is, $dx_1/dp_2 < 0$), then from (26), $\partial x_1/\partial p_2$ is negative. A rise in p_2 will result in a fall in x_1. Suppose on the other hand, good 1 is an inferior good (that is, $\partial x_1/\partial M < 0$). Then if good 1 is a net substitute for good 2 (that is, $dx_1/dp_2 > 0$), $\partial x_1/\partial p_2$ is positive. A rise in p_2 will result in a rise in x_1.

Net substitutes should be clearly distinguished from gross substitutes, presented in Section 1.3. Good 1 is said to be a *gross substitute* for good 2 if

$$\frac{\partial x_1}{\partial p_2} > 0$$

Similarly *net complements* should be distinguished from gross complements. Good 1 is said to be a *gross complement* of good 2 if

$$\frac{\partial x_1}{\partial p_2} < 0$$

In the gross concepts, no variation in income is made to compensate for the change in real income due to a change in the price.

THE SECOND-ORDER CONDITION

The second-order condition for maximum is that the matrix

$$S \equiv \begin{bmatrix} \dfrac{\Delta_{11}}{\Delta} & \dfrac{\Delta_{12}}{\Delta} & \dfrac{\Delta_{13}}{\Delta} & \dfrac{\Delta_{14}}{\Delta} \\ \vdots & \vdots & \vdots & \vdots \\ \dfrac{\Delta_{41}}{\Delta} & \dfrac{\Delta_{42}}{\Delta} & \dfrac{\Delta_{43}}{\Delta} & \dfrac{\Delta_{44}}{\Delta} \end{bmatrix} \tag{27}$$

is negative definite, where Δ and Δ_{ij} denote the determinant and cofactor of the coefficient matrix in (12).[13] That is, the quadratic form satisfies the inequality

$$(z_1\ z_2\ z_3\ z_4)\, S \begin{pmatrix} z_1 \\ z_2 \\ z_3 \\ z_4 \end{pmatrix} < 0 \tag{28}$$

for all z_i not zero. This condition is satisfied if the utility function is strictly quasi-concave.

DEMAND FOR A GOOD WHEN ITS OWN PRICE CHANGES

Inequality (28) means

$$\sum_{i=1}^{4} \sum_{j=1}^{4} \frac{\Delta_{ij}}{\Delta} \cdot z_i z_j < 0 \qquad \text{for all } z_i \text{ not zero} \tag{29}$$

Let z_1 be nonzero, and z_2, z_3, and z_4 be zero in (29). Then (29) is reduced to

$$\frac{\Delta_{11}}{\Delta} \cdot z_1^2 < 0 \tag{30}$$

Since z_1^2 is always positive,

$$\frac{\Delta_{11}}{\Delta} < 0 \tag{31}$$

which may be called the *negativity property*. The change in demand for good 1 when its own price changes is, as in (18)

$$\frac{\partial x_1}{\partial p_1} = \lambda \cdot \frac{\Delta_{11}}{\Delta} - x_1 \cdot \frac{\partial x_1}{\partial M} \tag{32}$$

[13] See MR5 and MR3.

In view of (31), the substitution term in (32), which may be called the *own-price substitution term*, is negative. Hence as long as good 1 is not an inferior good, *the demand for the good falls when its own price rises*. This relationship has been called the *law of demand*.[14]

If good 1 is inferior, then $\partial x_1 / \partial M < 0$. If the income effect dominates in (32), then $\partial x_1 / \partial M_1$ can become positive, bringing about an increase in demand as a result of a rise in its price. The effect has been called the *Giffen effect*.

HOMOGENEITY

From matrix (12), form the inner product of the last row and the cofactors of another row i. From the theory of determinants,[15] this sum equals zero:

$$-\sum_{j=1}^{3} p_j \cdot \frac{\Delta_{ij}}{\Delta} = 0 \qquad i \neq 4 \tag{33}$$

This equation implies that the substitution terms weighted by their respective prices add up to zero.

This equation has been called *homogeneity property* since it ensures that *an equal relative change in all prices and income leaves the amount of commodities purchased unchanged*. The proof is as follows. As in (18) and (19),

$$\frac{\partial x_1}{\partial p_i} = \lambda \cdot \frac{\Delta_{i1}}{\Delta} - x_i \cdot \frac{\partial x_1}{\partial M} \qquad i = 1, \dots, 3 \tag{34}$$

But from (8)

$$dx_1 = \sum_{i=1}^{3} \frac{\partial x_1}{\partial p_i} dp_i + \frac{\partial x_1}{\partial M} dM \tag{35}$$

Let $dp_1 = \alpha p_1$, $dp_2 = \alpha p_2$, $dp_3 = \alpha p_3$ and $dM = \alpha M$, where α is the proportionate change. Substituting these and (34) in (35),

$$dx_1 = \alpha \left[\lambda \sum_{j=1}^{3} p_j \cdot \frac{\Delta_{ij}}{\Delta} + (M - p_1 x_1 - p_2 x_2) \frac{\partial x_1}{\partial M} \right]$$

$$= \alpha(0 + 0)$$

$$= 0 \tag{36}$$

Thus the demand function is homogeneous of degree zero with respect to prices and income.

---

[14] See also the derivation of the law of demand in Section 11.2 from the revealed preference axiom.

[15] See MR2.

SUBSTITUTES AND COMPLEMENTS

The earlier expansion by alien cofactors, (33), showed

$$\sum_{j=1}^{3} p_j \frac{\Delta_{1j}}{\Delta} = 0$$

Therefore

$$p_2 \frac{\Delta_{12}}{\Delta} + p_3 \frac{\Delta_{13}}{\Delta} = -p_1 \frac{\Delta_{11}}{\Delta} \tag{37}$$

The right-hand side of (37) is positive because of (31). Therefore

$$p_2 \frac{\Delta_{12}}{\Delta} + p_3 \frac{\Delta_{13}}{\Delta} > 0 \tag{38}$$

This means that all Δ_{1j}/Δ appearing in the sum of the left-hand side of (38) can be positive. Since a good j has been defined as a substitute for good 1 if $\Delta_{ij}/\Delta > 0$, (38) means that *all other goods can be substitutes for good* 1.

Inequality (38) also means that all Δ_{1j}/Δ appearing in the sum cannot be negative. Since good j has been defined as a net complement of good 1 if $\Delta_{1j}/\Delta < 0$, (38) means that *all other goods cannot be complements for good* 1.[16,17]

THE COMPOSITE-COMMODITY THEOREM

Many economic models aggregate goods into a single good such as the consumption good, the future good, and the product of an industry. Hicks has derived the following condition required for justifying such aggregation. If the prices of a group of goods change in the same proportion, then the group of goods can be treated as a single good.

Consider the case of three goods, two of which change in price by the same proportion, which may be denoted by $d \ln p$ so that

$$d \ln p = \frac{dp_1}{p_1} = \frac{dp_2}{p_2} \tag{39}$$

Denote the expenditure on each good by

$$r_1 = p_1 x_1 \qquad r_2 = p_2 x_2 \tag{40}$$

and the total expenditures on these two goods by

$$r = r_1 + r_2 \tag{41}$$

---

[16] It is easily seen that if there exist only two goods, they cannot be a complement to each other.

[17] On the Slutsky equation and related topics, see Slutsky (1915); Hicks (1939), math app., secs. 6–10; Samuelson (1947), chaps. 5–7.

First, assume the price of only the first good changes by the proportion $d \ln p$, that is,

$$\frac{dp_1}{p_1} = d \ln p \tag{42}$$

In this case, the change in the expenditure on the first good dr_1 is

$$dr_1 = \frac{\partial r_1}{\partial p_1} dp_1 = p_1 \cdot \frac{\partial x_1}{\partial p_1} p_1 \, d \ln p \tag{43}$$

and the change in the expenditure on the second good dr_2 is

$$dr_2 = \frac{\partial r_2}{\partial p_1} dp_1 = p_2 \cdot \frac{\partial x_2}{\partial p_1} p_1 \, d \ln p \tag{44}$$

Using (18) in (43) and the analogue of (19) in (44)

$$dr_1 = \left[p_1 \, p_1 \, \lambda \cdot \frac{\Delta_{11}}{\Delta} - p_1 \, p_1 \, x_1 \cdot \frac{\partial x_1}{\partial M} \right] d \ln p \tag{45}$$

$$dr_2 = \left[p_1 \, p_2 \, \lambda \cdot \frac{\Delta_{12}}{\Delta} - p_1 \, p_2 \, x_1 \cdot \frac{\partial x_2}{\partial M} \right] d \ln p \tag{46}$$

Similarly, if the price of the second good only changes by $d \ln p$, that is,

$$\frac{dp_2}{p_2} = d \ln p \tag{47}$$

then

$$dr_1 = \frac{\partial r_1}{\partial p_2} dp_2 = p_1 \frac{\partial x_1}{\partial p_2} p_2 \, d \ln p \tag{48}$$

$$dr_2 = \frac{\partial r_2}{\partial p_2} dp_2 = p_2 \frac{\partial x_2}{\partial p_2} p_2 \, d \ln p \tag{49}$$

Using (18) and (19)

$$dr_1 = \left[p_1 \, p_2 \, \lambda \cdot \frac{\Delta_{21}}{\Delta} - p_1 \, p_2 \, x_2 \cdot \frac{\partial x_1}{\partial M} \right] d \ln p \tag{50}$$

$$dr_2 = \left[p_2 \, p_2 \, \lambda \cdot \frac{\Delta_{22}}{\Delta} - p_2 \, p_2 \, x_2 \cdot \frac{\partial x_2}{\partial M} \right] d \ln p \tag{51}$$

The change in the total expenditures when both p_1 and p_2 change by the proportion $d \ln p$ is

$$dr = \frac{\partial r_1}{\partial p_1} dp_1 + \frac{\partial r_1}{\partial p_2} dp_2 + \frac{\partial r_2}{\partial p_1} dp_1 + \frac{\partial r_2}{\partial p_2} dp_2$$

Using (45), (46), (50) and (51),

$$dr = \left\{ \sum_{i=1}^{2} \sum_{j=1}^{2} p_i p_j \lambda \cdot \frac{\Delta_{ij}}{\Delta} - (p_1 x_1 + p_2 x_2) \left[p_1 \frac{\partial x_1}{\partial M} + p_2 \frac{\partial x_2}{\partial M} \right] \right\} d \ln p \qquad (52)$$

Using (40) and (41),

$$\frac{dr}{d \ln p} = \sum_{i=1}^{2} \sum_{j=1}^{2} p_i p_j \lambda \cdot \frac{\Delta_{ij}}{\Delta} - r \cdot \frac{\partial r}{\partial M} \qquad (53)$$

This expression has the same form as (18). Because of (29) the first term of the right-hand side of (53), which is the substitution term, is negative. Thus the value of aggregate demand for the group of two goods falls when a proportionate price increase (compensated for income) takes place. In this sense these two goods can be treated as one good. The results can be generalized to the case of n goods.[18]

EXPENDITURE FUNCTION, INDIRECT UTILITY FUNCTION

Just as the firm minimizes the cost of a level of output in Chapter 2, the consumer can be considered to minimize the expenditures to attain a level of his utility index. This leads to the concept of the *expenditure function*, which corresponds to the cost function in the theory of the firm. Just as an output level corresponds to the minimized cost level, a level of the utility index corresponds to the minimized expenditure level. This leads to the concept of the so-called *indirect utility function*.

Suppose a consumer's preferences can be represented by a utility function

$$U = U(x_1, x_2) \qquad (54)$$

and he maximizes this function subject to the budget constraint

$$p_1 x_1 + p_2 x_2 = M \qquad (55)$$

As before, each good is infinitely divisible, the consumer is never satiated in any good, and therefore the consumer spends his entire income to maximize his utility.

Assume the consumer attempts to minimize his expenditures to attain various levels of his utility index, that is, chooses x_1 and x_2 so as to minimize

$$M = p_1 x_1 + p_2 x_2 \qquad (56)$$

subject to

$$U(x_1, x_2) = U^0 \qquad (57)$$

---

[18] *Cf.* Hicks (1946), p. 312f.

Solving the first-order condition yields the demand functions

$$x_1^0 = f^1(p_1, p_2, U^0) \tag{58}$$

$$x_2^0 = f^2(p_1, p_2, U^0) \tag{59}$$

These functions can be called the *income-compensated demand functions*. As U^0 changes, x_1^0 and x_2^0 change, which in turn causes the minimum expenditure $M = p_1 x_1^0 + p_2 x_2^0$ to change. Thus the minimum expenditure can be written

$$M = g(p_1, p_2, U^0) = p_1 x_1^0 + p_2 x_2^0 \tag{60}$$

This function g can be called the *expenditure function*, which denotes the minimum expenditure necessary to achieve various levels of utility for a given set of prices.

In Figure 1.4.3, let the indifference curve represent U^0, and the slope of the equal-expenditure lines represent the given prices p_1 and p_2. As U^0 is changed, x_1^0 and x_2^0 will also change, and cause the minimum expenditure to change.

One of the most important properties of the expenditure functions is that the partial derivative

$$\frac{\partial g}{\partial p_i} \tag{61}$$

equals the demand x_1^0 for good i in terms of prices and utility. Since U is held constant, x_i^0 gives the income-compensated demand for any change in p_i.

Figure 1.4.3

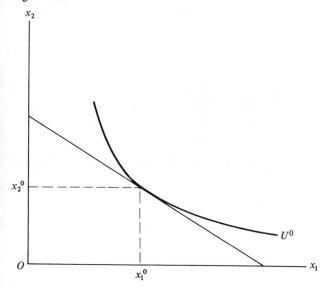

The expenditure function is a strictly monotone (increasing) function in utility. Hence the utility level can be expressed as a function of minimized expenditure as

$$U = h(p_1, p_2, M) \tag{62}$$

This function is called the *indirect utility function*. It represents maximum utility that can be attained as a function of prices and income.

One of the most important properties of the indirect utility function is that the ratio

$$-\frac{\dfrac{\partial h}{\partial p_i}}{\dfrac{\partial h}{\partial M}} \tag{62'}$$

equals the demand x_i for good i in terms of prices and income. This is the market demand function. By definition

$$M = g(p_1, p_2, U) = g(p_1, p_2, h(p_1, p_2, M))$$

Therefore by differentiation with respect to M,

$$1 = \frac{\partial g}{\partial U} \cdot \frac{\partial h}{\partial M}$$

and by differentiation with respect to p_1,

$$0 = \frac{\partial g}{\partial p_1} + \frac{\partial g}{\partial U} \cdot \frac{\partial h}{\partial p_1}$$

Therefore

$$\frac{\partial g}{\partial p_1} = -\frac{\dfrac{\partial h}{\partial p_1}}{\dfrac{\partial h}{\partial M}}$$

This represents demand for x_1 at $U = h(p_1, p_2, M)$, and therefore the market demand function of prices and income.

The Slutsky Equation Again
Consider the income-compensated demand function

$$x_1^0 = f^1(p_1, p_2, U^0) = \frac{\partial g}{\partial p_1} \tag{63}$$

Differentiating this function with respect to p_1 yields

$$f_1^1 = \frac{\partial^2 g}{\partial p_1^2} \tag{64}$$

where g is a concave function in prices,[19] and therefore the right-hand side of the above equation is nonpositive. Thus *the own-price substitution effect is nonpositive.* Differentiating the income-compensated demand function with respect to p_2 yields

$$f_2^1 = \frac{\partial^2 g}{\partial p_1 \, \partial p_2} = \frac{\partial^2 g}{\partial p_2 \, \partial p_1} \tag{65}$$

But

$$\frac{\partial g}{\partial p_2} = x_2^0 \tag{66}$$

Hence

$$f_2^1 = \frac{\partial x_2^0}{\partial p_1} = f_1^2 \tag{67}$$

Thus *the cross-substitution effects are symmetric.*

By definition

$$x_1 = f^1(p_1, p_2, h(p_1, p_2, M)) = \frac{\partial g}{\partial p_1}$$

Therefore

$$\frac{\partial x_1}{\partial M} = \frac{\partial}{\partial U}\left(\frac{\partial g}{\partial p_1}\right) \frac{\partial h}{\partial M} = \frac{\partial^2 g}{\partial U \, \partial p_1} \frac{\partial h}{\partial M} \tag{68}$$

Next, differentiate the same function with respect to p_2. Since x_1 is a function of p_2 and of U which in turn is a function of p_2,

$$\frac{\partial x_1}{\partial p_2} = \frac{\partial}{\partial p_2}\left(\frac{\partial g}{\partial p_1}\right) + \frac{\partial}{\partial U}\left(\frac{\partial g}{\partial p_1}\right) \frac{\partial h}{\partial p_2}$$

$$= \frac{\partial^2 g}{\partial p_2 \, \partial p_1} + \frac{\partial^2 g}{\partial U \, \partial p_1} \frac{\partial h}{\partial p_2} \tag{69}$$

---

[19] Let (x', p'), (x'', p''), and (x''', p''') be the cost-minimizing pairs of price and quantity vectors for the utility level U such that

$$p''' = ap' + (1 - a)p'' \qquad 0 < a < 1$$

Then

$$g(p''', U) = p'''x''' = ap'x''' + (1 - a)p''x'''$$

Because g is cost-minimizing

$$g(p', U) \leq p'x''' \qquad g(p'', U) \leq p''x'''$$

Hence

$$g(p''', U) \geq ag(p', U) + (1 - a)g(p'', U)$$

Using (68) in (69),

$$\frac{\partial x_1}{\partial p_2} = \frac{\partial^2 g}{\partial p_2 \, \partial p_1} + \frac{\dfrac{\partial x_1}{\partial M} \dfrac{\partial h}{\partial p_2}}{\dfrac{\partial h}{\partial M}} \tag{70}$$

Using the result (62'),

$$\frac{\partial x_1}{\partial p_2} = \frac{\partial^2 g}{\partial p_2 \, \partial p_1} - x_2 \frac{\partial x_1}{\partial M} \tag{71}$$

In the right-hand side, the first term represents the substitution effect and the second term the income effect.[20]

1.5 PRODUCT-FACTOR SUBSTITUTION AND FACTOR SUPPLIES

Let us use the following notation:
x_1 = the amount of a commodity consumed
p_1 = the price of the commodity
x_2 = the amount of leisure
v = the amount of labor time supplied
p_2 = the wage rate
V = the total time available

Let the utility function be

$$U = U(x_1, x_2) \qquad U_1 > 0 \quad U_2 > 0 \tag{1}$$

The budget equation for the commodity is

$$p_1 x_1 = p_2 v = p_2 \cdot (V - x_2) \tag{2}$$

This equation can be rewritten

$$p_1 x_1 + p_2 x_2 = p_2 V \tag{3}$$

Let

$$p_2 V = M \tag{4}$$

The new budget equation (3) states that the spending on the commodity and leisure cannot exceed the potential income, or *wealth*, M. The worker's problem

---

[20] On the expenditure function and indirect utility function see Houtthakker (1952), McKenzie (1957), and Karlin (1959).

is to maximize the utility function (1) subject to the constraint (3). Forming a Lagrangean function and writing the first-order condition for maximum utility,

$$U_1 - \lambda p_1 = 0 \tag{5}$$

$$U_2 - \lambda p_2 = 0 \tag{6}$$

$$p_1 x_1 + p_2 x_2 = M \tag{7}$$

From (5) and (6),

$$\frac{U_2}{U_1} = \frac{p_2}{p_1}$$

Thus *the marginal rate of substitution between the commodity and the factor is equal to the price ratio.*

Taking differentials of (5)–(7),

$$\begin{bmatrix} U_{11} & U_{12} & -p_1 \\ U_{21} & U_{22} & -p_2 \\ -p_1 & -p_2 & 0 \end{bmatrix} \begin{bmatrix} dx_1 \\ dx_2 \\ d\lambda \end{bmatrix} = \begin{bmatrix} \lambda dp_1 \\ \lambda dp_2 \\ x_1 dp_1 + x_2 dp_2 - dM \end{bmatrix} \tag{8}$$

Solving for dx_2,

$$dx_2 = \frac{\lambda dp_1 \Delta_{12} + \lambda dp_2 \Delta_{22} + (x_1 dp_1 + x_2 dp_2 - dM) \Delta_{32}}{\Delta} \tag{9}$$

But from (4),

$$dM = V dp_2 \tag{10}$$

Substituting (10) in (9) yields

$$dx_2 = \frac{\lambda dp_1 \Delta_{12} + \lambda dp_2 \Delta_{22} + [x_1 dp_1 - (V - x_2) dp_2] \Delta_{32}}{\Delta} \tag{11}$$

Therefore

$$\frac{\partial x_2}{\partial p_2} = \lambda \frac{\Delta_{22}}{\Delta} - (V - x_2) \frac{\Delta_{32}}{\Delta} \tag{12}$$

From (9),

$$\frac{\partial x_2}{\partial M} = -\frac{\Delta_{32}}{\Delta} \tag{13}$$

Hence

$$\frac{\partial x_2}{\partial p_2} = \lambda \frac{\Delta_{22}}{\Delta} + (V - x_2) \frac{\partial x_2}{\partial M} \tag{14}$$

By the negativity property the substitution term is negative, but the income term in this case is positive as long as leisure is not an inferior good. Hence, when the wage rate increases, the demand for leisure can increase, and the supply of labor can decrease.[21]

What has preceded may be summarized in the following model. Consider a consumer whose utility function can be written

$$U = U(x_1, x_2, x_3, x_4) \qquad U_1, U_2, U_3, U_4 > 0 \tag{15}$$

where positive numbers x_1 and x_2 denote the quantities of the two products consumed, and negative numbers $x_3 = -v_1$ and $x_4 = -v_2$ denote negative net demands, or supplies, of the two factors. His budget equation can be written

$$p_1 x_1 + p_2 x_2 = p_1 v_1 + p_2 v_2$$

That is, his consumption expenditures are just equal to his total income. This equation can be written

$$p_1 x_1 + p_2 x_2 + p_3 x_3 + p_4 x_4 = 0 \tag{16}$$

The Lagrangean expression for this maximization problem is

$$L = U + \lambda \cdot (p_1 x_1 + p_2 x_2 + p_3 x_3 + p_4 x_4) \tag{17}$$

The first-order condition is

$$\frac{\partial L}{\partial x_1} = U_1 + \lambda p_1 = 0 \tag{18}$$

$$\frac{\partial L}{\partial x_2} = U_2 + \lambda p_2 = 0 \tag{19}$$

$$\frac{\partial L}{\partial x_3} = U_3 + \lambda p_3 = 0 \tag{20}$$

$$\frac{\partial L}{\partial x_4} = U_4 + \lambda p_4 = 0 \tag{21}$$

$$\frac{\partial L}{\partial \lambda} = p_1 x_1 + p_2 x_2 + p_3 x_3 + p_4 x_4 = 0 \tag{22}$$

These five equations in five unknowns x_1, x_2, x_3, x_4, and λ can be solved in terms of p_1, p_2, p_3, p_4, providing the demand functions for each good in terms of the product and factor prices. From the form of equations (18)–(22) it is apparent that these demand functions will be homogeneous of degree zero in the product and factor prices.

---

[21] On the backward-bending supply curve of labor, see Robbins (1930).

Furthermore, equations (18)–(22) yield

$$\frac{U_1}{U_2} = \frac{p_1}{p_2} \tag{23}$$

$$\frac{U_3}{U_4} = \frac{p_3}{p_4} \tag{24}$$

$$\frac{U_3}{U_1} = \frac{p_3}{p_1} \tag{25}$$

$$\frac{U_3}{U_2} = \frac{p_3}{p_2} \tag{26}$$

$$\frac{U_4}{U_1} = \frac{p_4}{p_1} \tag{27}$$

$$\frac{U_4}{U_2} = \frac{p_4}{p_2} \tag{28}$$

In words, the marginal rate of product substitution equals the product-price ratio; the marginal rate of factor substitution equals the factor-price ratio. Further the marginal rate of substitution between product 1 and factor 1 equals the factor-product-price ratio; similarly between product 2 and factor 1, between product 1 and factor 2, and between product 2 and factor 2.

1.6 SUMMARY

The theory of consumer's resource allocation assumes a strictly quasi-concave utility function invariant under monotone-increasing transformation. The consumer's maximization of his utility function provides the structural equations determining his resource allocation behavior. These structural equations provide, among others, demand functions expressing the quantity of each good demanded at the given prices and income. The structural equations can also determine the marginal utility of income, which is the price of the limited income in terms of utility. The condition for optimality in terms of the structural equations is that the marginal rate of substitution is equal to the price ratio and the budget hyperplane is tangential to the highest indifference surface.

The demand function that is obtained from the structural equations has various properties. It is homogeneous of degree zero in prices and income. Its rate of change with respect to a commodity price can be decomposed into the income effect and the (income-compensated) substitution effect. While the income effect is usually positive (the exception is the inferior good), the substitution effect can be of either sign. The own-price substitution effect, however, is negative, and as long as the good is not an inferior good, the rise in the price causes a fall in demand.

The factor of production supplied by the consumer can be regarded as a negative net demand for the good. Thus the theory of demand developed above can provide the theory of supply for the consumer.

The above calculus approach can be generalized into a nonlinear programming approach which provides more general results. When the marginal utility of a good does not exceed the marginal utility of income of the price, the good may not be demanded.

The analysis here assumed the existence of a differentiable utility function representing the preference of the consumer. More rigorous formulation of the consumer's choice and preferences is presented in Chapter 11.

The preceding models can provide a basis for empirical testing and for the derivation of empirical demand functions.[22]

[22] For example, see Klein (1962), chap. 2; Kogiku (1967a).

2
MODELS OF THE
FIRM'S OPTIMUM

2.1 INTRODUCTION

This chapter examines the optimizing behavior of the firm or producer, and derives the supply functions of products and the demand functions for factors of production. It will be shown how the firm constrained by technology will change its commodity output when its market price changes, and if it is producing more than one commodity, how it will change its mix of commodity outputs when their relative prices change. The models will also examine how the firm will change its demand for a factor of production when its price changes and how it will change its mix of factor inputs when their relative prices change. In short, the chapter examines the firm's resource allocation behavior in response to the price system.

In this chapter it is assumed that

- The prices of products are given.
- The prices of factors are given.

Again the prices are assumed given, but in the model of general equilibrium in Chapter 4 it will be shown that they are determined by the conditions of demand and supply in the product and factor markets. The prices are signals which tell the firm the conditions of the markets, deal out profits or losses, and determine what quantity adjustments the firm will make.

2.2 THE PRODUCTION FUNCTION

The firm achieves an optimum under a given state of technology. The present marginalist analysis describes this technological relationship by the explicit *production function*, which shows the maximum product output obtainable from various levels of factor inputs. For simplicity, the present model considers the producer producing one product using two factors.

A product can usually be produced by several alternative techniques. Every producer faces this choice of technique. The model here supposes that he has chosen the most efficient technique from among a spectrum of available techniques (so that output cannot be increased without increasing at least one input), and proceeds to examine the relationship between factor inputs and product output.[1]

Suppose the maximum product of y units can be produced by using v_1 and v_2 units of factors 1 and 2, respectively. The above technical relationship can be written

$$y = f(v_1, v_2) \tag{1}$$

where v_1 and v_2 are assumed positive. Normally

$$f(0, 0) = 0 \tag{2}$$

That is, without inputs, no output. The relationship (1) is called the *production function*. Several plausible assumptions can be made: that factors are divisible and quantities v_1 and v_2 are continuous variables; that the product is divisible; and that the production function f is a continuous function. It is assumed further that the production function is twice-differentiable; that is, the following partial derivatives exist.

$$f_1, f_2, f_{11}, f_{22}, f_{12}, f_{21} \tag{3}$$

The first two partial derivatives are called the *marginal productivity* of factors 1 and 2, respectively. They represent the rates of change of total product with respect to each factor. The existence of the derivatives in (3) rules out kinks or jumps in the marginal product curve, such as encountered in Section 7.2. It is assumed that

$$f_1 > 0 \qquad f_2 > 0 \tag{4}$$

that is, *marginal productivity is always positive*, as in Figure 2.2.1. Because of the twice-differentiability of f, $f_{12} = f_{21}$.

[1] The choice of technique is more explicitly analyzed in Part II.

Figure 2.2.1

$f(v_1, v_2)$

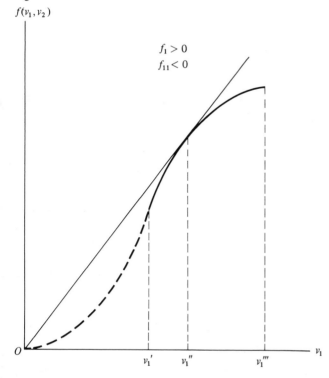

$f_1 > 0$

$f_{11} < 0$

v_1' v_1'' v_1'''

0 v_1

Examples

The *Cobb-Douglas production function* takes the form

$$y = b v_1^a v_2^{1-a} \tag{5}$$

where b is a positive constant, and a is a constant between 0 and 1. The marginal productivities are

$$\frac{\partial y}{\partial v_1} = ba\left(\frac{v_2}{v_1}\right)^{1-a} > 0 \tag{6}$$

$$\frac{\partial y}{\partial v_2} = b(1-a)\left(\frac{v_1}{v_2}\right)^{a} > 0 \tag{7}$$

The *CES production function* takes the form

$$y = [av_1^{-b} + (1-a)v_2^{-b}]^{-1/b} \qquad 0 < a < 1$$

$$-1 < b \tag{8}$$

where a can be referred to as the distribution parameter and b as the substitution parameter. The marginal productivities are

$$\frac{\partial y}{\partial v_1} = a\left(\frac{y}{v_1}\right)^{1+b} > 0 \tag{9}$$

$$\frac{\partial y}{\partial v_2} = (1 - a)\left(\frac{y}{v_2}\right)^{1+b} > 0 \tag{10}$$

These production functions are discussed again in Section 2.7.

STRICT QUASI-CONCAVITY AND THE DIMINISHING MARGINAL RATE OF FACTOR SUBSTITUTION

The models of production here assume that the production function is *strictly quasi-concave*, or, the level set of the production function is strictly convex. In other words, consider the various combinations of factor inputs for producing a fixed amount of the product. The graph of such combinations is called an *isoquant* and is shown in Figure 2.2.2. The models of production here assume that *the isoquant is strictly convex to the origin*.

Taking the differentials of (1) and setting $dy = 0$,

$$f_1 \, dv_1 + f_2 \, dv_2 = 0 \tag{11}$$

The *marginal rate of factor substitution* between factors 2 and 1, denoted by s, is the rate of change of factor 2 with respect to factor 1 along the isoquant. From (11),

$$s \equiv -\frac{dv_2}{dv_1} = \frac{f_1}{f_2} \tag{12}$$

This is the rate of increase in factor 2 required to maintain the same output when factor 1 is decreased. This rate is the negative of the slope of a tangent to the isoquant in Figure 2.2.2. Marginalist models of production assume that the *marginal rate of factor substitution smoothly diminishes as the input regarded as the independent variable is increased*. This is analogous to the assumption of a diminishing marginal rate of commodity substitution in consumption.

According to the theory in MR5 the bordered Hessian of the strictly quasi-concave production function satisfies the inequality

$$\begin{vmatrix} f_{11} & f_{12} & f_1 \\ f_{21} & f_{22} & f_2 \\ f_1 & f_2 & 0 \end{vmatrix} > 0$$

or

$$f_{11}f_2^2 - 2f_1 f_2 f_{12} + f_{22} f_1^2 < 0 \tag{13}$$

Figure 2.2.2

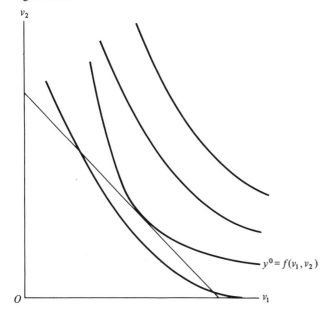

The production function can go through the stages of increasing and diminishing marginal productivity as shown in Figure 2.2.1. Marginal productivity is increasing between 0 and v_1', and decreasing thereafter. With respect to average productivity, y/v_1, it increases in the range 0 through v_1'', and decreases thereafter. Marginal productivity becomes negative after v_1'''.

STRICT CONCAVITY AND THE DIMINISHING RETURNS TO SCALE

A stronger assumption made concerning the production function (1) is that it is *strictly concave* as beyond v_1' in Figure 2.2.1. This implies not only the *diminishing marginal rate of factor substitution* but also the *law of decreasing returns to scale*, which means that multiplying both inputs by a number t which is greater than one results in output less than t times the original output. This is obvious from the definition of strict concavity in the Appendix. Furthermore, strict concavity implies that the Hessian matrix of the production function

$$\begin{bmatrix} f_{11} & f_{12} \\ f_{21} & f_{22} \end{bmatrix} \tag{14}$$

Figure 2.2.3

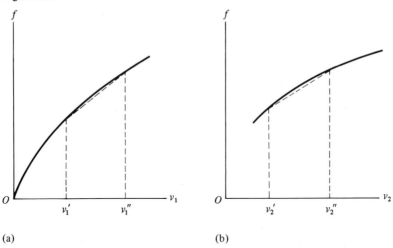

(a)   (b)

is negative definite. The necessary and sufficient condition for the negative definiteness of the Hessian matrix is that

$$f_{11} < 0 \qquad \begin{vmatrix} f_{11} & f_{12} \\ f_{21} & f_{22} \end{vmatrix} > 0 \tag{15}$$

or

$$f_{11} < 0 \qquad f_{22} < 0 \qquad f_{11}f_{22} - (f_{12})^2 > 0 \tag{16}$$

Hence strict concavity of the production function implies that the marginal product is diminishing. This has been called the *law of diminishing marginal productivity*.

Strict concavity implies strict quasi-concavity, but the latter does not imply the former.[2]

2.3 THE FIRM'S OPTIMUM

No matter what the level of output the firm wishes to produce it achieves an optimum by minimizing total cost of production. Let the level of output it wishes to produce be y^0, and the factor prices given by the markets be r_1 and r_2. Then the firm determines the factor inputs so as to minimize the total cost

$$C = r_1 v_1 + r_2 v_2 \tag{1}$$

subject to the technical constraint of the production function

$$f(v_1, v_2) = y^0 \tag{2}$$

[2] On empirical studies on production and cost functions, see Klein (1962), chap. 3.

Figure 2.3.1

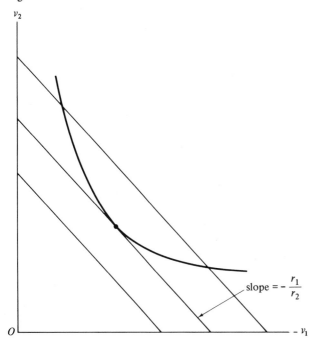

Various combinations of inputs for the given values of factor prices r_1, r_2, and cost C can be graphed as a straight line with the slope $-r_1/r_2$, as shown in Figure 2.3.1. A family of such straight lines can represent various levels of C. Each of these lines is called an *isocost line*. The farther away the isocost line is from the origin, the greater the cost it represents.

The Lagrangean function L for the minimization problem is

$$L = r_1 v_1 + r_2 v_2 + \lambda[y^0 - f(v_1, v_2)] \tag{3}$$

and the first-order condition is

$$\frac{\partial L}{\partial v_1} = r_1 - \lambda f_1 = 0 \tag{4}$$

$$\frac{\partial L}{\partial v_2} = r_2 - \lambda f_2 = 0 \tag{5}$$

$$\frac{\partial L}{\partial \lambda} = y^0 - f(v_1, v_2) = 0 \tag{6}$$

Equations (4), (5), and (6) are three equations in three unknowns v_1, v_2, and λ; from these the firm can determine the optimum values v_1, v_2, and λ, in terms of the given r_1, r_2, and y^0, provided that the condition of the implicit-function theorem is satisfied.[3] Then (1) determines C for each level of y^0. The expression for C as a function of r_1, r_2, and y is called the *total-cost function*, and can generally be written

$$C = C(r_1, r_2, y) \tag{7}$$

The producer's optimum conditions (4)–(6) imply

$$\frac{r_1}{f_1} = \frac{r_2}{f_2} (= \lambda) \tag{8}$$

In words, the firm must adjust factor inputs so that *the ratio of the price to marginal productivity will be the same for each factor*.

The λ in (8) is *marginal cost*, that is,

$$\frac{dC}{dy} = \lambda \tag{9}$$

in view of MR5.

Equation (8) can be rewritten, using (2.2.12):

$$\frac{r_1}{r_2} = s \tag{10}$$

That is, the producer will achieve optimum when he adjusts his inputs to those levels where *the marginal rate of factor substitution just equals the factor-price ratio*. When the factor-price ratio changes the firm will adjust inputs so as to maintain the above equality between the marginal rate of factor substitution and the factor-price ratio. In Figure 2.3.1 the equality (10) means that the lowest isocost line is tangential to the given isoquant.

The second-order condition for minimum is

$$\begin{vmatrix} L_{11} & L_{12} & -f_1 \\ L_{21} & L_{22} & -f_2 \\ -f_1 & -f_2 & 0 \end{vmatrix} < 0 \tag{11}$$

which can be written

$$\begin{vmatrix} -f_{11} & -f_{12} & -f_1 \\ -f_{21} & -f_{22} & -f_2 \\ -f_1 & -f_2 & 0 \end{vmatrix} < 0 \tag{12}$$

This implies

$$f_{11}f_2^2 - 2f_{12}f_1f_2 + f_{22}f_1^2 < 0 \tag{13}$$

---

[3] The Jacobian of the system (4)–(6) is nonzero by the second-order condition (11) below and the condition of the implicit-function theorem is satisfied.

which is the same as (2.2.13) for the quasi-concavity of the production function, or the *diminishing marginal rate of substitution*. In Figure 2.3.1 this means that the isoquant is convex to the origin at the point where the former touches the isocost line.

It can be shown that the cost function (7) is homogeneous of degree one in the factor prices, and an increasing function in the output. The unknown λ can be eliminated from (4) and (5) giving

$$\frac{f_1}{f_2} = \frac{r_1}{r_2}$$

This and (6) determine the optimum values of v_1 and v_2 for the minimization problem involving (1) and (2). Hence the values of v_1 and v_2 depend only on the factor price ratio r_1/r_2. Therefore, when r_1 and r_2 change by the same proportion in (1), v_1 and v_2 remain the same; C will rise by the same proportion. Hence *the cost function (7) is homogeneous of degree one in the factor prices*. From the assumption of positive marginal productivities, an increase in y calls for an increase in v_1 and/or v_2, which implies an increase in C in (1). Hence *the cost function (7) is an increasing function in y*.[4]

2.4 THE FIRM'S SUPPLY FUNCTION

SHORT RUN

In dealing with the cost function expressing total cost as a function of output, it is useful to consider two different time periods: short run and long run. The former has a fixed input independent of the level of output; in the latter all factor inputs are variable. In the short run the firm's problem is to minimize total cost

$$C = r_1 v_1 + r_2 v_2 + b \tag{1}$$

where b is the fixed cost due to the fixed input, subject to the constraint of the production function

$$y = f(v_1, v_2) \tag{2}$$

Solving the problem for v_1, v_2, and the Lagrangean multiplier in terms of r_1, r_2, and y will give a *cost function*

$$C = g(y) + b \tag{3}$$

The *average-cost function* is

$$\frac{C}{y} = \frac{g(y)}{y} + \frac{b}{y} \tag{4}$$

[4] On the producer's optimum, see Samuelson (1947), chap. 4; Hicks (1946), chaps. 6 and 7.

Figure 2.4.1

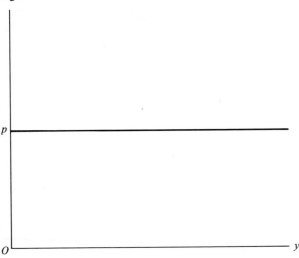

Figure 2.4.2

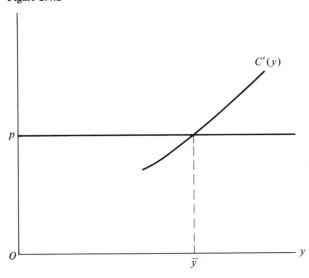

which is made up of the *average variable-cost function*

$$\frac{g(y)}{y} \qquad (5)$$

and the *average fixed-cost function*

$$\frac{b}{y} \qquad (6)$$

The *marginal-cost function* is

$$\frac{dC}{dy} = g'(y) \qquad (7)$$

The firm as a market agent is producing an optimum amount of output when it maximizes its profits, that is, the total revenue minus total cost, which can be written

$$\pi = py - g(y) - b \qquad (8)$$

The assumption that the firm regards the product prices p (and factor prices r_1 and r_2) as constant can be expressed by saying that the demand for its product is horizontal at p, as shown in Figure 2.4.1. Also profits in (8) are a function of output y alone.

For the firm to maximize its profits, the first-order condition is

$$\frac{d\pi}{dy} = p - g'(y) = 0$$

that is,

$$p = g'(y) \qquad (9)$$

Therefore, the firm should expand its production until *the marginal cost just equals the product price*. The optimum output is shown in Figure 2.4.2. The second-order condition for maximum profits is

$$\frac{d^2\pi}{dy^2} = -g''(y) < 0 \qquad (10)$$

that is

$$C'' > 0 \qquad (11)$$

Therefore, for optimum, the *marginal cost must be rising*.

THE FIRM'S SHORT-RUN SUPPLY FUNCTION

When the market price of the product changes, the firm will have to adjust its output to maintain the optimum. The function showing how the firm adjusts its output when the product price changes is called the firm's *supply function*.

Figure 2.4.3

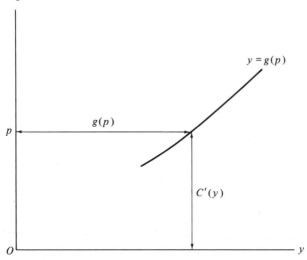

Equation (9) states this relationship implicitly. Equation (9) can be solved for y to obtain an explicit expression for y in terms of p, say

$$y = h(p) \tag{12}$$

This is the *supply function*. It is the inverse function of the rising portion of the marginal cost function (7), as shown in Figure 2.4.3. Therefore, it must be an increasing function of the price.

The following proposition has a bearing on the discussion in Section 4.7. In connection with average and marginal costs one can show that *when average cost is falling, average cost is above marginal cost.* For the falling average cost means

$$\frac{d}{dy}\left(\frac{C}{y}\right) = \frac{C'y - C}{y^2} < 0 \tag{13'}$$

That is,

$$\frac{C}{y} > C' \tag{13''}$$

If the firm equates marginal cost to the market price, then its profits will be negative. For

$$\pi = py - C$$
$$= C'y - C$$
$$= y\left(C' - \frac{C}{y}\right) < 0 \tag{13'''}$$

LONG RUN

Denote the plant size by k. The fixed cost associated with the plant size can be written $G(k)$. Then the firm's problem is to minimize

$$C = r_1 v_1 + r_2 v_2 + G(k) \qquad (14)$$

subject to the production function

$$y = F(v_1, v_2, k) \qquad (15)$$

The Lagrangean expression is

$$L = r_1 v_1 + r_2 v_2 + G(k) + \lambda[y - F(v_1, v_2, k)] \qquad (16)$$

The first-order condition is

$$\frac{\partial L}{\partial v_1} = r_1 - \lambda F_1 = 0 \qquad (17)$$

$$\frac{\partial L}{\partial v_2} = r_2 - \lambda F_2 = 0 \qquad (18)$$

$$\frac{\partial L}{\partial \lambda} = y - F(v_1, v_2, k) = 0 \qquad (19)$$

These three equations can be solved for each of v_1, v_2, and λ, in terms of r_1, r_2, k, and y. Assuming r_1 and r_2 to be constant, v_1 and v_2 can be expressed as a function of y and k. Hence the cost function (14) can be rewritten

$$C = H(y, k) + G(k) \qquad (20)$$

The long-run cost function $K(y)$ is an envelope of these short-run curves, as k is adjusted to minimize cost for each output.[5] To obtain the equation of the envelope, set the partial derivative of C with respect to k equal to zero:

$$\frac{\partial C}{\partial k} = 0 \qquad (21)$$

Solve (21) for k in terms of y, and substitute it in (20). Then C can be expressed as a function of y, giving the long-run cost function:

$$C = K(y) \qquad (22)$$

The long-run marginal-cost curve is

$$\frac{dC}{dy} = K'(y) \qquad (23)$$

[5] See Allen (1932), Samuelson (1947), p. 34.

As in the short run, the long-run marginal-cost curve will represent the long-run supply curve of the producer.

Example

Let the family of short-run cost functions be written

$$C = ay^3 - by^2 + (c - k)y + dk^2 \qquad (24)$$

with the restriction

$$b^2 < 3ac \qquad (25)$$

The last term represents the short-run fixed cost associated with the plant size. Set the partial derivative of C with respect to k equal to zero:

$$y - 2\,dk = 0 \quad \text{or} \quad k = \frac{y}{2d} \qquad (26)$$

This equation gives the plant size as a function of output. Substituting into (24) gives the long-run cost function

$$C = ay^3 - \left[b + \frac{1}{4d}\right]y^2 + cy \qquad (27)$$

The long-run marginal cost is

$$\frac{dC}{dy} = 3ay^2 - 2\left[b + \frac{1}{4d}\right]y + c \qquad (28)$$

If the price of the product is p, the producer will set y so that marginal cost equals p:

$$\frac{dC}{dy} = p \qquad (29)$$

that is, by solving (29) for y which maximizes profit. Let this solution be y^*. Then the optimum plant size is from (26)

$$k^* = \frac{y^*}{2d} \qquad (30)$$

The short-run cost function corresponding to this plant size is from (24)

$$C^* = ay^3 - by^2 + (c - k^*)y + (dk^*)^2 \qquad (31)$$

The profit per short-run period is

$$\pi = py - C^* \qquad (32)$$

Whether this size plant will be constructed or not will depend on whether π in (32) corresponding to the given p is positive or not.[6]

---

[6] On the supply functions of the firm, see Viner (1931).

2.5   FACTOR DEMAND AND PRODUCT SUPPLY

The profits in (2.4.7) can be rewritten

$$\pi = p \cdot f(v_1, v_2) - r_1 v_1 - r_2 v_2 \tag{1}$$

The firm controls π by controlling v_1 and v_2. The necessary condition for maximum profits is

$$\frac{\partial \pi}{\partial v_1} = p f_1 - r_1 = 0 \qquad p f_1 = r_1 \tag{2}$$

$$\frac{\partial \pi}{\partial v_2} = p f_2 - r_2 = 0 \qquad p f_2 = r_2 \tag{3}$$

The product price multiplied by the marginal product of a factor is called the *value of marginal product* of the factor. Equations (2) and (3) state that for optimum, *the value of marginal product must equal the factor price.* They imply

$$\frac{r_1}{f_1} = \frac{r_2}{f_2} = p \tag{4}$$

The factor price divided by the marginal product is marginal cost in view of (2.3.8) and (2.3.9). Hence, for optimum, *marginal cost is equal in terms of each factor, and the equalized marginal cost is equal to the product price.* This result, based on the production function, is the same as (2.4.9) derived from the cost function. The marginal productivities f_1 and f_2 in (2) and (3) are functions of v_1 and v_2. Hence they make up a system of two equations in two unknowns v_1 and v_2, and, because the Jacobian determinant is nonzero by (9) below, can be solved in terms of the parameters r_1, r_2, and p, to yield the *demand functions* for the two factors:

$$v_1^* = g(p, r_1, r_2) \qquad v_2^* = h(p, r_1, r_2) \tag{5}$$

and the product-supply function

$$y^* \equiv f(v_1^*, v_2^*) \equiv F(p, r_1, r_2) \tag{6}$$

The second-order sufficient condition for maximum profits is

$$\pi_{11} < 0 \qquad \begin{vmatrix} \pi_{11} & \pi_{12} \\ \pi_{12} & \pi_{22} \end{vmatrix} > 0 \tag{7}$$

This implies

$$\pi_{22} < 0 \tag{8}$$

That is, marginal profits of each factor are decreasing.

The inequalities in (7) and (8) can be restated in terms of f. From (2) and (3),

$$\pi_{11} = pf_{11} \qquad \pi_{12} = pf_{12}$$
$$\pi_{21} = pf_{21} \qquad \pi_{22} = pf_{22}$$

Therefore

$$f_{11} < 0 \qquad \begin{vmatrix} f_{11} & f_{12} \\ f_{21} & f_{22} \end{vmatrix} > 0 \tag{9}$$

which imply

$$f_{11} < 0 \qquad f_{22} < 0 \qquad f_{11}f_{22} - (f_{12})^2 > 0 \tag{10}$$

This is the same as (2.2.16) for the strict concavity of the production function, implying diminishing returns to scale and diminishing marginal rate of substitution (also the diminishing returns to each factor).[7]

PROPERTIES OF FACTOR-DEMAND AND PRODUCT-SUPPLY FUNCTIONS

The model can provide some properties of the factor-demand functions (5). Equations (2) and (3) can be written

$$f_1 = \frac{r_1}{p} \tag{11}$$

$$f_2 = \frac{r_2}{p} \tag{12}$$

Thus v_1 and v_2 depend only on r_1/p and r_2/p. Therefore, doubling all prices does not affect the solution values of v_1 and v_2. Therefore, the *factor-demand functions are homogeneous of degree zero in the product and factor prices*. Since doubling all prices does not change v_1^* and v_2^* in (6), *the product-supply function F is also homogeneous of degree zero in the product and factor prices*.

---

[7] A famous proposition in macroeconomics concerning demand for labor is "the wage is equal to the marginal product of labor." Keynes (1936), p. 5. This particular proposition can be obtained by rewriting, say, (2) as

$$f_1 = \frac{r_1}{p}$$

The left-hand side is the marginal product of labor, while the right-hand side represents the real wage. Of course, f must be regarded as an aggregate production function, expressing the aggregate output as a function of aggregate input of labor.

COMPARATIVE STATICS

Substituting (5) in the optimality conditions (11) and (12) gives identities

$$\frac{\partial f(v_1^*, v_2^*)}{\partial v_1} \equiv \frac{r_1}{p} \tag{13}$$

$$\frac{\partial f(v_1^*, v_2^*)}{\partial v_2} \equiv \frac{r_2}{p} \tag{14}$$

To obtain the effects of a change in the *product price*, partially differentiate (13) and (14) with respect to p:

$$f_{11} \cdot \frac{\partial v_1^*}{\partial p} + f_{12} \cdot \frac{\partial v_2^*}{\partial p} = -\frac{r_1}{p^2} = -\frac{f_1}{p} \tag{15}$$

$$f_{21} \cdot \frac{\partial v_1^*}{\partial p} + f_{22} \cdot \frac{\partial v_2^*}{\partial p} = -\frac{r_2}{p^2} = -\frac{f_2}{p} \tag{16}$$

In matrix notation

$$\begin{bmatrix} f_{11} & f_{12} \\ f_{21} & f_{22} \end{bmatrix} \begin{bmatrix} \dfrac{\partial v_1^*}{\partial p} \\ \dfrac{\partial v_2^*}{\partial p} \end{bmatrix} = \begin{bmatrix} -\dfrac{f_1}{p} \\ -\dfrac{f_2}{p} \end{bmatrix} \tag{17}$$

where the determinant of the coefficient matrix is positive by (9). Hence

$$\frac{\partial v_1^*}{\partial p} = \begin{vmatrix} -\dfrac{f_1}{p} & f_{12} \\ -\dfrac{f_2}{p} & f_{22} \end{vmatrix} \div \begin{vmatrix} f_{11} & f_{12} \\ f_{21} & f_{22} \end{vmatrix} \tag{18}$$

$$\frac{\partial v_2^*}{\partial p} = \begin{vmatrix} f_{11} & -\dfrac{f_1}{p} \\ f_{21} & -\dfrac{f_2}{p} \end{vmatrix} \div \begin{vmatrix} f_{11} & f_{12} \\ f_{21} & f_{22} \end{vmatrix} \tag{19}$$

Differentiating (6) with respect to p,

$$\frac{\partial y^*}{\partial p} = f_1 \cdot \frac{\partial v_1^*}{\partial p} + f_2 \cdot \frac{\partial v_2^*}{\partial p} \tag{20}$$

Substituting from (18) and (19),

$$\frac{\partial y^*}{\partial p} = \frac{\frac{1}{p} f(-f_1^2 f_{22} - f_2^2 f_{11} + 2 f_1 f_2 f_{12})}{\begin{vmatrix} f_{11} & f_{12} \\ f_{21} & f_{22} \end{vmatrix}}$$

From (2.3.13) and (9), the right-hand side is positive. Hence

$$\frac{\partial y^*}{\partial p} > 0$$

That is, *a rise in the product price brings about an increase in product supply.* Since the right-hand side of (20) is thus positive and f_1 and f_2 are positive, at least one of $\partial v_1^*/\partial p$ is positive. That is, *a rise in the product price increases the demand for some inputs.*

To obtain the effect of a change in a factor price, differentiate (13) and (14) with respect to r_1, obtaining

$$f_{11} \cdot \frac{\partial v_1^*}{\partial r_1} + f_{12} \cdot \frac{\partial v_2^*}{\partial r_1} = \frac{1}{p} \tag{21}$$

$$f_{21} \cdot \frac{\partial v_1^*}{\partial r_1} + f_{22} \cdot \frac{\partial v_2^*}{\partial r_1} = 0 \tag{22}$$

That is,

$$\begin{bmatrix} f_{11} & f_{12} \\ f_{21} & f_{22} \end{bmatrix} \begin{bmatrix} \dfrac{\partial v_1^*}{\partial r_1} \\ \dfrac{\partial v_2^*}{\partial r_1} \end{bmatrix} = \begin{bmatrix} \dfrac{1}{p} \\ 0 \end{bmatrix} \tag{23}$$

Hence

$$\frac{\partial v_1^*}{\partial r_1} = \begin{vmatrix} \frac{1}{p} & f_{12} \\ 0 & f_{22} \end{vmatrix} \div \begin{vmatrix} f_{11} & f_{12} \\ f_{21} & f_{22} \end{vmatrix} \qquad \text{also} \qquad \frac{\partial v_2^*}{\partial r_2} = \begin{vmatrix} f_{11} & 0 \\ f_{21} & \frac{1}{p} \end{vmatrix} \div \begin{vmatrix} f_{11} & f_{12} \\ f_{21} & f_{22} \end{vmatrix} \tag{24}$$

$$\frac{\partial v_2^*}{\partial r_1} = \begin{vmatrix} f_{11} & \frac{1}{p} \\ f_{21} & 0 \end{vmatrix} \div \begin{vmatrix} f_{11} & f_{12} \\ f_{21} & f_{22} \end{vmatrix} \qquad \text{also} \qquad \frac{\partial v_1^*}{\partial r_2} = \begin{vmatrix} 0 & f_{12} \\ \frac{1}{p} & f_{22} \end{vmatrix} \div \begin{vmatrix} f_{11} & f_{12} \\ f_{21} & f_{22} \end{vmatrix} \tag{25}$$

Hence, from (9) and (10)

$$\frac{\partial v_1^*}{\partial r_1} < 0 \qquad \frac{\partial v_2^*}{\partial r_2} < 0 \tag{26}$$

A rise in a factor price causes a fall in the profit-maximizing demand for it. The cross effects of input prices on input demands are symmetrical. The knowledge of the sign of f_{12} is needed to determine the sign of $\partial v_2^*/\partial r_1$. From (24), (25), and (18),

$$\frac{\partial y^*}{\partial r_1} = f_1 \frac{\partial v_1^*}{\partial r_1} + f_2 \frac{\partial v_2^*}{\partial r_1} = -\frac{\partial v_1^*}{\partial p} \qquad \frac{\partial y^*}{\partial r_2} = -\frac{\partial v_2^*}{\partial p} \qquad (27)$$

Thus *an increase in a factor price reduces optimum output if an increase in product price raises the demand for the factor.* The input price effects on output and output price effects on input are symmetrical.

Substituting (27) into (20),

$$\frac{\partial y^*}{\partial p} = -\left(f_1 \frac{\partial y^*}{\partial r_1} + f_2 \frac{\partial y^*}{\partial r_2} \right) \qquad (28)$$

Since the left-hand side is positive, and f_i are positive, *at least one of $\partial y^*/\partial r_i$ must be negative* in the general case of two or more goods.

WHEN A FACTOR IS NOT TO BE EMPLOYED

The preceding model must be modified in order to take into account the possibility of a factor not being used at all. Equations (2) and (3) must be written

$$\frac{\partial L}{\partial v_i} = pf_i - r_i = 0 \qquad \text{for } v_i > 0$$

$$\leqq 0 \qquad \text{for } v_i = 0$$

In the case of Figure 2.5.1,

$$\frac{\partial L}{\partial v_1} = pf_1 - r_1 = 0 \qquad \text{for } v_1 > 0$$

$$\frac{\partial L}{\partial v_2} = pf_2 - r_2 \leqq 0 \qquad \text{for } v_2 = 0$$

The value of marginal product does not exceed the factor price for factor 2. The preceding two expressions imply

$$\frac{f_1}{f_2} \geqq \frac{r_1}{r_2}$$

The price ratio does not exceed the marginal rate of factor substitution, which is also clear from the figure.

Figure 2.5.1

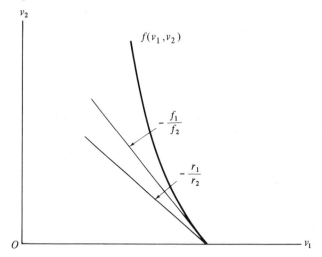

WHEN A SPECIALIZED FACTOR EXISTS

The preceding model must be modified also if one of the factors, say factor 2, is specialized and therefore is not priced in the market while limited in supply. Then the problem becomes: maximize

$$\pi = pf(v_1, v_2) - r_1 v_1$$

subject to

$$v_2 \leqq \bar{v}_2$$

The Lagrangean in this case is

$$L = pf(v_1, v_2) - r_1 v_1 + \lambda(\bar{v}_2 - v_2)$$

The first-order condition is

$$\frac{\partial L}{\partial v_1} = pf_1 - r_1 = 0 \qquad \text{if } v_1 > 0$$

$$\frac{\partial L}{\partial v_2} = pf_2 - \lambda = 0 \qquad \text{if } v_2 > 0$$

$$\frac{\partial L}{\partial \lambda} = (\bar{v}_2 - v_2) = 0 \qquad \text{if } \lambda > 0$$

$$\geqq 0 \qquad \text{if } \lambda = 0$$

That is, the value of marginal product of factor 1 equals the price of factor 1; the shadow price of factor 2 is equal to the value of the marginal product of the factor; if the shadow price is positive, the specialized factor is completely used up; if the shadow price is zero, the factor used does not exceed the available supply.

2.6 PRODUCT TRANSFORMATION

Consider a firm that produces two products, say wool (y_1) and mutton (y_2), using one factor, say labor (v). Denote its *implicit production function* by

$$f(y_1, y_2, v) = 0 \tag{1}$$

Equation (1) denotes the relation among output of one product, output of the other product, and input of the factor, assuming that production is *efficient* in the sense that no output can be increased without increasing input and that input cannot be decreased without decreasing at least one output. Equation (1) is assumed to be solvable explicitly for v:

$$v = g(y_1, y_2) \tag{2}$$

Figure 2.6.1

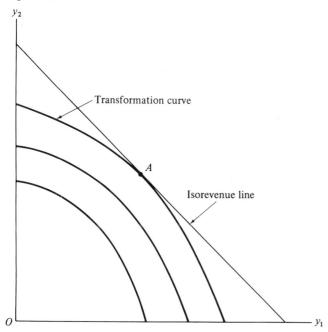

which gives the cost of producing various combinations of two outputs, wool and mutton, in terms of the factor, labor. For a fixed level of the factor input v^0,

$$v^0 = g(y_1, y_2) \tag{3}$$

This equation gives a *transformation curve*, giving the level of one output producible given the level of the other output.

The *transformation function* (2) is assumed to be strictly quasi-convex. According to MR5, this means that the bordered Hessian of g is negative, that is,

$$\begin{vmatrix} g_{11} & g_{12} & g_1 \\ g_{21} & g_{22} & g_2 \\ g_1 & g_2 & 0 \end{vmatrix} < 0 \tag{3'}$$

The strict quasi-convexity means that the graph of equation (3), called the *production-possibility frontier* or *transformation curve*, is strictly concave to the origin, as in Figure 2.6.1, or alternatively, the marginal rate of transformation is increasing.

The *marginal rate of transformation* is the rate of change of one output with respect to the other output holding the factor input constant, that is,

$$t = -\frac{dy_2}{dy_1} \tag{4}$$

It can be obtained by taking the total differential of (3)

$$g_1 \, dy_1 + g_2 \, dy_2 = 0 \tag{5}$$

and deriving the derivative

$$-\frac{dy_2}{dy_1} = \frac{g_1}{g_2} \tag{6}$$

The partial derivatives in (6) represent *marginal costs* of products 1 and 2 in terms of the factor. Equation (6) can be written

$$-\frac{dy_2}{dy_1} = \frac{\dfrac{\partial y_2}{\partial v}}{\dfrac{\partial y_1}{\partial v}} \tag{7}$$

since from (2)

$$dv = g_1 \, dy_1 + g_2 \, dy_2$$

and therefore

$$\frac{\partial y_1}{\partial v} = \frac{1}{g_1} \qquad \frac{\partial y_2}{\partial v} = \frac{1}{g_2} \tag{8}$$

each of which represents the *marginal productivity* of the factor in the production of each good.

The quasi-convexity means that the marginal rate of transformation is increasing. That is,

$$\frac{dt}{dy_1} = \frac{g_1^2 g_{22} + g_2^2 g_{11} - 2g_1 g_2 g_{12}}{g_2^3} > 0 \tag{9}$$

That is,

$$-g_1^2 g_{22} - g_2^2 g_{11} + 2g_1 g_2 g_{12} < 0 \tag{10}$$

as in (3').

A stronger assumption is that the transformation function is strictly convex. In this case the Hessian matrix of g

$$\begin{bmatrix} g_{11} & g_{12} \\ g_{21} & g_{22} \end{bmatrix}$$

is positive definite. In this case, not only is the production-possibility frontier strictly concave to the origin, but also marginal costs g_i are increasing, that is, g_{ii} are positive.

The firm achieves an optimum when it maximizes its revenue for a given level of input v^0 whose price is r. Its objective function is then profits

$$\pi = p_1 y_1 + p_2 y_2 - rg(y_1, y_2) \tag{11}$$

which must be maximized. The first-order condition is

$$p_1 - rg_1 = 0 \quad \text{or} \quad p_1 = rg_1 \tag{12}$$
$$p_2 - rg_2 = 0 \quad \text{or} \quad p_2 = rg_2 \tag{13}$$

Thus *the price is equal to marginal cost for each product.* Dividing (12) by (13) yields

$$\frac{p_1}{p_2} = \frac{g_1}{g_2} \tag{14}$$

that is, *the marginal rate of transformation must be equal to the price ratio,* as at A in Figure 2.6.1. At A, the *iso-revenue line* corresponding to the given prices p_1 and p_2 is tangential to the transformation curve corresponding to the given factor input v_0.

Second-order conditions require (see MR5)

$$-rg_{11} < 0 \quad -rg_{22} < 0 \quad \begin{vmatrix} -rg_{11} & -rg_{12} \\ -rg_{21} & -rg_{22} \end{vmatrix} > 0 \tag{15}$$

These conditions imply

$$g_{11} > 0 \quad g_{22} > 0 \quad g_{11}g_{22} - (g_{12})^2 > 0 \tag{16}$$

The transformation function (2) is strictly convex. Not only the marginal rate of transformation increases, but the marginal cost of each output in terms of the input is rising.

WHEN A PRODUCT IS NOT TO BE PRODUCED

A model allowing for the possibility of a product not produced must replace equations (12) and (13) by

$$\frac{\partial \pi}{\partial y_i} = p_i - rg_i \leq 0 \qquad \text{for } y_i = 0$$

or

$$= 0 \qquad \text{for } y_i > 0$$

The expression rg_i can be interpreted as the marginal cost as in (12) and therefore, *for the product not produced, the product price does not exceed the marginal cost.* In the case of Figure 2.6.2,

$$\frac{\partial \pi}{\partial y_1} = p_1 - \lambda g_1 = 0 \qquad \text{for } y_1 > 0$$

and

$$\frac{\partial \pi}{\partial y_2} = p_2 - \lambda g_2 \leq 0 \qquad \text{for } y_2 = 0$$

Figure 2.6.2

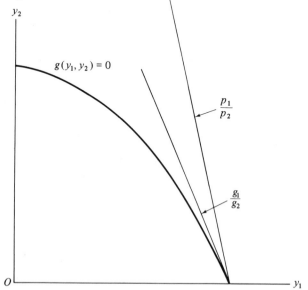

Hence

$$\frac{p_1}{p_2} \geqq \frac{g_1}{g_2}$$

That is, *the marginal rate of transformation does not exceed the price ratio.*

SUMMARY

What has preceded can be summarized in the following model of a producer producing two products using two factors. Let the firm's production function be written

$$F(y_1, y_2, y_3, y_4) = 0 \qquad F_i > 0 \qquad i = 1, \ldots, 4 \tag{17}$$

where $y_3 = -v_1$, and $y_4 = -v_2$ denote net outputs which are negative (indicating that they are inputs).[8] The profits of the firm is

$$\pi = p_1 y_1 + p_2 y_2 + p_3 y_3 + p_4 y_4 \tag{18}$$

The Lagrangean function for its maximization problem is

$$L = p_1 y_1 + p_2 y_2 + p_3 y_3 + p_4 y_4 - \lambda F \tag{19}$$

The first-order condition is

$$\frac{\partial L}{\partial y_1} = p_1 - \lambda F_1 = 0 \tag{20}$$

$$\frac{\partial L}{\partial y_2} = p_2 - \lambda F_2 = 0 \tag{21}$$

$$\frac{\partial L}{\partial y_3} = p_3 - \lambda F_3 = 0 \tag{22}$$

$$\frac{\partial L}{\partial y_4} = p_4 - \lambda F_4 = 0 \tag{23}$$

which give the following equations:

$$\frac{F_1}{F_2} = \frac{p_1}{p_2} \tag{24}$$

$$\frac{F_3}{F_4} = \frac{p_3}{p_4} \tag{25}$$

[8] The viewpoint taken here is that the firm is *supplied* with $V_i(=0)$ units of good i and *consumes* v_i units of it. Therefore, its *net supply or output* is $-v_i$, which is negative.

$$\frac{F_3}{F_1} = \frac{p_3}{p_1} \tag{26}$$

$$\frac{F_3}{F_2} = \frac{p_3}{p_2} \tag{27}$$

$$\frac{F_4}{F_1} = \frac{p_4}{p_1} \tag{28}$$

$$\frac{F_4}{F_2} = \frac{p_4}{p_2} \tag{29}$$

Solving five equations (17), (20)–(23) for five unknowns y_1, y_2, y_3, y_4, and λ gives the supply functions for products, and the demand functions for factors. The forms of these equations make it clear that *these demand and supply functions are homogeneous of degree zero in the product and factor prices.*

Equations (24)–(29) state that the marginal rate of transformation between the products is equal to the product-price ratio, and the marginal rate of substitution between the two factors is equal to the factor-price ratio. The marginal rate of transformation of factor 1 into product 1 is equal to the factor-product-price ratio, and similar equalities hold between product 2 and factor 1, between product 1 and factor 2, between product 2 and factor 2.

2.7 DISTRIBUTION

Factor 1's share in the value of the total output is $v_1 r_1$. Similarly factor 2's share in the value of total output is $v_2 r_2$. Will they add up to the value of total output pf so that the product will be just exhausted by distribution?

A production function $f(v_1, v_2)$ represents *constant returns to scale* if for any number $t > 1$,

$$f(tv_1, tv_2) = tf(v_1, v_2) \tag{1}$$

This means, for example, that the doubling of each input results in a doubling of output. Mathematically speaking, the function is homogeneous of degree one.

When the production function follows the rule of constant returns to scale if each input is paid its marginal product, then the total output is exactly exhausted. That is,

$$f_1 v_1 + f_2 v_2 = f \tag{2}$$

This follows from Euler's theorem concerning homogenous functions.[9] Multiplying (2) through by the outprice p, yields

$$pf_1 v_1 + pf_2 v_2 = pf \tag{3}$$

[9] See MR6.

In view of (2.5.2) and (2.5.3), equation (3) shows that the value of total output is just exhausted

If the production function has the property that, for $t > 1$,

$$f(tv_1, tv_2) > tf(v_1, v_2)$$

then it is said to follow the law of *increasing returns to scale*. It has already been said that production follows the law of *decreasing returns to scale* if the inequality is reversed, that is,

$$f(tv_1, tv_2) < tf(v_1, v_2)$$

ELASTICITY OF SUBSTITUTION

When the relative factor-prices change, one factor is substituted for another so as to maintain the equality between the factor-price ratio and the marginal rate of substitution. The extent of substitution of inputs in the production function is measured by the elasticity of substitution, which is defined by

$$\sigma \equiv \frac{d\left(\frac{v_2}{v_1}\right)}{\left(\frac{v_2}{v_1}\right)} = \frac{d\ln\left(\frac{v_2}{v_1}\right)}{d\ln s} \tag{4}$$

where s is the marginal rate of substitution along an isoquant, and is f_1/f_2 in magnitude. (It should be recalled that in equilibrium this marginal rate of substitution equals the factor-price ratio r_1/r_2.) Hence (4) can be rewritten

$$\sigma \equiv \frac{\dfrac{d\left(\frac{v_2}{v_1}\right)}{\left(\frac{v_2}{v_1}\right)}}{\dfrac{d\left(\frac{f_1}{f_2}\right)}{\left(\frac{f_1}{f_2}\right)}} = \frac{d\ln\left(\frac{v_2}{v_1}\right)}{d\ln\left(\frac{f_1}{f_2}\right)} \tag{5}$$

Now the ratio between the shares of input 2 and input 1 along the isoquant when each input is paid the value of its marginal product is

$$\frac{pf_2 v_2}{pf_1 v_1} = \frac{f_2 v_2}{f_1 v_1} = \frac{\dfrac{v_2}{v_1}}{\dfrac{f_1}{f_2}} \tag{6}$$

In view of (5), the share ratio in (6) increases, remains constant, or decreases, depending upon whether

$$\sigma \gtreqless 1 \tag{7}$$

For example, if $\sigma > 1$, the proportionate rate of increase of the numerator (v_2/v_1) in equation (6) is greater than that of the denominator (f_1/f_2) when r_1/r_2 is changed. Hence as v_1 is decreased and v_2 is increased, the distribution shifts toward the plentiful input v_2. If, on the other hand $\sigma < 1$ the proportionate rate of increase of the numerator (v_2/v_1) in equation (6) is smaller than that of the denominator (f_1/f_2) when r_1/r_2 changes. Hence as v_1 is decreased and v_2 is increased, the distribution shifts toward the scarce input v_1. When $\sigma = 1$, there is no change in the income shares of the inputs.

COBB-DOUGLAS PRODUCTION FUNCTION

For the Cobb-Douglas production function, Section 2.2 showed

$$s = \frac{a}{1-a} \frac{v_2}{v_1}$$

Hence

$$\frac{v_2}{v_1} = \frac{1-a}{a} s$$

$$\ln \frac{v_2}{v_1} = \ln \left(\frac{1-a}{a} \right) + \ln s$$

$$\sigma = \frac{d \ln \left(\dfrac{v_2}{v_1} \right)}{d \ln s} = 1$$

Thus as input 1 is increased and input 2 is decreased along an isoquant, the resulting changes in their marginal products leave their income shares constant.

CES PRODUCTION FUNCTION

The CES production function can be written

$$y = [av_1^{(\sigma-1)/\sigma} + (1-a)v_2^{(\sigma-1)/\sigma}]^{\sigma/(\sigma-1)}$$

where a, $\sigma > 0$. The marginal productivities are

$$\frac{\partial y}{\partial v_1} = \frac{\sigma}{\sigma-1} \left[\quad \right]^{[\sigma/(\sigma-1)]-1} a \frac{\sigma-1}{\sigma} v_1^{[(\sigma-1)/\sigma]-1}$$

$$= a \left[\quad \right]^{1/(\sigma-1)} v_1^{-1/\sigma} \left(= ay^{1/\sigma}v_1^{-1/\sigma} = a\left(\frac{y}{v_1}\right)^{1/\sigma} \right)$$

$$\frac{\partial y}{\partial v_2} = (1-a) \left[\quad \right]^{1/(\sigma-1)} v_2^{-1/\sigma} \left(= (1-a)\left(\frac{y}{v_2}\right)^{1/\sigma} \right)$$

Hence

$$s = \frac{a}{1-a} \left(\frac{v_2}{v_1}\right)^{1/\sigma}$$

That is,

$$\frac{v_2}{v_1} = \left(s\frac{1-a}{a}\right)^{\sigma}$$

$$\ln\left(\frac{v_2}{v_1}\right) = \sigma\left(\ln s + \ln\frac{1-a}{a}\right)$$

$$\frac{d\ln\left(\frac{v_2}{v_1}\right)}{d\ln s} = \sigma$$

Thus the elasticity of substitution is the constant σ.[10]

2.8 SUMMARY

The marginalist model of the firm assumes that in the neighborhood of equilibrium the production function is strictly concave; that is, not only the isoquant is convex to the origin, but also the marginal productivity is diminishing. The firm maximizes its profits with respect to the price system when it equates the value of marginal product to the factor prices, or equates the marginal rate of factor substitution to the price ratio. These equilibrium conditions provide the firm's product-supply and factor-demand functions that are

[10] On the elasticity of substitution, and the CES production function, see Allen (1938), chap. 12; and Arrow *et al.* (1961).

zero-degree homogeneous in the product and factor prices. For a multiproduct firm, it is assumed that the transformation function is strictly convex; that is, not only the transformation curve is concave to the origin, but also the marginal cost of each product in terms of the factor is rising. Equilibrium is reached when marginal cost is equal to price for each product, or the marginal rate of transformation is equal to the product-price ratio.

The cost-minimizing behavior of the firm under the given technology yields the cost function expressing the cost as a function of the product output. In terms of the cost function, the firm reaches equilibrium when the marginal cost is equal to the product price.

3
MODELS OF THE
COMPETITIVE MARKET

3.1 INTRODUCTION

The preceding two chapters examined the consumer's demand and supply of goods and the firm's demand and supply of goods, assuming each economic unit takes the prices of the goods as given. This chapter examines the determination of the price and quantity of a good that will be traded when these two groups of consumers and firms meet in a single market. By determining how much of the particular good will be demanded and supplied at what price, this chapter provides the partial equilibrium theory of the allocative function of the pricing system.

One of the most important concepts in price theory is that of *perfect competition*. The term has a specialized meaning peculiar to economics. If each buyer takes the market price as a given parameter, perfect competition is said to prevail on the buyer's side. If the buyer's purchase is very small relative to the total market, he cannot influence the price that will prevail in the market. Hence such a buyer plans his buying assuming that he cannot influence the market price by varying the amount he buys. Similarly, when the seller takes the market price as a given parameter, perfect competition is said to prevail on the seller's side. This can occur when the seller's sale is very small relative to the total market.

Other conditions that have been associated with perfect competition are *complete homogeneity* of the good being traded, *perfect knowledge* on the part of both the buyer and the seller regarding the markets, and *free mobility* of factors of production into and out of various productive activities.[1]

Chapters 3 and 4 assume that

- The consumers are all perfectly competitive buyers of products, and sellers of factors.
- The firms are all perfectly competitive sellers of products, and buyers of factors.

3.2 A STATIC MODEL OF A COMPETITIVE MARKET

Section 1.3 has shown that an individual's demand function is a function of prices and his income. In the static exchange economy an individual's disposable income is obtained by multiplying his initial holdings of goods (both products and factors) by their prices. Given the initial holdings of goods his income is a function of prices alone and the function is homogeneous of degree one.

Figure 3.2.1

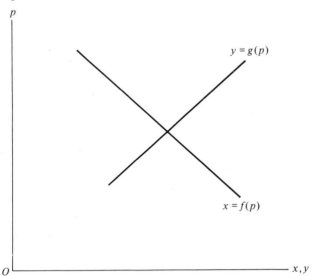

---

[1] Regarding what has been called a competitive solution to the resource allocation problem in socialist states see, for example, Bergson (1948).

Thus *an individual's demand can be regarded as a function of prices alone*, and furthermore, the function is homogeneous of degree zero in all prices. If not only exchange but also production in the economy is to be considered, this argument has to be made more elaborate by taking into account the consumer's share in the profits of the firms, as is done in Section 11.5. This chapter considers a single market, disregarding all other markets.

Assuming the prices of other commodities to be constant, the consumer's demand for a commodity is a function of its own price alone. When the buyers are all price-takers the market demand obtained as the sum of individual demands is a function of the price alone. This market demand function can be written

$$x = f(p) \tag{1}$$

where x denotes the quantity demanded, and p the price of the commodity. From the law of demand derived for the consumer in Section 1.4, under normal circumstances, the higher the price, the smaller the demand; mathematically

$$f' < 0 \tag{2}$$

This function is shown in Figure 3.2.1.

Other factors such as changes in the consumer's tastes, which mean changes in the preference maps and utility functions, affect the market demand function (1). In the interest of simplicity all these factors can be denoted by a parameter α whose increase means a rightward shift of the demand function; that is, an increase in x at the same level of p. Then (1) can be rewritten

$$x = f(p, \alpha) \qquad f_p < 0 \qquad f_\alpha > 0 \tag{3}$$

Similarly, where perfect competition prevails among sellers, the market supply function can be written

$$y = g(p, \beta) \qquad g_p > 0 \qquad g_\beta > 0 \tag{4}$$

where β is a shift parameter similar to α. It represents the effect of such factors as changes in technology, which in turn mean changes in the firm's production and supply functions.

In equilibrium, the quantity demanded equals the quantity supplied:

$$x = y \tag{5}$$

To analyze the effect of shifts of the demand and supply functions, use (5) in (4), and take the differentials of (3) and (4), as follows:

$$dx = f_p \, dp + f_\alpha \, d\alpha \tag{6}$$

$$dx = g_p \, dp + g_\beta \, d\beta \tag{7}$$

These equations can be written as a set of linear equations in dx and dp:

$$dx - f_p\, dp = f_\alpha\, d\alpha \tag{8}$$

$$dx - g_p\, dp = g_\beta\, d\beta \tag{9}$$

Using Cramer's rule,

$$dp = \frac{g_\beta\, d\beta - f_\alpha d\alpha}{f_p - g_p} \tag{10}$$

Setting $d\beta = 0$ and dividing both sides by $d\alpha$,

$$\frac{\partial p}{\partial \alpha} = \frac{-f_\alpha}{f_p - g_p} > 0 \tag{11}$$

In view of the assumed signs of the partial derivatives in the right-hand side of (11), the partial derivative in the left-hand side of (11) is positive. Thus, if demand rises (that is, if the quantity demanded at the same price level increases), then the price will increase, and vice versa. By setting $d\alpha = 0$ and dividing both sides of (10) by $d\beta$, and taking into account the signs of the partial derivatives in (3) and (4),

$$\frac{\partial p}{\partial \beta} = \frac{g_\beta}{f_p - g_p} < 0 \tag{12}$$

Thus, if the supply function shifts to the right (that is, if the quantity supplied at the same price level increases), then the price will fall, and vice versa.

The effects of exogenous factors upon the equilibrium quantity can be evaluated by solving (8) and (9) for dx, and computing the appropriate partial derivatives, as follows:

$$dx = \frac{f_p g_\beta\, d\beta - f_\alpha g_p\, d\alpha}{f_p - g_p} \tag{13}$$

Setting $d\beta = 0$,

$$\frac{\partial x}{\partial \alpha} = \frac{-f_\alpha g_p}{f_p - g_p} > 0 \tag{14}$$

Setting $d\alpha = 0$,

$$\frac{\partial x}{\partial \beta} = \frac{f_p g_\beta}{f_p - g_p} > 0 \tag{15}$$

The quantity traded increases when the demand and/or supply functions shift to the right.[2]

---

[2] On the comparative statics of market equilibrium, see Samuelson (1947), pp. 17–19.

SHIFTING OF THE EXCISE TAX AND SUBSIDY

The partial equilibrium analysis of this section can be applied to the shifting of an excise tax. Let the demand function be

$$x = f(p^b) \qquad f' < 0 \tag{16}$$

where p^b is the market price that the buyer pays. Let the supply function be

$$y = g(p^s) \qquad g' > 0 \tag{17}$$

Figure 3.2.2

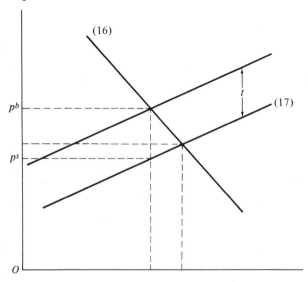

where p^s is the price that the seller receives. These functions are shown in Figure 3.2.2. Let t be the amount of the excise tax. Then

$$p^b = p^s + t \tag{18}$$

In the absence of the excise tax $p^b = p^s$. In equilibrium

$$x = y \tag{19}$$

From (16), (17), and (19),

$$f(p^b) - g(p^s) = 0 \tag{20}$$

Taking differentials of (20) and (18),

$$f' \, dp^b - g' \, dp^s = 0 \tag{21}$$

$$dp^b - dp^s = dt \tag{22}$$

Solving (21) and (22) for the unknowns dp^b and dp^s,

$$dp^b = \frac{g' \, dt}{g' - f'} \tag{23}$$

$$dp^s = \frac{f' \, dt}{g' - f'} \tag{24}$$

From (16) and (23),

$$dx = f' \, dp^b = \frac{f'g' \, dt}{g' - f'} \tag{25}$$

Hence

$$\frac{dx}{dt} = \frac{f'g'}{g' - f'} < 0 \tag{26}$$

$$\frac{dp^b}{dt} = \frac{g'}{g' - f'} > 0 \tag{27}$$

$$\frac{dp^s}{dt} = \frac{f'}{g' - f'} < 0 \tag{28}$$

Therefore an increase in the excise tax reduces the quantity traded, increases the market price, and reduces the price the producer receives. The ratio between the rise in p^b and the fall in p^s is equal to the ratio between the absolute values of the slopes of the supply and demand curves with respect to the price axis. The smaller the price sensitivity of the buyer (f') and the greater the price sensitivity of the seller (g'), the greater the share of the excise duty that is carried by the buyer.

If $t < 0$, then t can be regarded as a subsidy, and one can analyze the shifting of the subsidy.

3.3 MARKET EQUILIBRIUM IN THE SHORT RUN AND LONG RUN

SHORT-RUN EQUILIBRIUM OF THE INDUSTRY

Assume the competitive industry to be made up of identical size firms. The short run is the period in which the number and the plant size of the firms are fixed. The industry supply for this period is the sum of the supplies of individual producers who make up the industry. Therefore, if the ith firm's supply function is written

$$y^i = g^i(p) \tag{1}$$

then the industry supply function is

$$y = \Sigma \, y^i = \Sigma \, g^i(p) \tag{2}$$

which of course is an increasing function of the product price. Thus the higher the product price, the greater the product supply.

The short-run market equilibrium is given by the intersection of the short-run demand function, obtained by summing individual demand functions, with the short-run supply function as shown in Figure 3.3.1.

Figure 3.3.1

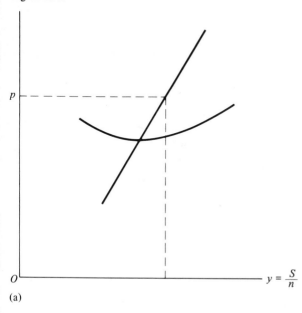

(a)

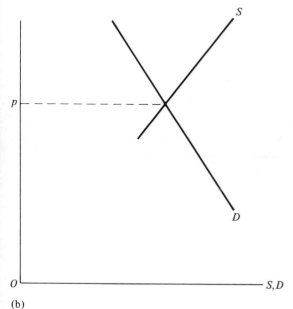

(b)

LONG-RUN EQUILIBRIUM OF THE INDUSTRY

In the long run the number of firms as well as the plant size is variable. Continuing to assume that the firms are of identical size and, therefore, the

Figure 3.3.2

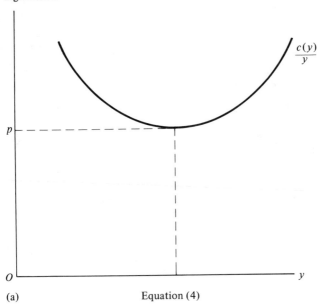

(a)   Equation (4)

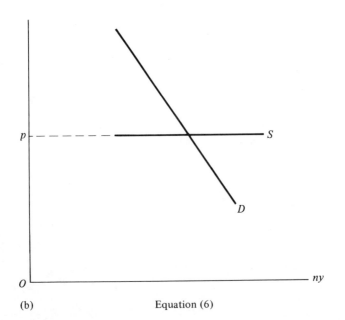

(b)   Equation (6)

long-run supply function of the firms is the same, the common supply function can be written

$$y = y(p)$$

Let the number of firms be n. Then the industry supply function can be written

$$ny(p) \tag{3}$$

In the equilibrium the number of firms will be such that each firm's profit, and therefore the total industry profit π, will be zero, that is,

$$\pi = pny(p) - nc(y(p)) = 0 \quad \text{or} \quad py(p) = c(y(p)) \tag{4}$$

where profit means that above the normal profits, and where $c(y)$ is the firm's long-run cost. Equation (4) gives p and therefore $y(p)$.

Let the long-run demand function be written

$$D = D(p) \tag{5}$$

In equilibrium

$$D = ny \tag{6}$$

Equation (6) gives n. Thus, the solution represents the long-run equilibrium in the industry and is as in Figure 3.3.2.

In the long-run equilibrium *the firm* has no profits or losses, and thus total cost equals total revenue, that is,

$$py = c \quad \text{or} \quad p = \frac{c}{y} \tag{7}$$

This is shown in Figure 3.3.2. Since the firm is maximizing profit,

$$p = \frac{dc}{dy} \tag{8}$$

From the preceding two equations,

$$\frac{dc}{dy} = \frac{c}{y} \tag{9}$$

This occurs at the point of minimum average cost, as at A in Figure 3.3.3.[3]

---

[3] At the minimum of average cost

$$\frac{d}{dy}\left(\frac{c}{y}\right) = 0 \quad \text{and} \quad \frac{d^2}{dy^2}\left(\frac{c}{y}\right) > 0$$

That is

$$\frac{c'y - c}{y^2} = 0 \quad \text{and} \quad \frac{c''}{y} - 2\frac{c'y - c}{y^3} > 0$$

Hence

$$c' = c/y \quad \text{and} \quad c'' > 0$$

That is, marginal cost equals average cost, and marginal cost is rising.

Figure 3.3.3

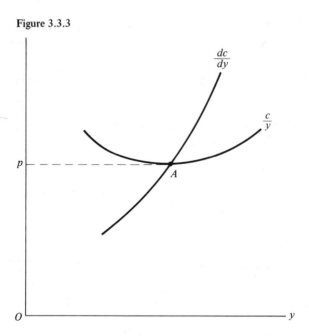

3.4 STABILITY OF MARKET EQUILIBRIUM

The market mechanism that leads to competitive equilibrium has been called a computer that solves the problem of optimum resource allocation. For the market mechanism to be able to solve this problem of optimum resource allocation, it must be *stable*, that is, the mechanism is such that beginning with any initial condition it will bring about equilibrium, and will restore equilibrium when it is disturbed. Hence it is essential to ascertain what conditions are sufficient for stability. Stability analysis of single market equilibrium is concerned with the adjustment process in the presence of disequilibrium between market demand and supply. The stability of general equilibrium is taken up in Chapter 4. The market is said to be *locally stable* if the market returns to equilibrium if displaced by a small amount. The market is said to be *globally stable* if the market approaches equilibrium from any starting point.

Various behavior assumptions have been made regarding the mechanism by which the market makes adjustments. The *Walrasian assumption* is that the price moves higher if there is positive excess demand (the quantity demanded exceeds the quantity supplied) and lower if there is negative excess demand. That is, the direction of the price change is the same as the sign of the excess demand. The *Marshallian assumption* is that the quantity increases if the excess demand price (the demand price minus the supply price for a level of output) is positive, and decreases if the excess demand price is negative. Both cases assume that no trade takes place until equilibrium is reached, that is, market participants contract and recontract until equilibrium is reached.

The Walrasian system can be described by a differential equation. Define

$$x = f(p) \tag{1}$$
$$y = g(p) \tag{2}$$
$$z = x - y \tag{3}$$
$$\frac{dp}{dt} = h(z) \qquad h' > 0 \quad h(0) = 0 \tag{4}$$

where t denotes time. Equations (1) and (2) are demand and supply equations, while equation (3) defines the *excess demand*. It is clear that z is a function of p.

$$z = f(p) - g(p) \tag{5}$$

Equation (4) describes how the price p changes when demand does not equal supply, that is, when the system is out of equilibrium. Thus, while all the preceding models assumed equality of demand and supply, the present one does not. The function h given in (4) states the Walrasian process that the price rises when demand exceeds supply and does not change when they are equal. The function h is shown in Figure 3.4.1. In the neighborhood of equilibrium value $\bar{z}$ of z, approximately,

$$h(z) - h(\bar{z}) = K \cdot (z - \bar{z}) \tag{6}$$

Figure 3.4.1

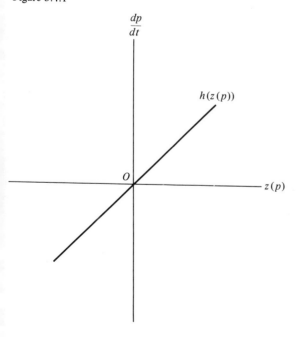

where

$$K = h' \, |_{z=\bar{z}} \tag{7}$$

and

$$K > 0 \tag{8}$$

by (4). In the neighborhood of equilibrium value $\bar{p}$ of p, approximately

$$z - \bar{z} = L \cdot (p - \bar{p}) \tag{9}$$

where

$$L = \frac{dz}{dp}\bigg|_{p=\bar{p}} = [f'(p) - g'(p)]\bigg|_{p=\bar{p}} \tag{10}$$

Substituting (9) and (6) into (4), and using the assumption in (4), that is,

$$h(\bar{z}) = 0 \qquad \text{for } \bar{z} = 0 \tag{11}$$

yields

$$\frac{dp}{dt} = K \cdot L \cdot (p - \bar{p}) \tag{12}$$

Carrying out the integration of

$$\int \frac{dp}{p - \bar{p}} = \int KL \, dt$$

Figure 3.4.2

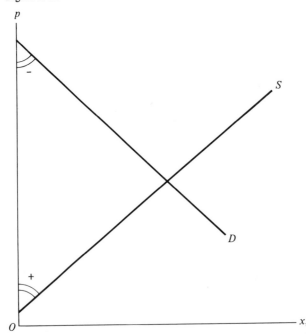

Figure 3.4.3

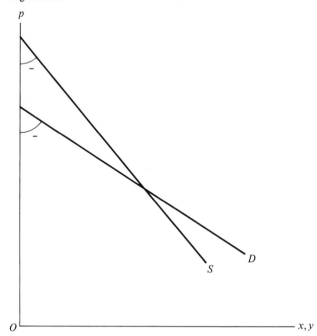

Figure 3.4.4

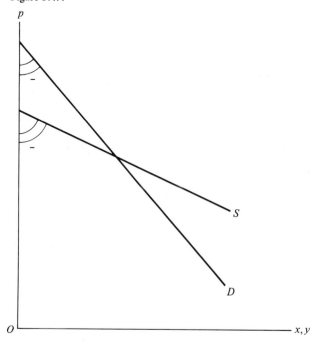

yields

$$\ln (p - \bar{p}) = KLt + c$$

or

$$p - \bar{p} = Me^{KLt} \tag{13}$$

where c is a constant of integration, and $M = e^c$. Let the initial condition be

$$p = p_0 \quad \text{for } t = 0 \tag{14}$$

Then substituting (14) in (13) yields

$$M = p_0 - \bar{p} \tag{15}$$

Substituting (15) into (13)

$$p = \bar{p} + (p_0 - \bar{p})e^{KLt} \tag{16}$$

From (8) and (10), p approaches $\bar{p}$ if and only if $KL < 0$, or by (8) if $L < 0$, which implies

$$f'(p)\Big|_{p=\bar{p}} < g'(p)\Big|_{p=\bar{p}} \tag{17}$$

That is, *with regard to the price axis, the slope of the supply function must be algebraically greater than that of the demand function.* In the normal case the former slope is positive while the latter slope is negative, satisfying the stability condition (17), as shown in Figure 3.4.2.

When both the supply and demand curves slope downward to the right, the algebraic comparison of the slopes shows that the stability condition (17) is not violated in Figure 3.4.3, but is violated in Figure 3.4.4.[4]

The Marshallian adjustment process in which quantity responds to price has been considered more characteristic of a long rather than short run, and of monopolistic rather than competitive markets.

3.5 A DYNAMIC MODEL OF THE COMPETITIVE MARKET— THE COBWEB THEOREM[5]

The model of Section 3.2 is static in that it does not bring in time explicitly. This section considers a dynamic model taking time explicitly into account, specifically the case where supply responds to price with a lag, as is typical in many markets for agricultural products.

---

[4] On the classical stability condition of market equilibrium, see Marshall (1920) and Walras (1926). Samuelson (1947), chap. 9 formulates a dynamic model for stability analysis.

[5] *Cf.* Samuelson (1947), p. 265.

Consider the market described by the following linear demand and supply functions:

$$x_t = a_1 + b_1 p_t \qquad b_1 < 0 \tag{1}$$

$$y_t = a_2 + b_2 p_{t-1} \tag{2}$$

The quantity demanded x_t in the current period is a function of the current price p_t. The suppliers made the production decisions for the current period on the basis of the price in the previous period, p_{t-1}. These decisions determine the quantity supplied y_t in the current period. Therefore supply is a function of p_{t-1}.

Assume that the market is in temporary equilibrium, that is, in each period the price settles at the level that equates demand and supply,

$$x_t = y_t \tag{3}$$

The three equations can be reduced to one first-order linear difference equation in p_t, as follows

$$p_t - \frac{b_2}{b_1} p_{t-1} = -\frac{a_1 - a_2}{b_1} \tag{4}$$

whose solution is

$$p_t = \left(p_0 - \frac{a_1 - a_2}{b_2 - b_1} \right) \left(\frac{b_2}{b_1} \right)^t + \frac{a_1 - a_2}{b_2 - b_1} \tag{5}$$

where p_0 is the price at $t = 0$.

Assume the supply curve is positively sloped, that is,

$$b_2 > 0 \tag{6}$$

then the price will stabilize as time goes on if

$$\left| \frac{b_2}{b_1} \right| < 1 \tag{7}$$

that is, if

$$|b_2| < |b_1| \tag{8}$$

as in Figure 3.5.1a. In this case, the path to equilibrium oscillates. If, on the other hand,

$$b_2 < 0 \tag{9}$$

then the price will stabilize as time goes on if

$$|b_2| < |b_1| \tag{10}$$

as in Figure 3.5.1b. In this case, equilibrium is approached without oscillation. Figure 3.5.1b is the same as Figure 3.4.3.

Figure 3.5.1

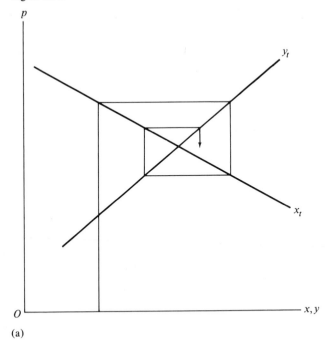

(a)

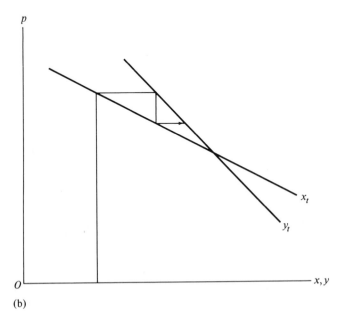

(b)

3.6 SUMMARY

The working of an individual market under competitive conditions can be understood in the following terms.

The demand for a commodity is obtained by summing individual demand functions, while the supply of the commodity is obtained by summing the supply functions of all the firms. The equilibrium price of the commodity is such that it equates the demand and supply. In the long run, in the competitive industry made up of identical-size firms, the number of firms as well as the plant size is adjusted so that each firm operates at the lowest point of the average-cost curve.

The market may be considered to "compute" the equilibrium price and quantity under the Walrasian dynamic adjustment process in which price rises if excess demand is positive, and vice versa, the process being able to converge to equilibrium if the slope of the demand function with respect to the price axis is algebraically smaller than that of the supply function.

4
MARGINALIST MODELS
OF GENERAL EQUILIBRIUM
AND WELFARE ECONOMICS

4.1 INTRODUCTION

The preceding analysis of the consumer and the firm proceeded as follows: The model of the consumer assumed that the product and factor prices were given and derived the equilibrium quantities of the products to consume and factors to supply. The model of the firm assumed that the product and factor prices were given and obtained the equilibrium quantities of the factors to demand and products to supply. The models of market equilibrium examined how the prices are determined in the product and factor markets where the buyers and sellers take the market prices as given and make appropriate quantity adjustments. The price and quantity of a good produced and exchanged were determined where the quantity demanded equals the quantity supplied, assuming that the prices of other goods remain constant. The demand and supply of one good was discussed independent of those of other goods. This analysis of a single market independent of other markets has been called *partial equilibrium analysis*. This analysis based on the *ceteris paribus* assumption serves a useful purpose, especially in the short run when such an assumption is usually valid. But it is unsatisfactory as a general explanation, since it disregards the interaction whereby a change in the price of one good (say wheat) affects the demand and supply of another good (say corn), and results in a change in the price of corn (which in turn will affect the demand and supply of wheat).

The study of the more general, simultaneous determination of prices and quantities in all markets has been called the *general equilibrium theory*. It is a study of resource allocation (allocation of products and factors to the consumers and firms) and the price system (determination of prices of products and factors) in the entire economy.

The marginalist microeconomic models are not as well suited to general equilibrium analysis of fundamental questions (such as existence) as the linear and set-theoretic microeconomic models are. Nevertheless the marginalist general equilibrium model assuming the utility and production functions with smoothly changing marginal utilities and productivities is presented here for comparison with the later models. The system of equations given here presents a simplified picture of the complicated functioning of the decentralized units making decisions by trial and error.

4.2 A MARGINALIST MODEL OF GENERAL COMPETITIVE EQUILIBRIUM

The model of general competitive equilibrium assumes that

• All consumers and producers are price-takers; that is, each of these economic units takes prices as given and therefore makes decisions assuming that market prices are not affected by its individual actions. Each unit assumes that the prices are set by the market which reflects the total demand and supply conditions. Each unit adjusts its quantities of factors and products, not their prices.
• Each consumer maximizes his utility while each producer maximizes his profits.
• Each market is in long-run equilibrium, and prices have been adjusted so as to equate demand and supply for each market.
• Each producer operates under the condition of *nonincreasing returns to scale*.
• The well-being of each economic unit (utility or profits) is not affected by that of other economic units except through their buying and selling on the markets, that is, except through the prices. To use the terminology to be introduced later, *technological external economies and diseconomies*, such as the effects of "keeping up with the Joneses" and interaction between the "foundry and laundry," are absent.

Competitive equilibrium here, in short, is defined as the state in which each consumer maximizes his utility index and each producer his profits, assuming prices given, and all markets are cleared.

The model here continues to assume two products and two factors, and twice-differentiability of all functions.

THE CONSUMING SECTOR

Consider consumer i whose utility function can be written

$$U^i = U^i(y_{i1}, y_{i2}, y_{i3}, y_{i4}) \qquad U^i_j > 0, \quad j = 1, \ldots, 4 \qquad (1)$$

where y_{i1} and y_{i2} denote the quantities of the two products consumed, and y_{i3} and y_{i4} denote the negative consumptions, or supplies, of the two factors. Assuming that the consumer is endowed with the two factors only and that there are no profits received from the firms since they are making no profits, the consumer's budget equation can be written

$$p_1 y_{i1} + p_2 y_{i2} + p_3 y_{i3} + p_4 y_{i4} = 0 \qquad (2)$$

That is, the consumer spends the entire factor income.

From the assumptions the utility function has the marginalist properties, that is, substitution of factors is infinitesimal; the marginal rate of substitution along any indifference curve smoothly diminishes; and therefore the product proportions are sensitive to the relative price ratio. The analysis of Section 1.5 makes it possible to express each of four unknowns y_{i1}, y_{i2}, y_{i3}, and y_{i4} in terms of p_1, p_2, p_3, and p_4. Aggregating the consumer demands for each good results in the *demand functions* that can generally be written

$$y_1 = F^1(p_1, p_2, p_3, p_4) \qquad (3)$$

$$y_2 = F^2(p_1, p_2, p_3, p_4) \qquad (4)$$

As was shown in Chapter 1, these demand functions are homogeneous of degree zero in the prices. The negative demand (factor-supply) functions for the factors can be written similarly

$$y_3 = F^3(p_1, p_2, p_3, p_4) \qquad (5)$$

$$y_4 = F^4(p_1, p_2, p_3, p_4) \qquad (6)$$

These functions are also homogeneous of degree zero.

THE PRODUCING SECTOR

Supplies of products are described by the industry *supply functions*,

$$y_1 = f^1(p_1, p_2, p_3, p_4) \qquad (7)$$

$$y_2 = f^2(p_1, p_2, p_3, p_4) \qquad (8)$$

The underlying production functions also possess the marginalist properties. As shown in Sections 2.5 and 2.6, these supply functions are homogeneous of degree zero in the product and factor prices.

As was shown in Section 2.5, the negative output (factor-demand) functions are also functions of product and factor prices:

$$y_3 = f^3(p_1, p_2, p_3, p_4) \tag{9}$$

$$y_4 = f^4(p_1, p_2, p_3, p_4) \tag{10}$$

As was shown in Sections 2.5 and 2.6, these equations are homogeneous of degree zero in p_1, p_2, p_3, and p_4.

The eight equations (3)–(10) contain eight variables: $p_1, p_2, p_3, p_4, y_1, y_2, y_3$, and y_4. Thus there are as many equations as variables. There remains, however, one problem: Since the demand and supply functions are homogeneous of degree zero with respect to prices p_1, p_2, p_3, and p_4, one of the prices, say p_1, can be chosen as 1, and all other prices made relative prices, thereby reducing the number of unknowns by one to seven while maintaining the same number of equations. It must be shown that one of the above eight equations is redundant. This is done by the well-known Walras' law.

WALRAS' LAW

Assume that the economy is not necessarily in equilibrium. Equations (3)–(10) are eight equations providing the consumers' demands and the firms' supplies for each of the four goods in terms of the four prices p_1, p_2, p_3, and p_4. Equations (3)–(6) can be rewritten

$$x_i = F^i(p_1, p_2, p_3, p_4) \qquad i = 1, \ldots, 4 \tag{11}$$

and equations (7)–(10)

$$y_i = f^i(p_1, p_2, p_3, p_4) \qquad i = 1, \ldots, 4 \tag{12}$$

F^i represents the consumers' demand functions. The ith good is a good demanded if F^i is positive, a good supplied if F^i is negative. f^i represents the firms' supply functions. The ith good is a good supplied if f^i is positive, a good demanded if f^i is negative. The firms' profits are not necessarily zero, and they are

$$\sum_{i=1}^{4} p_i y_i$$

since y_i is positive for outputs and negative for inputs. Since the consumers' expenditures are equal to their income including profits from the firms,

$$p_1 x_1 + p_2 x_2 \equiv -p_3 x_3 - p_4 x_4 + \sum_{i=1}^{4} p_i y_i$$

where x_3 and x_4 are negative. Therefore

$$\sum p_i x_i \equiv \sum p_i y_i \tag{13}$$

(total money value of demands is equal to that of supplies), or

$$\sum p_i(x_i - y_i) \equiv 0 \qquad (14)$$

(total money value of excess demands is zero). This identity holds true because of the budget constraints, regardless of whether p's are equilibrium prices or not. This has been called Walras' law. Hence, first, if excess demand $(x_i - y_i)$ is zero in three markets, then it must be zero in the remaining one market; that is if three markets are in equilibrium the remaining one must be in equilibrium also. Second, since the eight equations in (11)–(12) are bound together by (13), one of them is redundant.

Similarly, in the system of general equilibrium (3)–(10), one of the eight equations, say (3) providing the demand equation for y_1, can be dropped from the system. This reduces the number of equations by one to seven. Thus the number of equations is again equal to the number of unknowns.

EQUILIBRIUM PRICES

In the market economy the price system provides the mechanism which enables the utility-maximizing consumers and the profit-maximizing producers to buy that exact amount of each good which is offered for sale. Since the demand and supply plans of individual economic units depend on prevailing market prices alone, the dynamic market-clearing process, to be more closely examined later, operates as follows: If the demand is not equal to supply at the current market prices, then at least one economic unit will not be able to realize his planned purchase or sale. Under these circumstances, the market prices will rise in the markets where the quantity demanded exceeds the quantity supplied, and will fall in the markets where the opposite is true. When at the current market prices demand equals supply in every market, then all economic units can carry out their planned transactions; and the prevailing prices, current purchase, and sale plans represent general equilibrium.

Thus the model could determine the seven variables: the relative prices p_2, p_3, p_4; the quantities of products produced and consumed y_1 and y_2; the quantities of factors supplied and employed y_3 and y_4. This counting of variables and equations, however, gives no guarantee of the existence of a solution, not to mention the existence of nonnegative prices. A more rigorous analysis must await Parts II and III.[1]

STABILITY OF GENERAL EQUILIBRIUM

Chapter 3 considered models of stability of partial equilibrium. The models here analyze the stability of general equilibrium and the efficacy of the resource allocation mechanism of the price system.

[1] On general equilibrium in the marginalist framework, *cf.* Dorfman *et al.* (1958), (pp. 375–381); Brown (1963).

CASE OF TWO GOODS: WALRAS

Walras' stability condition was sufficient. The condition was that if the price in terms of the other good (*numéraire*) is above the equilibrium magnitude, then there will arise an excess supply for the good, and an excess demand in the opposite case; the price moved higher if the excess demand is positive and lower if the excess demand was negative. This stability condition introduces forces to restore equilibrium price.

HICKS

According to Hicks, equilibrium is *perfectly stable* if an excess supply results when a good's price is above the equilibrium value, and an excess demand in the opposite case, regardless of the condition of other markets, that is, regardless of whether the prices of other goods remain unchanged so that demand is unequal to supply, or change so as to equate demand and supply. More technically, write the excess-demand function

$$z^i = x^i - y^i = f^i(p_1, p_2) \qquad i = 1, 2 \tag{15}$$

Let the price p_1 vary so that the market for the first commodity is out of equilibrium while the other price is held constant so that the other market is also out of equilibrium. For Hicks' perfect stability defined above, the rate of change of the excess demand with respect to the price for each commodity must be negative, that is,

$$\frac{dz^1}{dp_1} = \frac{\partial z^1}{\partial p_1} = f_1^1 < 0 \tag{16}$$

and

$$f_2^2 < 0 \tag{17}$$

Next assume as p_1 is varied, p_2 also is varied to keep the second market in equilibrium; then

$$\frac{dz^1}{dp_1} < 0 \qquad \text{when} \qquad \frac{dz^2}{dp_1} = 0 \tag{18}$$

The first of these expressions can be written

$$\frac{\partial z^1}{\partial p_1} + \frac{\partial z^1}{\partial p_2} \frac{dp_2}{dp_1} = f_1^1 + f_2^1 \cdot \frac{dp_2}{dp_1} < 0 \tag{19}$$

Similarly, the second expression can be rewritten

$$f_1^2 + f_2^2 \cdot \frac{dp_2}{dp_1} = 0 \tag{20}$$

Expressions (19) and (20) imply

$$f_1^1 f_2^2 - f_2^1 f_1^2 > 0 \tag{21}$$

or

$$\begin{vmatrix} f_1^1 & f_2^1 \\ f_1^2 & f_2^2 \end{vmatrix} > 0 \tag{22}$$

Similarly

$$\begin{vmatrix} f_2^2 & f_1^2 \\ f_2^1 & f_1^1 \end{vmatrix} > 0 \tag{23}$$

which turns out to be equivalent to (22).

The results can be extended to the case of 3 goods as follows:

$$f_i^i < 0 \qquad \begin{vmatrix} f_i^i & f_j^i \\ f_i^j & f_j^j \end{vmatrix} > 0 \qquad \begin{vmatrix} f_i^i & f_j^i & f_k^i \\ f_i^j & f_j^j & f_k^j \\ f_i^k & f_j^k & f_k^k \end{vmatrix} < 0 \tag{24}$$

for $i, j, k = 1, 2, 3$, and $i \neq j \neq k \neq i$.

DYNAMIC STABILITY

Samuelson argued that the stability question belonged to dynamics, and that Hicks' concepts on stability are static-equilibrium oriented. He called a system *stable* if the variables converged to equilibrium values with the passage of time regardless of the initial condition. He set up the following dynamic system of equations

$$\frac{dp_i}{dt} = k_i f^i(p_1, p_2) \qquad k_i > 0 \quad i = 1, 2 \tag{25}$$

where f^i is the excess demand function and k_i is the speed of adjustment. These equations state that if the excess demand for a good is positive, its price will rise, and vice versa.

Expanding the right-hand side of the above equation around the equilibrium prices p_1^0 and p_2^0,

$$\frac{d(p_i - p_i^0)}{dt} = k_i f_1^i(p_1 - p_1^0) + k_i f_2^i(p_2 - p_2^0) \qquad i = 1, 2 \tag{26}$$

From the theory of linear differential equations, the system is stable, that is, $p_i \to p_i^0$ as $t \to \infty$, if the real parts of the characteristic roots of

$$\phi(\lambda) = \begin{vmatrix} k_1 f_1^1 - \lambda & k_1 f_2^1 \\ k_2 f_1^2 & k_2 f_2^2 - \lambda \end{vmatrix} \tag{27}$$

are all negative.

Define F by

$$F = \begin{bmatrix} f_1^1 & f_2^1 \\ f_1^2 & f_2^2 \end{bmatrix} \tag{28}$$

The Hicksian condition for perfect stability is (16), (17), (22), and (23). Samuelson showed that if F is symmetric, the Hicksian condition is equivalent to the dynamic stability.[2] Metzler, on the other hand, has proved that if the two goods are gross substitutes, that is,

$$f_2^1 > 0 \qquad f_1^2 > 0 \tag{29}$$

the Hicksian condition is equivalent to the dynamic stability.[3]

GLOBAL STABILITY

The preceding models of stability were concerned with local stability. The following model presents some features of more recent models concerned with global stability. They use such assumption as zero-degree homogeneity and gross substitutability.

Let x_j, $j = 1, 2$, denote the demands and x_j^*, $j = 1, 2$, denote the equilibrium demands for the two goods. The demand functions are homogeneous of degree zero in prices.

Let $\mathbf{p}^*$ be the equilibrium price vector, and $\mathbf{p}$ some other price vector such that

$$\frac{p_1}{p_1^*} < \frac{p_2}{p_2^*} \tag{30}$$

Since the demand function is homogeneous of degree zero,

$$x_1(p_1, p_2) = x_1\left(p_1^*, p_1^* \frac{p_2}{p_1}\right) \tag{31}$$

From (30)

$$\frac{p_1^*}{p_1} > \frac{p_2^*}{p_2} \tag{32}$$

that is,

$$p_1^* \frac{p_2}{p_1} > p_2^* \tag{33}$$

From the gross substitutability assumption,

$$x_1\left(p_1^*, p_1^* \frac{p_2}{p_1}\right) > x_1(p_1^*, p_2^*) \tag{34}$$

---

[2] *Cf.* Samuelson (1947). chap 9.
[3] *Cf.* Metzler (1945).

From (31) and (34)

$$x_1(p_1, p_2) > x_1(p_1^*, p_2^*) = x_1^* \tag{35}$$

Hence

$$x_1(p_1, p_2) - x_1^* > 0 \tag{36}$$

Thus there exists positive excess demand for good 1. By similar reasoning,

$$x_2(p_1, p_2) - x_2^* < 0 \tag{37}$$

Assume the *tâtonnement* process defined by (25). Then the price will fall for the good whose price is the highest relative to its equilibrium magnitude, while the price will rise for the good whose price is the lowest relative to its equilibrium magnitude. As long as p_1 and p_2 are different from p_1^* and p_2^*, respectively, this process continues. The process stops when $p_1/p_1^* = p_2/p_2^*$.

The case of three goods can be analyzed similarly.[4]

4.3 WELFARE ECONOMICS

In macroeconomic analysis welfare is usually measured by the size of aggregate real income, the stability of aggregate real income, the stability of the price level, aggregate distributive shares of factors, the growth of aggregate real income, and so on. In the more recent macroeconomic growth theory, welfare is often measured by the discounted sum of the future stream of per capita consumption. Microeconomic welfare analysis focuses its attention on the optimum allocation of products and factors among consumers.

PARETO OPTIMALITY

The New Welfare Economics embodied in the models discussed below differs from the old welfare economics in that it avoids interpersonal comparison of utility.

In an individualistic society, each individual's preferences are sovereign, and they exist side by side. Only under very rigid assumptions is it possible to find a single set of preferences for the society. Suppose a change in allocation brings about a rise in the utility index of one and a fall in that of another. So long as interpersonal comparison of utilities or judgment regarding the ranking of various states of consumption among persons is not introduced, one cannot say whether or not resource allocation in the economy as a whole has been improved. If, on the other hand, after the change in allocation no one experienced a fall in his utility index, and at least one individual's utility index rose, then such a

---

[4] For a survey of stability models, see Negishi (1962). Also *cf.* Arrow *et al.* (1959); Arrow and Hurwicz (1960).

change may be considered as an improvement in allocation in the economy. As long as there is room for such improvement, the economy may be considered not to have achieved optimum. The economy has achieved *Pareto optimality* when, by reallocation, it is impossible to make any one individual better off without making anyone else worse off.

This is an apparently conservative criterion, since it abstains from cases where one is better off but another is worse off than the initial allocation. The Pareto criterion avoids this difficulty by excluding such a change from consideration. But as long as the model respects the sovereignty of individuals and refrains from any judgment regarding interpersonal allocation of consumption, it must settle for such a criterion. Modern welfare economics has derived several theorems showing the role of perfectly competitive equilibrium in Pareto-optimum allocation of goods. They show that competitive market institutions— perfectly competitive consumers and firms maximizing their utility indices and profits, respectively, in response to market-determined prices (Adam Smith's invisible hand)—will produce a Pareto-optimum configuration of consumption and production.

A MODEL OF PARETO OPTIMALITY
IN AN EXCHANGE ECONOMY

Assume that

• All consumers are price-takers; that is, none of the consumers can set prices. The market-clearing prices are known to all consumers at no cost.
• Consumers maximize their utility.

The model continues the following assumptions:

• The utility function is characterized by the strictly diminishing marginal rate of substitution.
• The utility function is externality-free, that is, the level of the consumer's utility function depends only on the amounts of goods consumed by him.
• The marginal utility is always positive, that is, wants are never satiated.

Continuing to assume that there are two goods, consider a consumer whose twice-differentiable utility function can be written

$$U^i = U^i(x_{i1}, x_{i2}) \qquad U^i_1 > 0 \qquad U^i_2 > 0 \qquad i = 1, 2 \tag{1}$$

where x_{i1} and x_{i2} denote the quantities of two commodities consumed.
Let the second consumer's utility index be held at a constant level $\overline{U}^2$,

$$\overline{U}^2 = U^2(x_{21}, x_{22}) \tag{2}$$

Assume that the total quantities of two goods are fixed at x_1 and x_2:

$$x_{11} + x_{21} = x_1 \quad \text{and} \quad x_{12} + x_{22} = x_2 \tag{3}$$

Pareto optimality requires that for the level of utility for the second consumer, the first consumer's utility be maximum. The Lagrangean expression is

$$L = U^1 - \lambda_1(\overline{U}^2 - U^2) + \lambda_2(x_1 - x_{11} - x_{21}) + \lambda_3(x_2 - x_{12} - x_{22}) \tag{4}$$

The first-order condition is

$$U_1^1 - \lambda_2 = 0 \tag{5}$$

$$U_2^1 - \lambda_3 = 0 \tag{6}$$

$$\lambda_1 U_1^2 - \lambda_2 = 0 \tag{7}$$

$$\lambda_1 U_2^2 - \lambda_3 = 0 \tag{8}$$

From (5) and (6)

$$\frac{U_1^1}{U_2^1} = \frac{\lambda_2}{\lambda_3} \tag{9}$$

From (7) and (8)

$$\frac{U_1^2}{U_2^2} = \frac{\lambda_2}{\lambda_3} \tag{10}$$

Hence

$$\frac{U_1^1}{U_2^1} = \frac{U_1^2}{U_2^2} \tag{11}$$

The marginal rate of substitution must be equal between the two consumers, and should be equal to the ratio of the inputed marginal utilities of the two commodities that are fixed in supply. The equations (2), (3), (5)–(8) can determine the four x_{ij}, $i = 1, 2$, $j = 1, 2$. Thus for the given level of the second consumer's utility $\overline{U}^2$, assuming strictly quasi-concave utility functions, there exists a unique allocation of the goods to the individuals. For different values of $\overline{U}^2$, there exist different allocations.

The collection of all such allocations can be drawn as a *contract curve* in the *Edgeworth box diagram*, as shown in Figure 4.3.1. Construct a rectangle whose horizontal side equals x_1 and vertical side equals x_2. Any point in this rectangle represents an allocation (x_{11}, x_{12}) and (x_{21}, x_{22}). This diagram has been called the Edgeworth box diagram. Draw the first consumer's indifference curves with the origin at the lower left-hand corner, and the second consumer's indifference

Figure 4.3.1

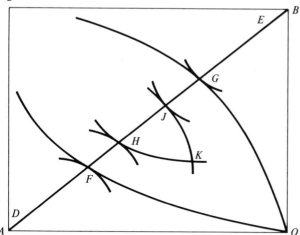

curves with the origin at the upper right-hand corner. The points of tangency represent Pareto-optimum allocation specified by (11) and form the contract curve.

A MODEL OF PARETO OPTIMALITY
IN EXCHANGE AND PRODUCTION

In a two-person, two-commodity, two-factor economy where production takes place, let the first consumer's utility function be written

$$U^1 = U^1(x_{11}, x_{12}, x_{13}, x_{14}) \qquad U_i^1 > 0 \quad i = 1, \ldots, 4 \qquad (12)$$

where x_{11} and x_{12} are the first consumer's consumptions of products 1 and 2, respectively; and x_{13} and x_{14} are his negative net consumptions, or supplies, of the factors 1 and 2, respectively. Let the second consumer's utility be a function of the quantities of products and factors pertaining to him, and let it be held constant at the level $\overline{U}^2$,

$$\overline{U}^2 = U^2(x_{21}, x_{22}, x_{23}, x_{24}) \qquad U_i^2 > 0 \quad i = 1, \ldots, 4 \qquad (13)$$

Society's aggregate transformation function giving the level of the maximum net output (when it is negative, it means an input) of each commodity that can be produced from the given levels of all other net outputs can be written implicitly

$$F(x_{11} + x_{21}, x_{12} + x_{22}, x_{13} + x_{23}, x_{14} + x_{24}) = 0 \quad F_i > 0 \quad i = 1, 2, 3, 4 \quad (14)$$

Assume further that

- The production function for each product is externality-free, that is, the output of a product depends only upon the inputs used in its production.
- The partial derivatives F_i (marginal costs or marginal products) are positive.

The transformation function is strictly quasi-convex.

Pareto optimality requires that for the given level of utility for the second consumer, the first consumer's utility must be maximum; the Lagrangean expression for this maximization problem is

$$L = U^1(x_{11}, x_{12}, x_{13}, x_{14}) \tag{15}$$
$$- \lambda_1[\overline{U}^2 - U^2(x_{21}, x_{22}, x_{23}, x_{24})]$$
$$- \lambda_2 F(x_{11} + x_{21}, x_{12} + x_{22}, x_{13} + x_{23}, x_{14} + x_{24})$$

The first-order condition is

$$\frac{\partial L}{\partial x_{11}} = U_1^1 - \lambda_2 F_1 = 0 \qquad U_1^1 = \lambda_2 F_1 \tag{16}$$

$$\frac{\partial L}{\partial x_{12}} = U_2^1 - \lambda_2 F_2 = 0 \qquad U_2^1 = \lambda_2 F_2 \tag{17}$$

$$\frac{\partial L}{\partial x_{13}} = U_3^1 - \lambda_2 F_3 = 0 \qquad U_3^1 = \lambda_2 F_3 \tag{18}$$

$$\frac{\partial L}{\partial x_{14}} = U_4^1 - \lambda_2 F_4 = 0 \qquad U_4^1 = \lambda_2 F_4 \tag{19}$$

$$\frac{\partial L}{\partial x_{21}} = \lambda_1 U_1^2 - \lambda_2 F_1 = 0 \qquad \lambda_1 U_1^2 = \lambda_2 F_1 \tag{20}$$

$$\frac{\partial L}{\partial x_{22}} = \lambda_1 U_2^2 - \lambda_2 F_2 = 0 \qquad \lambda_1 U_2^2 = \lambda_2 F_2 \tag{21}$$

$$\frac{\partial L}{\partial x_{23}} = \lambda_1 U_3^2 - \lambda_2 F_3 = 0 \qquad \lambda_1 U_3^2 = \lambda_2 F_3 \tag{22}$$

$$\frac{\partial L}{\partial x_{24}} = \lambda_1 U_4^2 - \lambda_2 F_4 = 0 \qquad \lambda_1 U_4^2 = \lambda_2 F_4 \tag{23}$$

Equations (13), (14), (16)–(23) are ten equations in ten unknowns: eight x's and two λ's. These equations can be solved to determine the Pareto-optimum x's for the given level of U^2.

The two λ's can be eliminated from the ten equations to give the necessary condition among x's. Dividing (16) by (17), and (20) by (21),

$$\frac{U_1^1}{U_2^1} = \frac{F_1}{F_2} = \frac{U_1^2}{U_2^2} \tag{24}$$

The marginal rate of substitution between two products is the same for all consumers. This common ratio must be equal to the marginal rate of transformation between products 1 and 2. This is shown graphically in Figure 4.3.2(a).

Figure 4.3.2

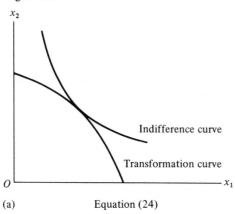

(a)   Equation (24)

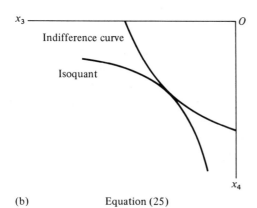

(b)   Equation (25)

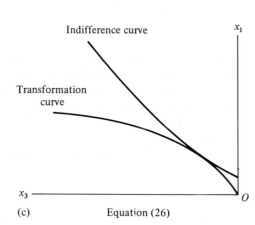

(c)   Equation (26)

Dividing (18) by (19), and (22) by (23),

$$\frac{U_3^1}{U_4^1} = \frac{F_3}{F_4} = \frac{U_3^2}{U_4^2} \tag{25}$$

The marginal rate of substitution between the (net consumptions of) two factors is the same for all individuals. This common ratio must be equal to the marginal rate of substitution between two factors in the production of each good. This is shown graphically in Figure 4.3.2(b).

Dividing (18) by (16), and (22) by (20),

$$\frac{U_3^1}{U_1^1} = \frac{F_3}{F_1} = \frac{U_3^2}{U_1^2} \tag{26}$$

This is shown graphically in Figure 4.3.2(c). Similarly, dividing (18) by (17), and (22) by (21),

$$\frac{U_3^1}{U_2^1} = \frac{F_3}{F_2} = \frac{U_3^2}{U_2^2} \tag{27}$$

The marginal rate of substitution between factor 1 and product 1 is the same for all individuals and is equal to the society's marginal productivity of factor 1 in producing commodity 1 in the economy. The marginal rate of substitution of factor 1 and product 2 is the same for all individuals, and is equal to the society's marginal productivity of factor 1 in producing commodity 2.

Dividing (19) by (16), and (23) by (20),

$$\frac{U_4^1}{U_1^1} = \frac{F_4}{F_1} = \frac{U_4^2}{U_1^2} \tag{28}$$

Similarly,

$$\frac{U_4^1}{U_2^1} = \frac{F_4}{F_2} = \frac{U_4^2}{U_2^2} \tag{29}$$

The marginal rate of substitution between factor 2 and product 1 is the same for all consumers and is equal to the society's marginal productivity of factor 2 in producing commodity 1. The marginal rate of substitution between factor 2 and product 2 is the same for all consumers, and is equal to the society's marginal productivity of factor 2 in producing commodity 2.

Section 1.8 showed that when under perfect competition each consumer cannot affect the prices of products and factors, he equates his marginal rates of substitution to the common price ratios (1.8.9–14). Therefore under perfect competition (24) and (25) are satisfied.

It was also shown in Chapter 2 that when under perfect competition each producer cannot affect the prices of products and factors, he equates the marginal rate of substitution between two factors to the factor-price ratio, the marginal rate of transformation between two products to the product-price ratio, and the marginal productivity of factors in the production of products to the product-factor-price ratio.

Therefore, under perfect competition equations (24)–(29), are satisfied. *The price system under perfect competition thus produces the condition necessary for Pareto optimality.* In other words, consumers and producers making independent, decentralized optimizing decisions in response to the signals of market prices bring about the productions and consumptions that are Pareto optimum.[5]

4.4 THE SOCIAL WELFARE FUNCTION

The Pareto-optimality criterion does not prescribe a unique allocation of products and factors. There are an infinite number of Pareto-optimal situations, ranging from one in which one individual enjoys all of the advantages to one in which another individual has all the advantages. In other words, all points on the contract curve are Pareto optimum in Figure 4.3.1, including the two end-points which represent an extreme inequality in income distribution. In the example of the preceding section there will exist a Pareto-optimum allocation corresponding to each value assigned to $\overline{U}^2$ for the second individual. (If the consumers are to start out with some initial endowments of two goods denoted by K in Figure 4.3.1, then only points on HJ are preferable under the Pareto-optimality criterion, and these preferable allocations are affected by the initial endowments of the two consumers, which may limit the final allocation to an extremely unfavorable one to one of the consumers.) This indeterminacy can be removed when the concept of the *social welfare function* is introduced, in essence bringing interpersonal comparison back into the argument. This idea has been considered by Bergson in order to choose a point on the contract curve as the best position.

Bergson's social welfare function is an index of social welfare based on a certain value judgment, for example, that of an economic policy-maker or of a legislature. In general its independent variables are all variables indicating the states of the economy, which can be described by the allocation of various goods $j(j = 1, 2)$ to each individual $i(i = 1, 2)$. The social welfare function can be written

$$W = V(x_{11}, x_{12}, x_{21}, x_{22}) \tag{1}$$

[5] For a graphical presentation of some of these theorems, see Bator (1957), especially pp. 23–36. The principles of the New Welfare Economics are presented in Lange (1942b), Reder (1947), and Samuelson (1947), chap. 8. Mishan (1960) provides a survey of welfare economics while American Economic Association (1969) contains classics in welfare economics.

The social welfare function is said to be the *individualist* type when social welfare depends on x_{ij} through individual utility U^i, that is, when it can be written

$$W = W(U^1, U^2) \qquad W_1 > 0 \quad W_2 > 0 \tag{2}$$

meaning that the society recognizes individuals' preferences. The social welfare function is said to be *Paretian* when an increase in an arbitrary U^i, while holding the remaining U^i constant, results in an increase in W, that is,

$$\frac{\partial W}{\partial U^i} > 0 \qquad i = 1, 2 \tag{3}$$

Lange has called this partial derivative the *marginal social significance* of the individual i.

OPTIMUM RESOURCE ALLOCATION GIVEN THE BERGSONIAN SOCIAL WELFARE FUNCTION

Assume that the society's social welfare function W is defined by (2). The function states that the society's well-being is determined by each individual's utility level, and that the former is an increasing function of the latter. Once this function is introduced, the Pareto optimum can be replaced by the social optimum of maximizing the social welfare function. The Lagrangean function for the exchange-optimum problem of Section 4.3 becomes

$$L = W(U^1, U^2) + \lambda_1(x_1 - x_{11} - x_{21}) + \lambda_2(x_2 - x_{12} - x_{22}) \tag{4}$$

The first-order condition becomes

$$\frac{\partial L}{\partial x_{11}} = W_1 U_1^1 - \lambda_1 = 0 \qquad W_1 U_1^1 = \lambda_1 \tag{5}$$

$$\frac{\partial L}{\partial x_{12}} = W_1 U_2^1 - \lambda_2 = 0 \qquad W_1 U_2^1 = \lambda_2 \tag{6}$$

$$\frac{\partial L}{\partial x_{21}} = W_2 U_1^2 - \lambda_1 = 0 \qquad W_2 U_1^2 = \lambda_1 \tag{7}$$

$$\frac{\partial L}{\partial x_{22}} = W_2 U_2^2 - \lambda_2 = 0 \qquad W_2 U_2^2 = \lambda_2 \tag{8}$$

The two equations in (4.3.3) and the preceding four equations are six equations in six variables: four x's and two λ's. They can be solved to determine the optimum values of x's and λ's.

Just as in the preceding section, combining the four equations will produce the same condition as (4.3.11). This means that the optimum occurs on the contract curve on which these marginal optimality conditions are satisfied.

The above optimality condition additionally gives

$$W_1 U_1^1 = W_2 U_1^2 \tag{9}$$

$$W_1 U_2^1 = W_2 U_2^2 \tag{10}$$

Equations (9)–(10) state that each individual's marginal utility of net consumptions of each good, weighted by his marginal social significance must be the same for all individuals and goods.

These two conditions introduce assumptions involving interpersonal comparison. Equations (9)–(10) can be rewritten:

$$\frac{W_1}{W_2} = \frac{U_1^2}{U_1^1} = \frac{U_2^2}{U_2^1} \tag{11}$$

Thus these conditions determine a single point on the contract curve as the best point.

Equations (5) and (7) imply also

$$\frac{\partial W}{\partial x_{11}} = \frac{\partial W}{\partial x_{21}} \tag{12}$$

Similarly for commodity 2.

$$\frac{\partial W}{\partial x_{12}} = \frac{\partial W}{\partial x_{22}} \tag{13}$$

Similarly for factor 2. Equations (12) and (13) state the equality of marginal social utility for all individuals and all goods. This specifies optimum distribution of incomes through such redistribution means as lump-sum taxes and subsidies.[6]

4.5 EXTERNALITY IN PRODUCTION AND CONSUMPTION

The model of Section 4.3 shows that under the assumptions regarding the consumer's tastes and the producer's technology, equilibrium under perfect competition represents Pareto-optimum patterns of production and consumption. One of the obstacles which prevent Adam Smith's invisible hand from serving as the optimum allocator of products and factors has been called *externality*. In the presence of externality it turns out that competitive equilibrium is not Pareto optimal. The following models examine the effects of this obstacle in production and consumption, and see if there exist any remedies.

[6] On the social welfare function, see Bergson (1938), Lange (1942b), Samuelson (1947), chap. 8, and Graaff (1957).

OWNERSHIP EXTERNALITY IN PRODUCTION

External economy and diseconomy mean that the profits of a producer are affected not only by the actions of his own such as his inputs and outputs of goods, but also by those of other producers. External economy and diseconomy can be classified into two types: pecuniary and technological.[7] *Pecuniary* externality is concerned with effects through the markets and the price mechanism. For example, the profits of the firms in one industry increase because they use as raw materials the product of another industry which has expanded and whose product has declined in price as a result of the economy of scale. *Techno-logical* externality means that the production function of a firm takes as arguments the inputs and outputs of goods by another firm, that is, the technical possibility of one firm is affected by another firm's activity.

In the preceding models the prices were attached to all variables that affect profits. But a first firm's output may be affected by the output of a second firm for which the first firm does not pay or is compensated for. Under these circumstances the price system does not take into account all the relevant factors, and there arises a divergence between the private marginal cost and social marginal cost, the price system focusing its attention on the former. Compensation for benefits or damage is not paid, and the market mechanism is bypassed. Competitive equilibrium under such circumstances will be shown to be not Pareto optimum.

Consider a three-good economy where two products y_1 (say apples) and y_2 (say honey) are produced using a given amount of one factor v_1 (say labor). Assume further that the level of output y_2 is affected by the level of output y_1, because the bees collect honey from apple blossoms. Thus the production functions are

$$y_1 = f^1(v_{11}) \qquad f_1^1 > 0 \tag{1}$$

$$y_2 = f^2(v_{21}, y_1) \qquad f_1^2 > 0 \quad f_2^2 > 0 \tag{2}$$

$$v_1 = v_{11} + v_{21} \tag{3}$$

The marginal rate of transformation can be computed as follows. Taking the differentials of (1)–(3)

$$dy_1 = f_1^1 \, dv_{11} \tag{4}$$

$$dy_2 = f_1^2 \, dv_{21} + f_2^2 \, dy_1 \tag{5}$$

$$0 = dv_{11} + dv_{21} \tag{6}$$

[7] *Cf.* Viner (1931), Scitovsky (1954).

Using (4) and (6) in (5)

$$dy_2 = -f_1^2 \, dv_{11} + f_2^2 f_1^1 \, dv_{11}$$

Therefore, the marginal rate of transformation t is

$$t = -\frac{dy_2}{dy_1} = \frac{f_1^2}{f_1^1} - f_2^2 \tag{7}$$

At social optimum, v_{11} and v_{21}, and therefore y_1 and y_2, should be so adjusted that the marginal rate of product substitution p_1/p_2 should equal the marginal rate of transformation, whose value should be the right-hand side of (7).

In Figure 4.5.1 the curve A_1A_2 gives the transformation curve, whose tangent gives the marginal rate of transformation equal to (7). At social optimum this must be equal to the price ratio and the marginal rate of substitution as at B. That is, the transformation curve must be tangent to an indifference curve.

In competitive equilibrium, each producer maximizes his profit by equating the value of marginal product to the factor price:

$$p_1 f_1^1 = r_1 \tag{8}$$

Since producer 2 has to pay only for labor input,

$$p_2 f_1^2 = r_1 \tag{9}$$

Figure 4.5.1

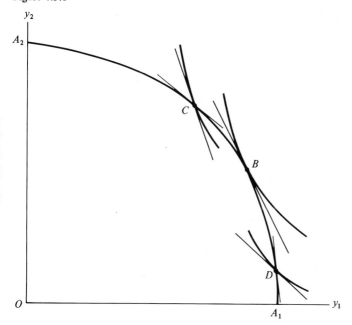

Hence in competitive equilibrium, v_{11} and v_{21}, and therefore y_1 and y_2, will be so adjusted that

$$\frac{p_1}{p_2} = \frac{f_1^2}{f_1^1} \tag{10}$$

At these values of y_1 and y_2 in competitive equilibrium, the marginal rate of product transformation which is given by the right-hand side of (7) will be smaller than the marginal rate of substitution given by the right-hand side of (10).

In Figure 4.5.1 since the total available labor is being used, production will be still on the transformation curve, and at that point the price ratio and therefore the marginal rate of substitution will be greater than the marginal rate of transformation, as at C. The point C clearly gives a lower value of the utility index than point B.

This means that too little of commodity 1 (apples) and too much of commodity 2 (honey) is being produced. Thus in the presence of a positive externality effect, too little of the externality-causing commodity is produced. Thus the competitive pricing mechanism does not produce optimum resource allocation.

Consider the case of external diseconomy, by assuming y_1 to be a chemical which has an ill effect on the bees and hence the honey production. In this case, f_2^2 is negative. At the competitive equilibrium, the price ratio and the marginal rate of substitution given by (10) will be less steep than the slope of the tangent to the transformation curve given by (7). This can occur only at a point like D, which is to the right of B. Thus y_1 will be overproduced, while y_2 will be underproduced. The utility index at D is clearly lower than at B.

Example

Consider the model with the utility function of the economy,

$$U = U(y_1, y_2) = y_1 y_2$$

the production functions for two producers,

$$y_1 = v_{11}$$
$$y_2 = 10v_{21}^{1/2} y_1^{1/2}$$

and the factor endowment,

$$v_{11} + v_{21} = 20$$

In competitive equilibrium the price ratio p_1/p_2 should equal the marginal rate of substitution, that is,

$$\frac{p_1}{p_2} = -\frac{dy_2}{dy_1}$$

From the utility function, along an indifference curve,

$$y_2\, dy_1 + y_1\, dy_2 = 0$$

Therefore

$$-\frac{dy_2}{dy_1} = \frac{y_2}{y_1}$$

Hence

$$\frac{p_1}{p_2} = \frac{y_2}{y_1}$$

From the production function

$$f_1^1 = 1$$
$$f_1^2 = 5v_{21}^{-1/2}v_{11}^{1/2}$$

From (10)

$$5v_{21}^{-1/2}v_{11}^{1/2} = \frac{y_2}{y_1} = 10v_{21}^{1/2}v_{11}^{-1/2}$$

Hence

$$v_{11} = 2v_{21}$$

This together with the factor-endowment equality

$$v_{11} = \frac{40}{3} \qquad v_{21} = \frac{20}{3}$$

Hence

$$y_1 = \frac{40}{3}$$

$$y_2 = 10\left(\frac{20}{3}\right)^{1/2}\left(\frac{40}{3}\right)^{1/2} = 94.3$$

$$U = 10\left(\frac{20}{3}\right)^{1/2}\left(\frac{40}{3}\right)^{3/2} = 1260$$

For Pareto optimality, the marginal rate of transformation must equal the marginal rate of substitution. From (7)

$$5v_{21}^{-1/2}v_{11}^{1/2} - 5v_{21}^{1/2}v_{11}^{-1/2} = \frac{y_2}{y_1} = 10v_{21}^{1/2}v_{11}^{-1/2}$$

that is,

$$v_{11} = 3v_{21}$$

From the factor-endowment equality

$$v_{11} = 15 \qquad v_{21} = 5$$

Hence

$$y_1 = 15$$
$$y_2 = 10 \cdot 5^{1/2} \cdot 15^{1/2} = 86 \cdot 6$$
$$U = 150 \cdot 5^{1/2} \cdot 15^{1/2} = 1295$$

Remedy 1: Market for Apples as Factor

The effect of this type of externality can be corrected by introducing a market for the externality-causing good (apples) as a factor of production. Let q be the price of the first product as a factor of production, and let the first producer get paid for apples not only as output but also as input into the production of honey. Then the profits functions of the two producers are

$$\pi_1 = (p_1 + q)y_1 - r_1 v_{11} \tag{11}$$

$$\pi_2 = p_2 y_2 - r_1 v_{21} - q \cdot y_1 \tag{12}$$

Under competition each producer maximizes his profits by equating the derivatives of the profit function with respect to independent variables equal to zero,[8] that is,

$$\frac{\partial \pi_1}{\partial v_{11}} = (p_1 + q)f_1^1 - r_1 = 0 \tag{13}$$

$$\frac{\partial \pi_2}{\partial v_{21}} = p_2 f_1^2 - r_1 = 0 \tag{14}$$

$$\frac{\partial \pi_2}{\partial y_1} = p_2 f_2^2 - q = 0 \tag{15}$$

Therefore

$$f_1^1 = \frac{r_1}{p_1 + q} \tag{16}$$

$$f_1^2 = \frac{r_1}{p_2} \tag{17}$$

$$f_2^2 = \frac{q}{p_2} \tag{18}$$

[8] That is, q will be determined so that the demand for y_1 by the second producer will be equal to the supply of y_1 by the first producer.

Then the marginal rate of transformation given by (7) is

$$\mathrm{MRT} = \frac{f_1^2}{f_1^1} - f_2^2$$

$$= \frac{p_1 + q}{p_2} - \frac{q}{p_2}$$

$$= \frac{p_1}{p_2} \tag{19}$$

that is, the marginal rate of transformation is equated to the marginal rate of substitution.

Remedy 2: Excise Tax on Honey

Another remedy is taxation. Let t be the rate of an excise tax on honey to be collected from the beekeepers and transferred to the apple producers. The profits functions of the two producers are

$$\pi_1 = p_1 y_1 - r_1 v_{11} + t p_2 y_2 \tag{20}$$

$$\pi_2 = p_2 y_2 - r_1 v_{21} - t p_2 y_2 \tag{21}$$

Under competition, the profit-maximizing producers will adjust v_{11} and v_{21} so that

$$\frac{\partial \pi_1}{v_{11}} = p_1 f_1^1 - r_1 = 0 \tag{22}$$

$$\frac{\partial \pi_2}{v_{21}} = p_2 f_1^2 - r_1 - t p_2 f_1^2 = 0 \tag{23}$$

Therefore

$$f_1^1 = \frac{r_1}{p_1} \tag{24}$$

$$f_1^2 = \frac{r_1}{(1 - t) p_2} \tag{25}$$

If t is such as to equate the marginal rate of transformation given by (7) to the marginal rate of substitution, then

$$\frac{f_1^2}{f_1^1} - f_2^2 = \frac{p_1}{(1 - t) p_2} - f_2^2 = \frac{p_1}{p_2} \tag{26}$$

Solving the last equality for t,

$$t = \frac{f_2^2 p_2}{p_1 + f_2^2 p_2} \tag{27}$$

Hence this rate of tax will produce a Pareto-optimum resource allocation.

EXTERNALITY IN CONSUMPTION

The consumer's utility has been assumed to depend only upon the quantities of commodities he consumes (and factor services he supplies). Assume now that an envious consumer's utility is affected not only by the quantities he consumes, but also by the quantities other consumers consume. For example, assume that in a two-person economy the consumers' utility functions are

$$U^1 = U^1(x_{11}, x_{12}, x_{21}) \tag{28}$$

$$U^2 = U^2(x_{21}, x_{22}) \tag{29}$$

Let the economy's transformation function be

$$F(x_{11} + x_{21}, x_{12} + x_{22}) = 0 \tag{30}$$

For Pareto optimality, maximize the first consumer's utility holding the second consumer's utility at a constant level $\overline{U}^2$. The Lagrangean function for this constrained maximum problem is

$$
\begin{aligned}
L = \ &U^1(x_{11}, x_{12}, x_{21}) \\
&- \lambda_1 [\overline{U}^2 - U^2(x_{21}, x_{22})] \\
&- \lambda_2 F(x_{11} + x_{21}, x_{12} + x_{22})
\end{aligned}
\tag{31}
$$

The first-order condition is

$$\frac{\partial L}{\partial x_{11}} = U_1^1 - \lambda_2 F_1 = 0 \tag{32}$$

$$\frac{\partial L}{\partial x_{12}} = U_2^1 - \lambda_2 F_2 = 0 \tag{33}$$

$$\frac{\partial L}{\partial x_{21}} = U_3^1 + \lambda_1 U_1^2 - \lambda_2 F_1 = 0 \tag{34}$$

$$\frac{\partial L}{\partial x_{22}} = \lambda_1 U_2^2 - \lambda_2 F_2 = 0 \tag{35}$$

$$\frac{\partial L}{\partial \lambda_1} = \overline{U}^2 - U^2(x_{21}, x_{22}) = 0 \tag{36}$$

$$\frac{\partial L}{\partial \lambda_2} = F(x_{11} + x_{21}, x_{12} + x_{22}) = 0 \tag{37}$$

From (34)

$$\lambda_1 U_1^2 = -U_3^1 + \lambda_2 F_1 \tag{38}$$

From (35)

$$\lambda_1 U_2^2 = \lambda_2 F_2 \tag{39}$$

Dividing (38) by (39) and using (32) and (33) gives

$$\frac{U_1^2}{U_2^2} = \frac{U_1^1 - U_3^1}{U_2^1} \tag{40}$$

rather than (4.3.13), the optimality condition in the no-externality case

$$\frac{U_1^2}{U_2^2} = \frac{U_1^1}{U_2^1} \tag{41}$$

Under perfect competition, each consumer equates his own marginal rate of substitution to the price ratio and therefore (41) results, rather than the optimal condition (40). Thus perfect competition fails to lead to Pareto optimality.[9]

4.6 DECREASING AVERAGE COST

The models so far ruled out increasing returns to scale, which means falling average cost. Although the models so far assumed all goods to be perfectly divisible, some goods, such as facilities provided by public utilities, are indivisible. Providing services using these facilities entail a large fixed cost, and involves falling average costs over a wide range of output. A falling average cost means that the average cost exceeds marginal cost, and the producer operating on the marginal-cost pricing principle will not engage in the production of this good, as was shown in Section 2.4. The following models examine problems involved in this situation of decreasing average cost.

Suppose that there are two goods in the economy: a commodity y and labor v (negative of which $-v$ is leisure), and that the utility or welfare function is

$$U = U(y, -v) \qquad U_1, U_2 > 0 \tag{1}$$

while the transformation function is

$$y = F(v) = \begin{cases} 0 & \text{for } v \leq c \\ a(v - c) & \text{for } v > c \end{cases} \tag{2}$$

In other words, to obtain y, the society must incur the fixed cost of c units of labor, in which case, for each unit of labor expended beyond c, the amount of the commodity produced is a. The average variable cost, and the marginal cost, in terms of labor is $1/a$. Thus the total-cost function in terms of labor is

$$C = C(y) = \begin{cases} 0 & \text{when } y = 0 \quad (v \leq c) \\ \left(c + \frac{1}{a}y\right) & \text{when } y > 0 \quad (v > c) \end{cases} \tag{3}$$

[9] On the problem of externality discussed in this section, see Meade (1952), Buchanan and Stubblebine (1962), Bator (1958).

where the wage rate is taken as unity. If the commodity is produced at all, the average cost is

$$\frac{C}{y} = \left(\frac{c}{y} + \frac{1}{a}\right) \tag{4}$$

while the marginal cost is

$$\frac{dC}{dy} = \frac{1}{a} \tag{5}$$

The average- and marginal-cost functions in terms of labor can be shown as AC and MC in Figure 4.6.1(b). The average cost consists of the average fixed cost and average variable cost.

SOCIAL OPTIMUM

If the commodity is to be produced at all, then the optimum of the economy is achieved when the marginal rate of substitution in consumption equals the marginal rate of transformation in production. The former is given by (1):

$$-\frac{d}{dy}(-v) = \frac{U_1}{U_2} \tag{6}$$

while the latter is given by (2).

$$-\frac{d}{dy}(-v) = \frac{1}{a} \tag{7}$$

Hence the optimality condition is

$$\frac{U_1}{U_2} = \frac{1}{a} \tag{8}$$

Equations (2) and (8) are two equations in y and $(-v)$, which can be solved for the optimum labor input $\bar{v}$. The price ratio p equals the equalized marginal rates:

$$p = \frac{1}{a} \tag{9}$$

The output corresponding to $\bar{v}$ is

$$\bar{y} = a(\bar{v} - c) \tag{10}$$

and the level of utility is

$$\bar{U} = U(a(\bar{v} - c), -\bar{v}) \tag{11}$$

In Figure 4.6.1(a), the point A represents the Pareto-optimum allocation.

Figure 4.6.1

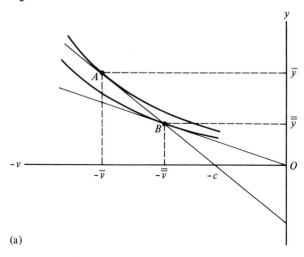

(a)

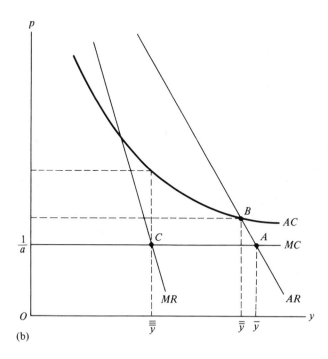

(b)

In terms of the cost function, the marginal cost is equated to the price. That is,

$$\frac{dC}{dy} = \frac{1}{a} = p \tag{12}$$

which gives the same results as (9).

The Pareto-optimum output and price are shown in Figure 4.6.1(b). AR denotes the demand function for y, showing the demand as a function of the price p. The intersection A of AR and MC (marginal cost) represents the Pareto-optimum output and price.

Equation (4) clearly shows that the average cost is a decreasing function of output. Equation (5) and the discussion of Section 2.4 show that a decreasing average cost means that average cost exceeds marginal cost and that the firm equating marginal cost to price incurs loss, and therefore will not engage in the production of the commodity whose optimum output is $\bar{y}$ in Figure 4.6.1 (a) and (b).

Alternative pricing formulas are discussed below.

AVERAGE-COST PRICING

One alternative is to set the price of the commodity equal to the average cost, that is,

$$p = \frac{c}{y} + \frac{1}{a} \qquad \text{or} \qquad py = c + \frac{y}{a} \tag{13}$$

assuming the level of demand y is predictable. In Figure 4.6.1 (a) and (b), the output y and the price p are given by the point B. The firm does not incur losses. Apparently, the output is lower and the price higher than in the case of Pareto optimum. The level of output is shown by $\bar{y}$.

MONOPOLISTIC FIRM

Another alternative is to set up a monopoly and let it produce the commodity. The consumers own the firm and receive the profits as nonwage income. The monopoly will set the price p so as to maximize profits, that is, equate marginal revenue to marginal cost (see Chapter 5). The firm does not incur losses either. The output ($\bar{\bar{y}}$) and prices are given by point C in Figure 4.6.1(b). In this solution also, the output is lower and the price is higher than in the Pareto-optimum case.

THE LANGE-LERNER FIRM

The Lange-Lerner firm sets the price equal to marginal cost and receives a subsidy to finance the deficit.[10] This should obviously give the Pareto-optimum

---

[10] Lange (1938); Lerner (1946), chaps. 15–17; Bergson (1948).

solution, represented again by point A. The price ratio is $p = 1/a$. The subsidy needed is

$$C - py = v - py$$
$$= v - \frac{1}{a} y$$

Using (10)

$$C - py = c$$

THE DECISION TO PRODUCE OR NOT

Whether to produce the good involving a large fixed cost and therefore a falling average cost must be determined by direct comparison of the choices available.

The domain for the quantity variables are

$$v > c \qquad y = a(v - c) > 0$$

and

$$v = 0 \qquad y = 0$$

Assume the good is to be produced and determine the optimum values $\bar{v}$ and $\bar{y}$. Compare $U(\bar{y}, -\bar{v})$ with $U(0, 0)$. If the former is greater than the latter, then the good should be produced.

4.7 THEORY OF PUBLIC GOODS

Another case of the "failure" of the competitive pricing mechanism to produce Pareto-optimum allocation of resources is the existence of public goods in the economy. Even a market economy cannot operate without such public goods as a lighthouse. Consider an economy made up of two consumers consuming two goods, the first being a private good and the second a public good. With respect to the private good x_1, the sum of the consumptions by the two consumers is equal to the total available quantity of the good, that is,

$$x_1 = x_{11} + x_{21}$$

A *public good* is defined to be a good the consumption of which by one consumer does not reduce the consumption by the other. Therefore

$$x_2 = x_{12} = x_{22}$$

Samuelson's analysis of this situation can be presented in a simplified form as follows.

Let the ith individual's utility function be

$$U^i = U^i(x_{i1}, x_2) \qquad i = 1, 2 \tag{1}$$

For Pareto optimality the first consumer's utility index U^1 must be maximized subject to the constraint

$$U^2(x_{21}, x_2) = \overline{U}^2 \tag{2}$$

where $\overline{U}^2$ is an arbitrary level of the second consumer's utility index, and subject to the transformation function for the two types of goods of the economy,

$$F(x_{11} + x_{21}, x_2) = 0 \tag{3}$$

The Lagrangean function for this maximization problem is

$$L = U^1(x_{11}, x_2) - \lambda_1 [\overline{U}^2 - U^2(x_{21}, x_2)] - \lambda_2 F \tag{4}$$

The first-order condition is

$$U_1^1 - \lambda_2 F_1 = 0 \tag{5}$$

$$\lambda_1 U_1^2 - \lambda_2 F_1 = 0 \tag{6}$$

$$U_2^1 + \lambda_1 U_2^2 - \lambda_2 F_2 = 0 \tag{7}$$

From (6)

$$\lambda_1 U_1^2 = \lambda_2 F_1 \tag{8}$$

From (7)

$$U_2^1 + \lambda_1 U_2^2 = \lambda_2 F_2 \tag{9}$$

Dividing (9) by (8)

$$\frac{U_2^1}{\lambda_1 U_1^2} + \frac{U_2^2}{U_1^2} = \frac{F_2}{F_1} \tag{10}$$

From (5) and (6)

$$\lambda_1 U_1^2 = U_1^1 \tag{11}$$

Substituting (11) in (10)

$$\frac{U_2^1}{U_1^1} + \frac{U_2^2}{U_1^2} = \frac{F_2}{F_1} \tag{12}$$

That is, for Pareto optimality, the sum of the two consumers' marginal rates of substitution between the two goods should be equal to the marginal rate of transformation between the two goods.

Assuming the concave transformation curve (increasing marginal rate of transformation), F_2/F_1 is an increasing function of x_2, while assuming the convex indifference curve (diminishing marginal rate of substitution), U_2^i/U_1^i is a decreasing function of x_2, and so is the vertical sum of U_2^i/U_1^i. The equality represents the intersection of the two curves at P in Figure 4.7.1.

A model of competitive equilibrium involving a public good, say TV programs, can be formulated as follows. Assume that the two goods are produced by identical competitive producers. If F is the aggregate-product function, then the producers equate the marginal rate of transformation of two goods to the price ratio, that is,

$$\frac{F_2}{F_1} = \frac{p_2}{p_1}$$

In competitive equilibrium, consumers choose their consumptions so that

$$\frac{U_2^1}{U_1^1} = \frac{p_2}{p_1} \tag{13}$$

$$\frac{U_2^2}{U_1^2} = \frac{p_2}{p_1} \tag{14}$$

Figure 4.71

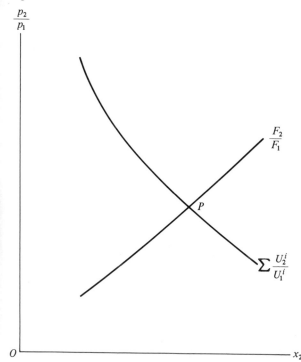

This gives

$$\frac{U_2^1}{U_1^1} + \frac{U_2^2}{U_1^2} = 2\frac{p_2}{p_1} > \frac{F_2}{F_1} \tag{15}$$

implying that the U_2^i are too large relative to the U_1^i, and therefore less than an optimal amount of good 2 is being produced.

The equality of the sum of marginal utilities to the marginal cost cannot be realized by the competitive mechanism. If every consumer is expected to declare the marginal utility of an additional unit of a public good, the left-hand side of (12) can be computed. But if the public good is to be financed by voluntary contributions according to his valuation, then it pays each citizen to understate his preference for the public good in order to reduce the contribution he will have to make. Thus the price mechanism fails to bring about the optimum allocation of resources.[11]

Example

Let x_{i1} be negative numbers denoting labor supplies,

$$U^1 = U^1(x_{11}, x_2) = -x_{11}^2 + 3x_2$$
$$U^2 = U^2(x_{21}, x_2) = -x_{21}^2 + 4x_2$$
$$x_2 = -7(x_{11} + x_{21})$$

For competitive equilibrium

$$\frac{3}{-2x_{11}} = \frac{1}{7}$$

$$\frac{4}{-2x_{21}} = \frac{1}{7}$$

Therefore

$$x_{11} = -10.5$$
$$x_{21} = -14$$

Thus

$$x_{11} + x_{21} = -24.5 \qquad x_2 = 171.5$$
$$U^1 = 404.25$$
$$U^2 = 490$$

---

[11] On the theory of public goods, see Samuelson (1954a, 1955, 1958).

Pareto optimality can be realized under any division of labor between the two individuals. Let

$$\frac{x_{11}}{x_{11} + x_{21}} = a$$

Then

$$x_{11} = \frac{a}{1 - a} x_{21}$$

The optimality condition is

$$\frac{3}{-2x_{11}} + \frac{4}{-2x_{21}} = \frac{1}{7}$$

Therefore

$$\frac{3(1 - a)}{-2ax_{21}} + \frac{4}{-2x_{21}} = \frac{1}{7}$$

$$-\left(\frac{3(1 - a)}{2a} + 2 \right) \frac{1}{x_{21}} = \frac{1}{7}$$

$$-\frac{3 + a}{2a} \frac{1}{x_{21}} = \frac{1}{7}$$

Therefore

$$x_{21} = -\frac{7(3 + a)}{2a} \qquad x_{11} = -\frac{7(3 + a)}{2(1 - a)}$$

For example,

$$a = \tfrac{1}{2} \qquad x_{11} = -24.5 \qquad x_{21} = -24.5$$
$$x_2 = 343 \qquad U^1 = 428.75 \qquad U^2 = 771.75$$

Thus competitive equilibrium is not Pareto optimum.

4.8 INDIRECT TAXATION

The effects of indirect taxation upon optimum resource allocation can be analyzed in the present context. This analysis can answer the question: What types of indirect taxation should be preferred in order to avoid a certain distortion of optimum resource allocation? The following will show that an indirect tax introduces a distortion unless it is proportional to the price.

Assume that the two goods are being produced and consumed, and that the total consumption of each good consists of the private and public portions.

Let:

x_i = the total quantity of the ith good produced and consumed

x_{1i} = the quantity of the ith good consumed by the private sector

x_{2i} = the quantity of the ith good consumed by the public sector

Then

$$x_1 = x_{11} + x_{21} \tag{1}$$

$$x_2 = x_{12} + x_{22} \tag{2}$$

Let the technological possibility be represented by the transformation function

$$F(x_1, x_2) = 0 \tag{3}$$

Also let the preferences of the private sector be represented by the utility function of that sector

$$U(x_{11}, x_{12}) \tag{4}$$

Assume that the quantities of public consumption are absolutely needed constants and therefore can be disregarded. The model thus concentrates upon the utility function of the private sector, (4).

SOCIAL OPTIMUM

To see what is required for the maximum of (4) subject to (3), form the Lagrangean function

$$L = U(x_{11}, x_{12}) - \lambda F(x_{11} + x_{21}, x_{12} + x_{22}) \tag{5}$$

and equate the partial derivatives with respect to x_{11} and x_{12} to zero

$$U_1 - \lambda F_1 = 0 \tag{6}$$

$$U_2 - \lambda F_2 = 0 \tag{7}$$

Therefore

$$\frac{U_1}{U_2} = \frac{F_1}{F_2} \tag{8}$$

Thus the marginal rate of substitution in private consumption should be equal to the marginal rate of transformation in the economy.

COMPETITIVE EQUILIBRIUM

The behavior of the private sector under perfect competition can be examined beginning with its producing activity. The firm will maximize its income

$$R = p_1 x_1 + p_2 x_2 \tag{9}$$

subject to (3), where

p_i = the price of the ith good excluding the excise tax

The relevant Lagrangean function gives

$$L = p_1 x_1 + p_2 x_2 - \lambda F(x_1, x_2) \tag{10}$$

The first-order condition gives

$$\frac{F_1}{F_2} = \frac{p_1}{p_2} \tag{11}$$

That is, the producer will be equating the marginal rate of transformation to the commodity-price ratio.

The consumer under perfect competition will maximize (4) subject to his budget equation,

$$(p_1 + t_1)x_1 + (p_2 + t_2)x_2 = R - T \tag{12}$$

where

t_i = tax per unit of the ith good

T = income tax

The Lagrangean function involved is

$$L = U(x_{11}, x_{12}) + \lambda[R - T - (p_1 + t_1)x_1 - (p_2 + t_2)x_2] \tag{13}$$

and the first-order condition is

$$U_1 - \lambda(p_1 + t_1) = 0 \tag{14}$$

$$U_2 - \lambda(p_2 + t_2) = 0 \tag{15}$$

so that

$$\frac{U_1}{U_2} = \frac{p_1 + t_1}{p_2 + t_2} \tag{16}$$

That is, the consumer will be equating his marginal rate of substitution to the commodity-price ratio including the excise taxes.

Therefore, for the economy to satisfy the optimum condition (8), the excise taxes must be such that

$$\frac{p_1}{p_2} = \frac{p_1 + t_1}{p_2 + t_2} \tag{17}$$

That is, *the excise taxes should be proportional to the prices so that they will not distort the relative prices.*

Figure 4.8.1

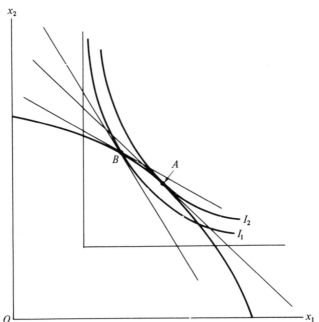

Note that a sales tax which levies the same proportion of the value of the two goods does not violate this rule (17). However, an excise on one good only, or excises on the two goods with different rates, does violate the optimum condition (17).

If, for example, an excise of t_1 is placed on commodity 1 and no excise on commodity 2, then competitive equilibrium will be reached on a point of the transformation curve, where the marginal rate of substitution $(p_1 + t_1)/p_2$ will be greater than the marginal rate of substitution p_1/p_2, as at B in Figure 4.8.1. At this point the economy is underproducing the taxed commodity and overproducing the untaxed commodity, compared with the Pareto-optimum point A. The economy is on a lower indifference curve.

4.9 SUMMARY

The marginalist models of competitive general equilibrium enumerate the demand and supply equations for all goods, count the number of equations and the number of variables, and assure that they are equal. This does not guarantee that a solution with nonnegative prices will exist. The more rigorous analysis must await Part III.

This model of general competitive equilibrium under the *tâtonnement* process can be shown to be dynamically stable if it satisfies several assumptions. This shows the need for alternative formulations of dynamic behavior.

The so-called New Welfare Economics derives, in terms of marginal adjustments in consumption and production, conditions for Pareto optimality (which abstains from judgment upon income distribution and interpersonal comparison of well-being). Competitive equilibrium is shown to be Pareto optimum, but the market mechanism fails to produce such optimality in the presence of externality, decreasing average cost, and public goods.

5
IMPERFECT
COMPETITION

5.1 INTRODUCTION

The partial equilibrium analysis of the firm of Chapter 2 does not apply when competition is not perfect; that is, when each producer or factor owner does not take the prices as given. The situation is referred to under various names, depending on the number of buyers or sellers. When there is only one seller, the situation is called *monopoly*; if there are only two sellers, it is *duopoly*; when there are only a few sellers it is *oligopoly*. The corresponding situations with respect to the buyer are called *monopsony*, *duopsony*, and *oligopsony*, respectively. When there is only one seller and only one buyer in the market the situation is called *bilateral monopoly*. This chapter discusses several models describing these situations, beginning with monopoly.

5.2 MONOPOLY

If a producer is a single seller of the product, namely, a monopolist, then the market-clearing price he can charge is a function of the amount he offers, given by the market demand function

$$p = g(y) \qquad g' < 0 \qquad (1)$$

which slopes downward to the right, as shown in Figure 5.2.1. Let his cost function be

$$C = h(y) \qquad h' > 0 \tag{2}$$

Then his profit function is total revenue R less total cost C, that is,

$$\pi = R(y) - C(y) \tag{3}$$

The first-order condition for maximum profit is

$$\frac{d\pi}{dy} = R'(y) - C'(y) = 0 \tag{4}$$

that is,

$$R'(y) = C'(y) \tag{5}$$

That is, *marginal revenue* is equal to *marginal cost*. This occurs at point A in Figure 5.2.1, where the monopolist produces y' and sells it at p'.

Figure 5.2.1

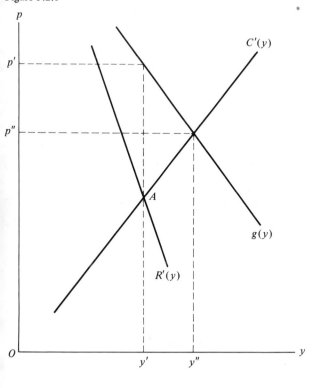

The marginal revenue can be rewritten

$$\frac{d}{dy} py = \frac{dp}{dy} y + p$$

$$= p\left(\frac{dp}{dy} \frac{y}{p} + 1\right) \tag{6}$$

Defining

$$-\frac{dy}{dp} \frac{p}{y} = \eta \tag{7}$$

where η is the absolute value of the price elasticity of demand, marginal revenue equals

$$p\left(1 - \frac{1}{\eta}\right) \tag{8}$$

If the seller is perfectly competitive, then the elasticity of demand for his product η is infinitely large, and the marginal revenue (8) is equal to p, the *average revenue*. As long as the seller is a monopolist, that is, the elasticity of demand for his product is not infinitely large, the marginal revenue (8) is less than the average revenue at all output levels.

The *degree of monopoly* has been defined as

$$\text{degree of monopoly} = \frac{AR - MR}{AR}$$

$$= 1 - \frac{MR}{AR} \tag{9}$$

Using (6), the degree of monopoly equals

$$-\frac{dp}{dy} \frac{y}{p} \tag{10}$$

The right-hand side is the reciprocal of the price elasticity of demand and is called the *price flexibility*.

The second-order condition is

$$\frac{d^2\pi}{dy^2} = R''(y) - C''(y) < 0 \tag{11}$$

that is,

$$R''(y) < C''(y) \tag{12}$$

This condition is satisfied if marginal revenue is falling (the demand curve slopes downward to the right), while marginal cost is rising.

If the monopolist followed the rule of the perfectly competitive firm (that is, a firm that produces the amount at which marginal cost equals price) this would result in a greater output y'' and a lower price p'', as also shown in Figure 5.2.1.

5.3 DUOPOLY AND OLIGOPOLY

Assume that the number of sellers is neither one nor very many. Then this situation of imperfect competition is either duopoly or oligopoly. In the former the number is two, while in the latter the number is more than two but a few. In these situations, each seller must act making some assumptions regarding the reaction of the other seller or sellers. No assumptions have been universally acceptable regarding the reactive behavior. Different assumptions produce different solutions.

There are two types of policy the duopolist or oligopolist can follow: Either the duopolist can adjust his own price, or he can adjust his quantity. The models of the latter policy can be further classified according to the following scheme:

1. Cournot's Duopoly Model

Duopolist A is passive and duopolist B is passive, "passive" here meaning that the seller does not know the rival's reaction pattern and assumes the rival to make no change.

2. Stackelberg's Model of Asymmetric Duopoly

A is passive and B is active or A is active and B is passive, "active" here meaning that the seller knows the rival's reaction pattern.

3. Indeterminate Case

A is active and B is active.

4. Collusive Duopoly

A is collusive, and B is collusive.

COURNOT'S DUOPOLY

Let:

y_1 = supply by duopolist A
y_2 = supply by duopolist B
p = market price of the commodity

Let the market demand function be written

$$p = f(y_1 + y_2) \qquad f' < 0 \tag{1}$$

and let the cost of these supplies be zero for simplicity. The duopolists' profits π_1 and π_2 are

$$\pi_1 = py_1 \qquad \pi_2 = py_2 \tag{2}$$

When each duopolist determines his supply so as to maximize his profits, the first-order conditions are

$$\frac{\partial \pi_1}{\partial y_1} = p + y_1 \cdot \frac{\partial p}{\partial y_1} = f + y_1 f' \cdot \left(1 + \frac{dy_2}{dy_1}\right) = 0 \tag{3}$$

$$\frac{\partial \pi_2}{\partial y_2} = p + y_2 \cdot \frac{\partial p}{\partial y_2} = f + y_2 f' \cdot \left(1 + \frac{dy_1}{dy_2}\right) = 0 \tag{4}$$

The change assumed by one duopolist in the competitor's output, for example dy_2/dy_1 in the case of the first duopolist, is called the *conjectural variation*. In Cournot's analysis, in Cournot (1838), each duopolist, assumes the other to continue to supply the same quantity, and determines his quantity so as to

Figure 5.3.1

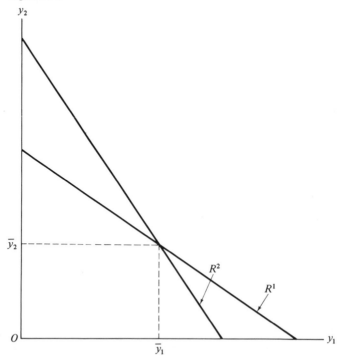

maximize his profits under that assumption. In short, Cournot's analysis assumes conjectural variation to be zero. Hence (3) and (4) can be written

$$\frac{\partial \pi_1}{\partial y_1} = f + y_1 f' = 0 \tag{5}$$

$$\frac{\partial \pi_2}{\partial y_2} = f + y_2 f' = 0 \tag{6}$$

Equation (5) can be solved for y_1 in terms of y_2, and the solution can be written

$$y_1 = R^1(y_2) \tag{7}$$

and called the *reaction function* for A. It gives the supply by A at different levels of supply by B. Similarly the reaction function for B can be written

$$y_2 = R^2(y_1) \tag{8}$$

The values of y_1 and y_2, say $\bar{y}_1$ and $\bar{y}_2$, which satisfy simultaneous equations (7) and (8), are the equilibrium supplies. In the present case assuming zero costs for both sellers, (5) and (6) are symmetric, and therefore (7) and (8) are identical. Figure 5.3.1 shows the equilibrium supplies of the duopolists determined by the intersection of the reaction equations.

Example

Let the demand function (1) be

$$p = a - b \cdot (y_1 + y_2) \qquad a, b > 0 \tag{9}$$

Hence the profit of the first producer (2) will be

$$[a - b \cdot (y_1 + y_2)]y_1 \tag{10}$$

The condition for maximum profit (5) is

$$a - b(y_1 + y_2) - by_1 = 0 \tag{11}$$

$$y_1 = \frac{a - by_2}{2b} \tag{12}$$

This corresponds to the reaction function (7) for the first producer. The reaction function for the second producer can be similarly derived:

$$y_2 = \frac{a - by_1}{2b} \tag{12'}$$

Solving the two reactions equations for y_1 and y_2,

$$y_1 = y_2 = \frac{a}{3b} \tag{13}$$

The price will be

$$p = a - b \cdot \left(\frac{2a}{3b}\right) = \frac{a}{3} \tag{14}$$

In this case, if the number of firms is n, then it can be easily seen

$$y_i = \frac{a}{(n+1)b} \qquad i = 1, \ldots, n \tag{15}$$

$$p = \frac{a}{n+1} \tag{16}$$

As n is increased to infinity, each firm's output approaches zero, while the price also approaches zero, which is the marginal cost under the assumption of the model. This situation of infinitely large n represents perfect competition.

Compare the Cournot solution with perfect competition and monopoly. Under perfect competition where the price is equated to the marginal cost of zero, an output of a/b is supplied, as can be seen in Figure 5.3.2. The present solution (13) supplies 2/3 of the supply under perfect competition. Under monopoly where the marginal revenue

$$a - 2by$$

Figure 5.3.2

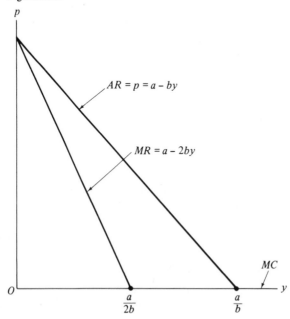

is set equal to a marginal cost of zero, the supply will be one half of the perfect competition case.

The dynamic analysis of the Cournot duopoly calls for the reaction functions with a time lag. Introducing a one-period time lag into the reaction function (12) of duopolist A to the rival's supply

$$y_1(t + 1) = \frac{a - by_2(t)}{2b} \tag{17}$$

Similarly

$$y_2(t + 1) = \frac{a - by_1(t)}{2b} \tag{18}$$

The system of two difference equations (17) and (18) gives the paths of the outputs of the outputs of the two firms toward the Cournot equilibrium.

ASYMMETRIC DUOPOLY

In this formulation, due to Stackelberg (1934), one duopolist is active, while the other is passive. Duopolist A is active in the sense that A knows B's reaction pattern corresponding to every action A takes, that is, A knows B's reaction function. Equilibrium exists in this case also.

Let duopolist B be passive, and his reaction function be (8). The maximum-profits condition for A can be obtained as follows. A's profits function (2) now can be written

$$\pi_1 = py_1 = f(y_1 + y_2) \cdot y_1 = f(y_1 + R^2(y_1)) \cdot y_1 \tag{19}$$

This is a function in one variable, y_1. Thus the maximum-profits condition (3) becomes

$$\frac{d\pi_1}{dy_1} = f + y_1 f' \cdot \left(1 + \frac{dR^2}{dy_1}\right) = 0 \tag{20}$$

Equation (20) in one variable, y_1, can be solved for y_1. The solution $\bar{y}_1$ can be substituted in (8) to obtain $\bar{y}_2$.

For example, let B's reaction function be in the form of (12'), that is,

$$y_2 = \frac{a - by_1}{2b} \tag{21}$$

The conjectural variation dR^2/dy_1 is

$$\frac{dy_2}{dy_1} = -\frac{1}{2} \tag{22}$$

Therefore, using (20),

$$a - b(y_1 + y_2) + (1 - \tfrac{1}{2}) \cdot (-b)y_1 = 0 \qquad (23)$$

That is, A's reaction function is

$$y_1 = \frac{2(a - by_2)}{3b} \qquad (24)$$

Substituting (21) in (24) yields

$$y_1 = \frac{a}{2b} \qquad (25)$$

Substituting this solution into (21) yields

$$y_2 = \frac{a}{4b} \qquad (26)$$

Comparing (25) and (26) with (12), duopolist A's profits have increased, and duopolist B's profits have declined, relative to the Cournot solution.

INDETERMINATE CASE

Suppose A and B are both active, that is, each duopolist thinks he knows the other's reaction patterns and determines the profits-maximizing supply based on the other's reaction function. Then the reaction functions will never be observed. Thus there will exist no equilibrium.

COLLECTIVE MONOPOLY

Here the duopolists know that their profits are interdependent, they avoid rivalry and act collusively so as to maximize the total industry profits. For the purpose of exposition here, suppose that A's and B's cost functions are given by

$$C_1 = C^1(y_1) \qquad (27)$$
$$C_2 = C^2(y_2) \qquad (28)$$

respectively. In this case, the profits functions are

$$\pi_1 = f(y_1 + y_2) \cdot y_1 - C^1(y_1) \qquad (29)$$
$$\pi_2 = f(y_1 + y_2) \cdot y_2 - C^2(y_2) \qquad (30)$$

and the total-profits function is

$$\pi = \pi_1 + \pi_2 = f(y_1 + y_2) \cdot (y_1 + y_2) - C^1(y_1) - C^2(y_2) \qquad (31)$$

The maximum conditions are

$$\frac{\partial \pi}{\partial y_1} = (y_1 + y_2) \cdot f' + f - \frac{dC^1}{dy_1} = 0 \tag{32}$$

$$\frac{\partial \pi}{\partial y_2} = (y_1 + y_2) \cdot f' + f - \frac{dC^2}{dy_2} = 0 \tag{33}$$

Equations (32) and (33) can be solved for y_1 and y_2. These equations show that the marginal cost of one duopolist is equal to that of the other, the common value being the marginal revenue for the industry. They also indicate that the duopolist with the more slowly rising marginal cost will have a greater output and hence a greater share of the market. The more profitable duopolist will have to make a payment to the other for the collective monopoly to be more satisfactory than an alternative market form.

5.4 PRODUCT DIFFERENTIATION

So far the product has been assumed completely homogeneous. When the product is differentiated, two market situations can exist: in one the sellers are few, in the other the sellers are many. The former case has been called *differentiated duopoly or oligopoly*; and the latter, simply, *monopolistic competition*.

DIFFERENTIATED DUOPOLY

When the product is differentiated, each duopolist faces a different demand function. Then writing the demand functions

$$p_1 = f^1(y_1, y_2) \qquad f^1_1 < 0 \quad f^1_2 < 0 \tag{1}$$

$$p_2 = f^2(y_1, y_2) \qquad f^2_1 < 0 \quad f^2_2 < 0 \tag{2}$$

the preceding analysis of Cournot, Stackelberg, and others can be applied *mutatis mutandis*.

MONOPOLISTIC COMPETITION: SHORT RUN (MONOPOLY)

Assume that the number of sellers is large, but each seller's product is distinct so that he faces a demand curve not completely elastic. Assume further that each firm has the same demand and cost functions, and the demand function is

$$p_i = a_0 - a_1 y_i - a_2 \sum_{\substack{j=1 \\ j \neq i}}^{n} y_j \qquad i = 1, \ldots, n \tag{3}$$

Assume further that $a_1 \neq a_2$, and a_2 is very small. This assumed demand function is shown as (3) in Figure 5.4.1. Denote the cost function by $C(y_i)$. The profit of the firm is

$$\pi_i = y_i \cdot \left(a_0 - a_1 y_i - a_2 \sum_{\substack{j=1 \\ j \neq i}}^{n} y_j\right) - C(y_i) \qquad i = 1, \ldots, n \qquad (4)$$

Figure 5.4.1

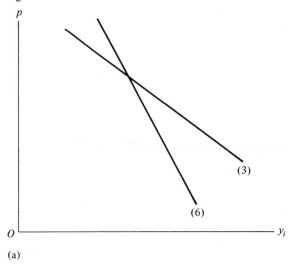

(a)

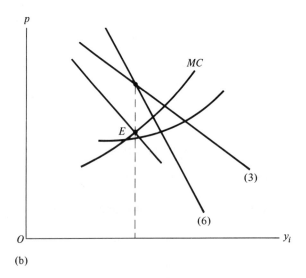

(b)

Since there are many sellers, the firm assumes the effect of its output on other firms to be small, and maximizes its profits disregarding the influences on others. Taking the derivative of (4) with respect to y_i and setting it equal to zero, that is, equating marginal revenue to marginal cost,

$$a_0 - 2a_1 y_i - a_2 \sum_{\substack{j=1 \\ j \neq i}}^{n} y_j = C'(y_i) \tag{5}$$

A quantity variation by the ith firm will be accompanied by other firms who find it advantageous for the same reason. Therefore the actual demand curve for the ith firm will turn out to be, setting $y_j = y_i (j = 1, \ldots, n)$ in (3),

$$p_i = a_0 - [a_1 + (n-1)a_2]y_i \qquad i = 1, \ldots, n \tag{6}$$

This demand function with a steeper slope than (3) is shown as (6) in Figure 5.4.1. The actual profits function is, setting $y_i = y_j$ in (4),

$$\pi_i = a_0 y_i - [a_1 + (n-1)a_2]y_i^2 - C(y_i) \qquad i = 1, \ldots, n \tag{7}$$

The industry reaches a short-run equilibrium when (5) is satisfied by all n firms. Because the firms are identical the equilibrium quantity of each firm is given by setting $y_i = y_j$ in (5),

$$a_0 - [2a_1 + (n-1)a_2]y_i = C'(y_i) \tag{8}$$

and solving (8) for y_i. This equilibrium position is shown as E in Figure 5.4.1(b).

LONG RUN (COMPETITION)

In the long run, the number of firms n changes until profit is driven down to zero. Therefore, (7) is set equal to zero:

$$a_0 y_i - [a_1 + (n-1)a_2]y_i^2 = C(y_i) \tag{9}$$

Equations (8) and (9) provide two equations in two unknowns y_i and n. Dividing (9) through by y_i and subtracting (8) from the result,

$$\frac{C}{y_i} - C' = a_1 y_i \tag{10}$$

Since average cost exceeds marginal cost, the solution $\bar{y}$ is to the left of the minimum point of the average-cost curve. Use $\bar{y}$ in (8) to obtain

$$n = \frac{a_0 - C'}{a_2 \bar{y}} - 2\frac{a_1}{a_2} + 1 \tag{11}$$

This equilibrium position is shown in Figure 5.4.2. The firm produces output short of the minimum average-cost output.[1]

---

[1] *Cf.* Chamberlin (1933), chap. 5.

Figure 5.4.2

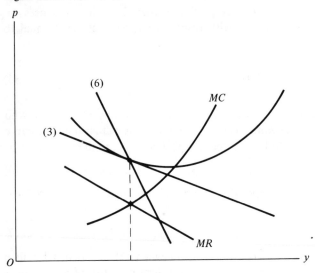

5.5 MONOPSONY

If the producer is a monopsonist of a factor, then the price he pays, the *average-factor cost*, is a function of the amount he buys, which can be written

$$r = f(v) \quad , \quad f'(v) > 0 \tag{1}$$

From the discussion of Section 2.5, it slopes upward to the right as *AFC* does in Figure 5.5.1. Then the firm's total-factor cost is

$$C = rv = vf(v) \tag{2}$$

and the marginal-factor cost is

$$\frac{dC}{dv} = r + vf'(v) \tag{3}$$

Hence it exceeds the factor price. It is shown as *MFC* in Figure 5.5.1. This equation can be written

$$\frac{dC}{dv} = r\left(1 + \frac{v}{r}\frac{dr}{dv}\right) \tag{4}$$

Defining the *elasticity of supply* as

$$e = \frac{r}{v}\frac{dv}{dr} \tag{5}$$

Figure 5.5.1

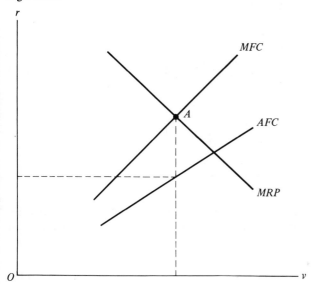

(4) can be rewritten

$$\frac{dC}{dv} = r\left(1 + \frac{1}{e}\right) \tag{6}$$

The monopsonist of a factor, who is also a monopolist of his product, determines the price and quantity of the factor as follows.

Let:

p = the price of the product he sells
y = the amount of the product he sells

Then his profit is

$$\pi = py - rv \tag{7}$$

The necessary condition for maximum profits is

$$\frac{d\pi}{dv} = p\frac{dy}{dv} + y\frac{dp}{dy}\frac{dy}{dv} - \left(\frac{dr}{dv}v + r\right) = 0 \tag{8}$$

That is,

$$\left(p + y\frac{dp}{dy}\right)\frac{dy}{dv} = \frac{dr}{dv}v + r \tag{9}$$

The left-hand side is marginal revenue times marginal product, called *marginal-*

revenue product, while the right-hand side is *marginal-factor cost*. This equality occurs at A in Figure 5.5.1.

Using (5.2.8) and (6), (9) can be rewritten

$$\left(1 - \frac{1}{\eta}\right) p \frac{dy}{dv} = \left(1 + \frac{1}{e}\right) r \tag{10}$$

Therefore

$$r = p \frac{dy}{dv} \left(1 - \frac{1}{\eta}\right)\left(1 + \frac{1}{e}\right)^{-1}$$

$$= p \frac{dy}{dv} \frac{\eta - 1}{\eta} \frac{e}{1 + e} \tag{11}$$

If the producer is a perfectly competitive seller of his product and a perfectly competitive buyer of the factor, then η and e are infinitely large. Therefore from (11),

$$r = p \cdot \frac{dy}{dv} \tag{12}$$

that is, the value of marginal product equals the factor price, as was shown in Chapter 2. If the producer is a monopolist only, then $e = \infty$, and

$$r = \left(1 - \frac{1}{\eta}\right) p \cdot \frac{dy}{dv} \tag{13}$$

This expression is less than (12) by the amount

$$\frac{1}{\eta} p \cdot \frac{dy}{dv} \tag{14}$$

which Robinson has called the amount of "monopolistic exploitation." If monopsony alone exists, then the factor price is given by

$$r = \frac{p \cdot \dfrac{dy}{dv}}{1 + \dfrac{1}{e}} \tag{15}$$

which is smaller than the value of marginal product by

$$\frac{p \cdot \dfrac{dy}{dv}}{1 + e} \tag{16}$$

This has been called the amount of "monopsonistic exploitation." If both monopoly in the product market and monopsony in the factor market exist, then the factor price will be less than the value of marginal product by the sum of (14) and (16).[2]

MONOPOLY AND RESOURCE ALLOCATION

Assume that two commodities y_1 and y_2 are produced using one factor v, the former by a monopoly and the latter by a competitive producer, and that both producers are competitive buyers of the factor. The producer 1 equates the marginal-revenue product to the factor price, that is,

$$\frac{dy_1}{dv_1}\left(p_1 + y_1 \frac{dp_1}{dy_1}\right) = r \tag{17}$$

while producer 2 equates the value of marginal product to the factor price

$$\frac{dy_2}{dv_2} p_2 = r \tag{18}$$

Since the total amount of labor is fixed

$$dv_1 + dv_2 = 0 \tag{19}$$

Since $dy_1/dp_1 < 0$ (the demand function is negatively sloped), (17) and (18) imply

$$\frac{dy_1}{dv_1} p_1 > \frac{dy_2}{dv_2} p_2$$

Using (19),

$$-\frac{dy_2}{dy_1} < \frac{p_1}{p_2}$$

that is, the marginal rate of transformation is less than the price ratio, to which the consumers equate their marginal rate of substitution. Since the marginal rate of transformation is less than the marginal rate of substitution, as shown in Figure 4.8.1, the economy again is at B, rather than at the Pareto-optimum A. Similar analysis can be made of the welfare aspects of monopsony.

5.6 BILATERAL MONOPOLY

The ability of the monopoly to "exploit" the factor discussed in the preceding section, is limited or nullified by the sellers who organize themselves into a monopoly. An example is a labor market where a federation of employers is the

[2] Robinson (1933), chaps. 25–26.

Figure 5.6.1

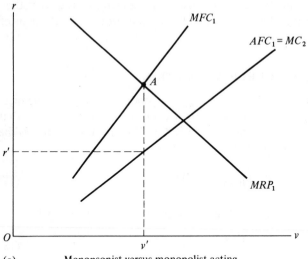

(a)   Monopsonist versus monopolist acting
as perfectly competitive seller

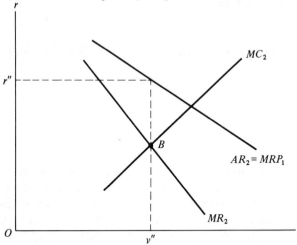

(b)   Monopolist versus monopsonist acting
as perfectly competitive buyer

monopsonist and a trade union is the monopolist. The situation has been called a *bilateral monopoly*. It can be analyzed by the device of the contract curve of Figure 4.3.1.

The point O indicates the initial holdings of the two individuals; that is, individual 1 owns x_1 units of money and individual 2 owns x_2 units of a factor (say, labor). Let OF be the indifference curve of individual 1, and OG be that

Figure 5.6.2

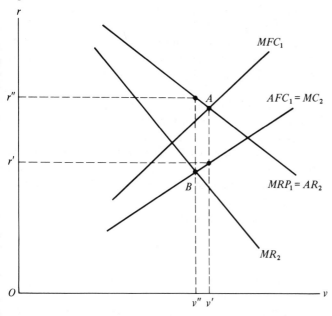

of individual 2, both through O. Let the intersection of OF and OG with the contract curve be F and G, respectively. Then, to both individuals, any point on FG (between F and G) is preferable to O. Hence their trade can end up on a point on FG (between F and G). The terms of exchange at that point are given by the common slope of the two individuals' indifference curves (they are tangential to each other on the contract curve). The closer the point is to F, the worse to individual 1, and vice versa. Which point on FG will in fact be chosen by the two parties will depend on the bargaining process, and cannot be determined theoretically.

ANALYSIS IN TERMS OF REVENUE AND COST FUNCTIONS

The monopsonist's demand for the factor is a derived demand in the sense that it is derived from the demand for the product in the production of which the factor is used. The factor-demand curve will be the value of marginal-product curve if the monopsonist is a perfectly competitive seller of the product, as was shown in Section 2.5, and will be the marginal-revenue-product curve (MRP_1) if the monopsonist is a monopolist in the product market, as was shown in Section 5.5 and in Figure 5.5.1.

The monopolist of the factor, the other party in the exchange, does not have a supply curve. But if he is forced to act as a perfectly competitive seller, then he will sell at marginal cost. Then his marginal-cost curve (MC_2) will be his supply curve. To the monopsonist of the factor this curve is the average-factor-cost curve (AFC_1), and his marginal-factor-cost curve (MFC_1) can be drawn as in Figure 5.6.1. Thus if the seller's monopoly power is ignored, the monopsonist's equilibrium is reached where his marginal-revenue-product curve intersects with his marginal-factor-cost curve at A. Thus he will purchase v' units of the factor at the price r'.

On the other hand, if the buyer of the factor is forced to act like a perfectly competitive buyer and the monopoly power of the sellers alone is considered, then the monopsonist's marginal-revenue-product curve is the monopolist's average-revenue curve (AR_2; see figure 5.6.2). The curve marginal to this represents the monopolist's marginal-revenue curve (MR_2). The monopolist's optimum is obtained where his marginal-cost curve intersects with his marginal-revenue curve at B. Thus he will sell v'' units of labor at r''. The final outcome can be between r' and r'', but is theoretically indeterminate.

5.7 SUMMARY

Models of imperfect competition analyze the behavior of imperfectly competitive sellers and buyers. A monopolist achieves optimum when he equates marginal-revenue product to the factor price in contrast to the perfectly competitive seller who equates the value of marginal product to the factor price. A monopolist of a product who also is a monopsonist of a factor achieves optimum when he equates marginal-revenue product to marginal-factor cost. In terms of the product-cost function, equilibrium is achieved when marginal revenue is equated to marginal cost. Models of competition among the few make various assumptions and produce indeterminate as well as determinate results.

6
INTERTEMPORAL RESOURCE ALLOCATION

6.1 INTRODUCTION

The models of this chapter distinguish the commodity by the time period. For simplicity assume that there exists only one commodity, say wheat, and only two periods : period 1, the present, and period 2, the future. The aggregation of commodities into a single commodity is justified if the hypothesis of the composite commodity theorem in Section 1.4 is satisfied. Assume that the commodity is traded perfectly competitively, that is, each economic unit buys or sells the commodity assuming the prices are given; and that there exists a future market for the commodity in which contracts for future delivery of the commodity are traded. All transactions take place in period 1, and the resulting relative prices for the two periods are defined as follows: The *forward price* of a commodity for period 2, denoted by p_2, is the price that must be paid in period 1 in order to get a unit of the commodity delivered in period 2. The forward price for period 1, denoted by p_1, is the *spot price*. We may take $p_1 = 1$. The *real rate of interest r* in terms of this commodity from period 1 to period 2 is defined as

$$r = \frac{p_1 - p_2}{p_2} = \frac{1 - p_2}{p_2} \tag{1}$$

and the *interest factor* as

$$1 + r = \frac{p_1}{p_2} = \frac{1}{p_2} \tag{2}$$

The relative price p_2, therefore, can be written

$$\frac{1}{1+r} \tag{3}$$

The interest factor can alternatively be defined

$$1 + r = \frac{\text{units of period 2 commodity delivered}}{\text{units of period 1 commodity loaned}} \tag{4}$$

6.2 INTERTEMPORAL CONSUMPTION: SAVING AND DISSAVING

Assume that the consumer has perfect foresight and complete certainty about the future income stream. The consumer then can be assumed to know his preference map over his commodity plane for all times, and therefore he can be assumed to make once-and-for-all decisions in period 1 regarding his consumption plans for periods 1 and 2. Assume these preferences to be represented by a utility function

$$U(C_1, C_2) \tag{1}$$

The utility function has the following properties: U is twice-differentiable; U is increasing, that is, U_1 and U_2 are positive and therefore there is no satiation; U is strictly quasi-concave, that is,

$$\begin{vmatrix} U_{11} & U_{12} & U_1 \\ U_{21} & U_{22} & U_2 \\ U_1 & U_2 & 0 \end{vmatrix} > 0 \tag{2}$$

that is, indifference curves are strictly convex to the origin, or the marginal rate of substitution is strictly diminishing, as is shown in Figure 6.2.1.

Suppose the consumer has fixed endowments Y_1 and Y_2 of a commodity for periods 1 and 2, respectively, and maximizes his utility out of his consumptions C_1 and C_2 for periods 1 and 2, respectively. His problem can be formulated as follows: Maximize

$$U = U(C_1, C_2) \qquad U_1, U_2 > 0 \tag{3}$$

subject to

$$C_1 + \frac{C_2}{1+r} = Y_1 + \frac{Y_2}{1+r} \tag{4}$$

Figure 6.2.1

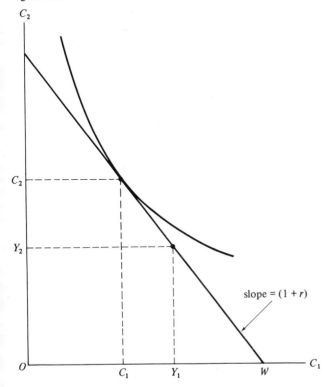

Equation (4) assumes that consumption is generally different from income in each period. The excess of consumption over income, $C_t - Y_t$ represents *saving* when it is negative, and *dissaving* when it is positive. The right-hand side can be called the *wealth* of the consumer and denoted by W, and (4) can be rewritten

$$C_1 + \frac{C_2}{1 + r} = W \qquad (5)$$

Hence the problem can be stated as that of maximizing the utility function (1) subject to the budget equation (5). The same procedure as was applied to equations (1.3.1) and (1.3.2) can be applied, the only difference being that the prices p_1 and p_2 have been replaced by 1 and $(1/(1 + r))$, respectively, and income M by wealth W. Upon forming the Lagrangean function and deriving the first-order condition, one obtains the analogue of (1.3.7) as the optimum condition:

$$\frac{U_1}{U_2} = \frac{p_1}{p_2} = 1 + r \qquad (6)$$

That is, the marginal rate of substitution between two consumptions equals the interest factor $1 + r$. In other words, for optimum, the marginal utility of current consumption must be $(1 + r)$ times as large as that of consumption next year.

From (5) and (6), C_1 and C_2 can be determined in terms of the wealth W and the interest rate r. Then $C_t - Y_t$, the saving or dissaving depending on whether it is negative or positive, also can be obtained as a function of r and W.

The same procedure as in Section 1.4 can be applied to the present problem to obtain the price and income effects on the consumptions C_1 and C_2. By deriving the analogue of the Slutsky equation (1.4.15), one can show that the effect of the rise in the relative price of current consumption, that is, a fall in $1/(1 + r)$, or a rise in the rate of interest r, can be broken up into the substitution and income effects. From the negativity property (1.4.32) of the demand function, one can conclude that a rise in the interest rate means a fall in current consumption and a rise in saving.[1]

6.3 INTERTEMPORAL PRODUCTION: INVESTMENT AND DISINVESTMENT

In the same fashion, the consumer can be assumed to have perfect foresight and complete certainty about technology, that is, the production function transforming the commodity of period 1 (wheat used as seeds) into the commodity of period 2.

The individual having the endowments Y_1 and Y_2 of the commodity in the two periods will take advantage of production opportunities by setting up a firm which undertakes to transform Y_1 and Y_2 into available amounts of the commodity in two periods, A_1 and A_2, in accordance with the technology that may be represented by a production-possibility frontier

$$f(Q_1, Q_2) = 0 \qquad (1)$$

where *net output* $Q_t = A_t - Y_t$ is input if it is negative, representing *investment*; and output if it is positive, representing *disinvestment*. The production function has the following properties: f is twice-differentiable; the function is increasing in the net outputs Q_t, that is, f_1 and f_2 are positive; the function is strictly convex and therefore the function is strictly quasi-convex, that is,

$$\begin{vmatrix} f_{11} & f_{12} & f_1 \\ f_{21} & f_{22} & f_2 \\ f_1 & f_2 & 0 \end{vmatrix} < 0 \qquad (2)$$

That is, the production-possibility frontier is strictly concave to the origin, and marginal products are decreasing.

---

[1] On the intertemporal allocation by the consumer, see Fisher (1930).

The *wealth* of the consumer who engages in production is the present value W:

$$A_1 + \frac{A_2}{1+r} = W \qquad (3)$$

The wealth of the consumer depends not only on the initial endowments, but also on the production which transforms these into available amounts A_1 and A_2.

The present value of the initial endowments is called *capital* and denoted by K:

$$Y_1 + \frac{Y_2}{1+r} = K \qquad (4)$$

Thus the consumer as a producer can be said to first set up a firm with the initial capital K, and subject to technology f, engage in production so as to maximize the firm's present value W, and then choose his consumption plan so as to maximize his utility U subject to the present value W of total expenditures possible from production.

Graphically speaking, in Figure 6.3.1 the endowments are given by Y_1 and Y_2, which can be transformed into A_1 and A_2 according to the transformation curve. Given the interest rate, the production optimum is chosen at E, which maximizes the present value of A_1 and A_2. Now A_1 and A_2 can be traded along the straight-line budget equation, that is, some A_2 is traded for equivalent A_1, until the line touches the highest indifference curve at F.

Figure 6.3.1

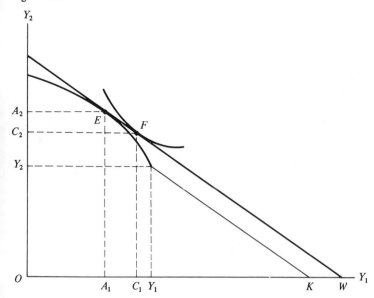

FIRM

When the productive activity is undertaken by the firm, it can be described by Figure 6.3.2. The optimum investment of period 1 commodity and disinvestment of period 2 commodity are given by point Q.

The excess of the present value of the period 2 output over the period 1 input may be considered the firm's profit. The firm can be considered to choose point Q so as to maximize the profit

$$Q_1 + \frac{Q_2}{1 + r} = p_1 Q_1 + p_2 Q_2 \tag{5}$$

subject to the technological constraint

$$f(Q_1, Q_2) = 0$$

The optimum-production problem can be solved by means of the Lagrangean function

$$L = p_1 Q_1 + p_2 Q_2 - \lambda f(Q_1, Q_2) \tag{6}$$

Assuming that Q_1 is negative and Q_2 is positive,

$$\frac{\partial L}{\partial Q_t} = p_t - \lambda f_t = 0 \qquad t = 1, 2 \tag{7}$$

Figure 6.3.2

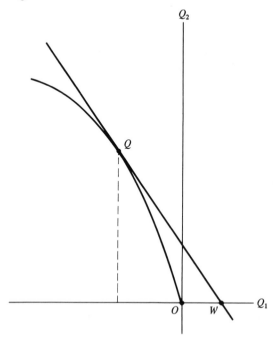

Taking the ratio of the above marginal conditions,

$$\frac{p_1}{p_2} = \frac{f_1}{f_2} = -\frac{dQ_2}{dQ_1} \tag{8}$$

The marginal rate of transformation between net outputs is equal to the price ratio. The price ratio can be written as

$$1 : \frac{1}{1+r} = (1+r) : 1$$

INTERNAL RATE OF RETURN

Criteria alternative to the maximization of the firm's profit appear in the literature. One such criterion is the *internal rate of return* ρ, which can be defined for two periods as

$$\rho = -\frac{Q_2}{Q_1} - 1$$

or such ρ as to satisfy

$$Q_1 + \frac{Q_2}{1+\rho} = 0$$

that is, ρ such that the present value of net outputs in terms of the rate is equal to zero.

In the present case of two periods, the alternate criterion of equating the internal rate of return to the market rate of interest gives the same result as maximizing the wealth.[2]

6.4 SUMMARY

As was shown in Chapter 4 on general equilibrium, under the assumption of perfect competition, the economy can have a competitive equilibrium where, at the prevailing prices of the commodity for the two periods, the demand and supply are equal for the commodity in two periods, and the consumers maximize their utility and the firms their wealth.

Such competitive equilibrium is Pareto optimum in the sense that no consumer can be made better off without making another consumer worse off.[3]

---

[2] The internal rate of return concept has a number of theoretical difficulties. See Hirschleifer (1958).

[3] *Cf.* Fisher (1930), and Hicks (1946), chaps. 9, 15, 18. For a more general model, see Malinvaud (1953).

PART II
LINEAR MICROECONOMIC MODELS

The marginalist models of Part I were formulated in general terms. The properties of the production function were specified only in terms of its derivatives. The models are in fact so general that the theorems derived therefrom are often concerned with implicit optimality conditions and are not specific enough to be used in actual decision-making. By making these models more specific, one can derive results less implicit and more useful in specific decision-making.

Part II particularizes the models of Part I by linearizing the production relationships. That this has been done for good reasons will become clear. Linear models of production are used not only in the management of the individual producer's operations but also in the analysis of entire economies, and not only in market-oriented but also in planned economies. They are suitable to computations of explicit solutions to numerically specified allocation problems. These models make optimization operational, and they can be efficiently handled by computers. The models of Part II serve as practical devices for control and planning.

The development of this field has been in progress for some time. At the level of the firm, linear programming has been developed by mathematicians and applied by economists since World War II. At the level of the whole economy, attempts to improve on Cassel's theory of Walrasian general equilibrium have been made since the early 1930s by many economists. Leontief's input-output models have made linear models of the economy empirical and operational.

7
LINEAR MODELS
OF THE FIRM

7.1 INTRODUCTION

ACTIVITY ANALYSIS

The marginalist model of the producer's optimum was based on a *production function*, which expressed the *maximum* amount of a single output as a function of the amounts of several inputs. The concept of the production function therefore assumes that the choice of the most efficient production technique for each combination of input quantities has been made. Most marginalist models fail to examine the choice of optimum technique.

This chapter replaces the overall production function of Part I with a number of partial production relationships represented by *linear activites*, each of which represents a different combination of inputs and outputs given by a different technique. Hence the model here can explicitly analyze the choice of optimum technique and optimum combination of techniques.

FIXED PROPORTIONS

In so doing the law of variable proportions of the marginalist model is replaced by the *law of fixed proportions*. The law of variable proportions was an apt description of production in agriculture. It is also a good description of production in the long run when enough time elapses to allow the ratios between inputs to be adjusted. The law of fixed proportions is, however, an increasingly useful description of production in modern industrial society, where producible capital goods are more important and fixed proportions between specialized inputs are more characteristic of technology. It is also more applicable in the short run when input proportions cannot be changed readily. The substitution theorem below shows that some linear models do not necessarily rule out substitution in spite of the assumption of fixed coefficients of production.

REDUCED SIGNIFICANCE OF MARGINAL CALCULATIONS

The marginalist models assumed that the production function was twice-differentiable, and that there existed a smooth marginal-productivity curve. Properties of technology could then be described by the continuous derivatives of the production function, as by the law of diminishing marginal productivity and increasing marginal rate of transformation. In the linear activity analysis, however, the properties of production possibilities are described not so much by marginal changes as by fixed ratios between inputs and outputs.

The introduction of fixed proportions gives rise to discontinuity in the marginal functions used in the marginalist analysis. Marginal rates of factor substitution and marginal productivity are less useful as the central concepts. This point may be seen from the following.

Suppose the producer's inputs v_1 and v_2 are related to the output y in the fixed proportions as

$$v_1 = a_1 y$$
$$v_2 = a_2 y$$

so that the technically feasible ratio between two inputs is $a_1 : a_2$. Then the maximum amount of the output producible from the inputs v_1 and v_2 is

$$y = \min\left(\frac{v_1}{a_1}, \frac{v_2}{a_2}\right)$$

Then, in general, y is not a differentiable function. Consider the situation described by

$$y = \min\left(\frac{v_1}{2}, \frac{v_2}{3}\right)$$

and, holding v_2 at 6, let v_1 change from 0. The graph of the function is as given in Figure 7.1.1. The marginal productivity changes from positive to zero suddenly at $v_1 = 4$. This function is not differentiable at $v_1 = 4$. This reduces the usefulness of the optimality conditions derived in term of derivatives in Part I.

Figure 7.1.1

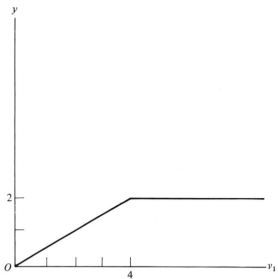

7.2 A LINEAR PROGRAMMING MODEL OF THE FIRM

Instead of a twice-differentiable production function, a set of *linear activity* vectors can be used to describe the technological condition. The linear activity specifies *the constant ratios among various inputs and outputs.* Thus in each linear activity, production follows the *law of fixed proportions,* or, the *law of constant returns to scale.*

In this section, it is assumed that

• each activity produces one output, that is, there is no joint production of more than one output in one activity.

Assume further that

• the first activity uses a_{11} units of the first input and a_{21} units of the second input to produce one unit of the output. Then the technological coefficients of the first activity can be represented by the activity vector,

$$P_1 = \begin{pmatrix} 1 \\ a_{11} \\ a_{21} \end{pmatrix}$$

Similarly, the activity vector for the second activity can be written

$$P_2 = \begin{pmatrix} 1 \\ a_{12} \\ a_{22} \end{pmatrix}$$

To produce y_1 units of output will require $a_{11}y_1$ units of input 1 and $a_{21}y_1$ units of input 2. Similarly for the other activity. Suppose in the short run *the available quantities of inputs 1 and 2 are fixed* at v_1 and v_2, respectively.

Assume further that

- the producer is a perfectly competitive seller and takes the price of the output as given, and that the average variable cost associated with each additional increment in the output of each activity is constant. Then *the profits per unit of the output are constant*; let this be π_1 for activity 1 and π_2 for activity 2. Then the producer's problem is to maximize his profit π

$$\pi = \pi_1 y_1 + \pi_2 y_2 \qquad (1)$$

subject to constraints

$$a_{11}y_1 + a_{12}y_2 \leq v_1 \qquad (2)$$

$$a_{21}y_1 + a_{22}y_2 \leq v_2 \qquad (3)$$

This linear programming problem[1] can be written in matrix notation: Maximize

$$\pi' y \qquad (4)$$

subject to

$$Ay \leq v \qquad (5)$$

$$y \geq 0 \qquad (6)$$

where

$$\pi = \begin{pmatrix} \pi_1 \\ \pi_2 \end{pmatrix} \qquad y = \begin{pmatrix} y_1 \\ y_2 \end{pmatrix} \qquad A = \begin{pmatrix} a_{11} & a_{12} \\ a_{21} & a_{22} \end{pmatrix} \qquad v = \begin{pmatrix} v_1 \\ v_2 \end{pmatrix}$$

IMPUTATION OF VALUES TO RESOURCES: SHADOW PRICES

According to the theory of linear programming given in MR5, the above linear programming maximization problem has a dual, that is, a linear programming minimization problem: Minimize

$$v' \lambda \qquad (7)$$

subject to

$$A' \lambda \geq \pi \qquad (8)$$

$$\lambda \geq 0 \qquad (9)$$

[1] If the price of the total output and the variable cost of each activity are functions of the output of the activity, then the profits function (1) becomes nonlinear in y_1 and y_2. Then the nonlinear programming formulation of the theory of the firm will be required.

where λ = column vector (λ_1, λ_2). According to the theory of MR11, *if* (4)–(6) *have a solution,* (7)–(9) *also have a solution; and the minimand* $\mathbf{v}'\bar{\lambda}$ *equals the maximand* $\boldsymbol{\pi}'\bar{\mathbf{y}}$*, that is, profits, for optimum values* $\bar{\mathbf{y}}$ *and* $\bar{\lambda}$. As is shown in (MR11.16),

$$\frac{d(\boldsymbol{\pi}'\bar{\mathbf{y}})}{dv_i} = \frac{d(\mathbf{v}'\bar{\lambda})}{dv_i} = \bar{\lambda}_i$$

In other words, $\bar{\lambda}$ is the accounting price (or shadow price) system evaluating the fixed resources of the firm. The constant $\bar{\lambda}_i$ here is the rate of change of the maximand $\boldsymbol{\pi}'\bar{\mathbf{y}}$ with respect to a change in v_i. In the present context, therefore, λ_i *represents the marginal profit of relaxing the input constraints* v_i.

According to (MR.11.10), if $\bar{y}_j$ is positive, then

$$\pi_j - \sum_i \bar{\lambda}_i a_{ij} = 0 \tag{10}$$

and according to (MR11.20) if $\bar{y}_j$ is zero, then

$$\pi_j - \sum_i \bar{\lambda}_i a_{ij} \leqq 0 \tag{11}$$

That is, *for the output being produced, the profit equals the cost (rent) of the limited resources, while for the output not being produced, the profit does not exceed the cost (rent) of the limited resources.*

Similarly, if $\bar{\lambda}_i > 0$, then

$$a_{i1}\bar{y}_1 + a_{i2}\bar{y}_2 = v_i$$

and if $\lambda_i = 0$, then

$$a_{i1}\bar{y}_1 + a_{i2}\bar{y}_2 \leqq v_i$$

Either the shadow price is positive and the constraint is effective, or the shadow price is zero and the resource requirement does not exceed the availability.

To graphically present the comparison with the marginalist theory, consider the case with two activities and two fixed resources. Assuming each activity to be producing the same product, the transformation curve or production-possibility frontier can be obtained.

The first constraint can be represented by the part of the first quadrant below the straight line (2), whose slope is $-a_{11}/a_{12}$, y_1-intercept is v_1/a_{11}, and y_2-intercept is v_1/a_{12}, in Figure 7.2.1. Similarly, the second constraint can be represented by the part of the first quadrant below the straight line (3). Thus the *production-possibility set* representing all possible combinations of activity levels is the shaded area. In three dimensions, the figure will be more complicated. This set generalizes the *production-possibility frontier* of the marginalist microeconomic theory by including not only equalities but also inequalities.

Figure 7.2.1

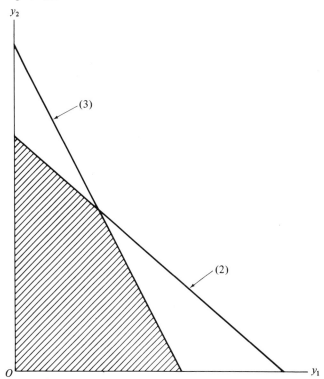

Figure 7.2.2

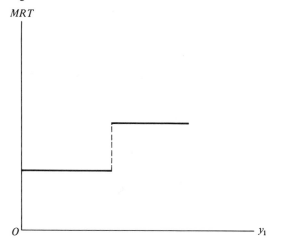

Figure 7.2.3

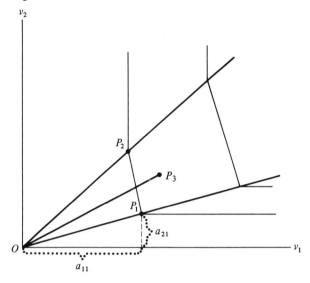

Figure 7.2.4

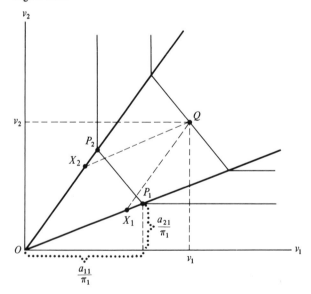

The marginal rate of transformation can be observed in Figure 7.2.2. It is nondecreasing. It is not increasing smoothly, but rises with a jump.

One can next construct the isoquant. In Figure 7.2.3, P_1 represents (a_{11}, a_{21}) and P_2 represents (a_{12}, a_{22}). Connect P_1 and P_2, extend a horizontal line to the right from P_1 and a vertical line upward from P_2. Then the kinked line segments represent all combinations of inputs 1 and 2 producing one unit of output, and are convex to the origin by excluding all inefficient activities, such as P_3.

Under the fixed-proportions assumption, doubling OP_1 and OP_2 outward and connecting the end points in the same manner yields another isoquant for two units of output.

One can also construct isoprofit curves as in Figure 7.2.4. On each vector it is possible to find the point which produces a unit of profits. On OP_1 that point will be

$$\left(\frac{a_{11}}{\pi_1}, \frac{a_{21}}{\pi_1} \right)$$

and similarly for activity 2. Connecting these points yields an *isoprofit curve* for unit profit. There are an infinite number of these isoprofit curves.

The optimum levels of these activities are obtained as follows. Locate (v_1, v_2) as Q in this diagram. The isoprofit curve going through this point represents the maximum profits. From Q, draw a parallel line to OP_2 and let it cut OP_1 at X_1, and draw a parallel line to OP_1 and let it cut OP_2 at X_2. Then X_1 and X_2 represent the profits which each activity should be contributing.[2]

7.3 JOINT PRODUCTION

The model of the preceding section can be expanded to the case of joint production. Let the producer's j^{th} *activity* be represented by $\mathbf{P}_j$ whose i^{th} element is a_{ij}, representing an output if positive and an input if negative for operating the jth activity at unit level. If a_{ij} is zero, then the ith good has nothing to do with activity j. Divide the m goods into two categories: those which are marketable and whose market prices are $p_i(i = 1, \ldots, s)$; and those which are not (factors of production peculiar to the producer), and whose supplies are fixed at b_i. Suppose there are r different linear activities. Let the jth activity be operated at y_j. Then the profits function is

$$\sum_{i=1}^{s} p_i \sum_{j=1}^{r} a_{ij} y_j \qquad (1)$$

---

[2] On the linear programming theory of the firm see Dorfman (1951) and Dorfman *et al.* (1958), chaps. 6 and 7.

This expression denotes profit, that is, revenue minus cost, since a_{ij} is positive if the ith good is output and negative if the ith good is input. The constraints are

$$- \sum_{j=1}^{r} a_{ij} y_j \leq b_i \qquad i = s + 1, \ldots, m \qquad (2)$$

$$y_j \geq 0 \qquad j = 1, \ldots, r \qquad (3)$$

The left-hand side of (2) denotes net input required because of the sign convention on a_{ij}. The producer's problem is to maximize (1) subject to (2) and (3). The dual of this problem is formulated in terms of the dual variables λ_i, whose solution value represents the rate of change of the maximand (1) with respect to b_i. In the present case, each solution value of the dual variable represents the marginal profit productivity of the corresponding limitational factor of production. Further, at optimum,

$$\sum_i b_i \lambda_i \qquad (4)$$

will be equal to the value of (1). That is, the dual variables represent a system of accounting (shadow) prices evaluating the producer's limitational factors of production. From (MR11.10), if y_j is positive, then

$$\sum_{i=1}^{s} p_i a_{ij} + \sum_{i=s+1}^{m} \lambda_i a_{ij} = 0 \qquad (5)$$

that is, in terms of accounting prices, revenue equals cost for the activity in operation. If, on the other hand, y_j is zero, then from (MR11.14)

$$\sum_{i=1}^{s} p_i a_{ij} + \sum_{i=s+1}^{m} \lambda_i a_{ij} \leq 0 \qquad (6)$$

that is, revenue does not exceed cost for the idle activity.[3]

---

[3] If $a_{ij} \geq 0$ for all j, then the ith good is a final product; if $a_{ij} \gtreqless$ for all j, the ith good is an intermediate product; and if $a_{ij} \leq 0$ for all j, the ith good is a primary input.

8
INPUT-OUTPUT
ANALYSIS

8.1 INTRODUCTION

Wassily Leontief spent a number of years in an effort to construct input-output tables for the U.S. economy for 1919 and 1929. His results, which he used to analyze the working of the American economy, were published in Leontief (1941, 1951).

His idea was as follows: An economy consists of a large number of consumers and producers who conduct among themselves transactions—sales and purchases of goods. Statistical measurement of these transactions will make clear in what manner individual economic units are dependent on one another.

Leontief focused his attention on interindustry relations, and based his system upon Walrasian general equilibrium theory. While the general equilibrium theory of Walras did not go beyond writing down a set of equations with literary coefficients, Leontief estimated such a system with empirically obtained numerical coefficients. (On the other hand, the Walrasian model of general equilibrium is more comprehensive, covering such aspects as credit.)

In this chapter the following changes are made from the marginalist model of Part I.

• The marginalist model of Part I considered final commodities to be produced directly from primary factors. The linear model here considers in addition intermediate commodities, that is, commodities that are used in the further production of commodities.

• The marginalist model of Part I used the neoclassical production function for each industry. The linear model of Part II assumes the linear activity for each industry and takes into account explicitly the interdependence between industries, that is, interindustry flows of goods.

8.2 INPUT-OUTPUT ACCOUNTING

TRANSACTIONS MATRIX

Assume that one industry produces only one commodity, that is, there is no joint production. Hence, the number of industries is the same as the number of commodities. Assume further that no changes occur in inventories of the commodities.

Use the following notation:

X_i = gross output of industry; $i = 1, \ldots, n$
x_{ij} = intermediate demand for the ith industry's output by the jth
      industry; $i, j = 1, \ldots, n$
x_i = final demand by consumers for the ith industry's output; $i = 1, \ldots, n$

By definition

$$\sum_{j=1}^{n} x_{ij} + x_i = X_i \qquad i = 1, \ldots, n \tag{1}$$

The sources of inputs for the jth industry are as follows:

x_{ij} = input of intermediate products from the ith industry, $i = 1, \ldots, n$
x_{0j} = input of the primary factor, assumed to be labor

The x_{ij} form a *transactions matrix*.

	1	2	$\cdots$	n		
1	x_{11}	x_{12}		x_{1n}	x_1	X_1
2	x_{21}	x_{22}		x_{2n}	x_2	X_2
$\vdots$						$\vdots$
n	x_{n1}	x_{n2}		x_{nn}	x_n	X_n
	x_{01}	x_{02}	$\cdots$	x_{0n}		

Let the prices of n commodities be p_i, $i = 1, \ldots, n$; and the price of labor be w. Then, for each commodity

$$\sum_{i=1}^{n} p_i x_{ij} + w x_{0j} = p_j X_j \tag{2}$$

INPUT COEFFICIENTS

The Leontief models assume constant proportions among inputs and output for each industry. This production relationship rules out factor substitutability. The ratios between input from each industry and the output,

$$a_{ij} = \frac{x_{ij}}{X_j} \qquad i, j = 1, \ldots, n \tag{3}$$

are called *input coefficients*, and can be arranged in a matrix as follows:

	1	2	...	n
1	a_{11}	a_{12}		a_{1n}
2	a_{21}	a_{22}		a_{2n}
$\vdots$				$\vdots$
n	a_{n1}	a_{n2}		a_{nn}
	a_{01}	a_{02}	...	a_{0n}

The ratio between the labor input and the output is denoted by

$$a_{0j} = \frac{x_{0j}}{X_j} \tag{4}$$

a_{0j} are called the *employment coefficients*. It should be noted that all these coefficients are nonnegative.

GROSS OUTPUTS NEEDED TO PRODUCE GIVEN FINAL OUTPUTS

From (3),

$$x_{ij} = a_{ij} X_j \qquad i, j = 1, \ldots, n \tag{5}$$

Substituting (5) into (1),

$$\sum_{j=1}^{n} a_{ij} X_j + x_i = X \qquad i = 1, \ldots, n \tag{6}$$

Let:

$\mathbf{X}$ = column vector of X_i, $i = 1, \ldots, n$
$\mathbf{x}$ = column vector of x_i, $i = 1, \ldots, n$

Then in matrix notation, (6) can be written

$$\mathbf{AX} + \mathbf{x} = \mathbf{X} \tag{7}$$

Therefore

$$(\mathbf{I} - \mathbf{A})\mathbf{X} = \mathbf{x} \tag{8}$$

Whether $(\mathbf{I} - \mathbf{A})$ is nonsingular or not is considered later. If $(\mathbf{I} - \mathbf{A})$ is nonsingular,

$$\mathbf{X} = (\mathbf{I} - \mathbf{A})^{-1}\mathbf{x} \tag{9}$$

In the formula

$$\mathbf{X} = (\mathbf{I} - \mathbf{A})^{-1}\mathbf{x}$$

the (i, j) element of the Leontief inverse $(\mathbf{I} - \mathbf{A})^{-1}$ indicates by how much the gross output of the ith industry has to be changed corresponding to a unit change in the jth industry's final demand. In this sense each element of the Leontief inverse can be called a multisector multiplier. In macroeconomic analysis the multiplier represents the income propagation effects; in the present interindustry analysis, the multiplier represents the propagation effects through intermediate demands. For example,

$$X_1 = \frac{1}{\Delta}(B_{11}x_1 + B_{21}x_2 + \cdots + B_{n1}x_n)$$

where Δ is the determinant of $(\mathbf{I} - \mathbf{A})$, and B_{i1} are the cofactors of the $(i, 1)$ elements of $(\mathbf{I} - \mathbf{A})$. The rate of change of the first industry's gross output with respect to the ith industry's final demand is

$$\frac{\partial X_1}{\partial x_i} = \frac{B_{i1}}{\Delta}$$

It should be noted that outputs that provide equilibrium between demand and supply for each commodity are determined by the technological condition represented by $\mathbf{A}$, and independently of the prices of these commodities.

HAWKINS-SIMON CONDITION

The feasible gross-output vector must be a positive vector:

$$\mathbf{X} > 0$$

The necessary and sufficient condition for there to be a positive solution $\mathbf{X}$ for the vector equation (8) to produce positive net outputs $\mathbf{x}$ is that all principal minors of $\mathbf{I} - \mathbf{A}$ be positive. This is known as the Hawkins-Simon condition. That is, let

$$\mathbf{L} = \mathbf{I} - \mathbf{A}$$

Then

$$L_{11} > 0 \qquad \begin{vmatrix} L_{11} & L_{12} \\ L_{21} & L_{22} \end{vmatrix} > 0 \qquad \begin{vmatrix} L_{11} & L_{12} & L_{13} \\ L_{21} & L_{22} & L_{23} \\ L_{31} & L_{32} & L_{33} \end{vmatrix} > 0 \qquad \cdots$$

$$\begin{vmatrix} L_{11} & L_{12} & \cdots & L_{1n} \\ \vdots & & & \vdots \\ L_{n1} & L_{n2} & \cdots & L_{nn} \end{vmatrix} > 0$$

where L_{ij} denotes the (i, j) element of $\mathbf{L}$.

In the case of two industries, a graphical illustration of sufficiency is possible. Consider the case of two industries whose technology can be represented by the Leontief matrix:

$$\mathbf{L} = \begin{pmatrix} 1 - a_{11} & -a_{12} \\ -a_{21} & 1 - a_{22} \end{pmatrix}$$

Let the two columns be represented by vectors $\mathbf{A}^1$ and $\mathbf{A}^2$ in Figure 8.2.1.

Let the two activities be operated at positive levels X_1 and X_2, respectively. Then the corner Q of the parallelogram formed by $X_1\mathbf{A}^1$ and $X_2\mathbf{A}^2$ represents

Figure 8.2.1

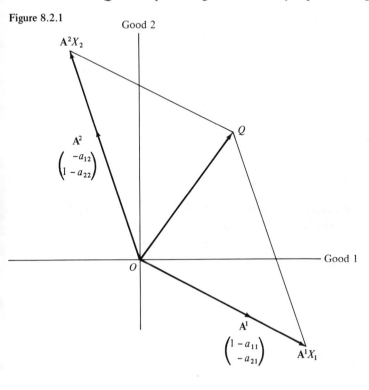

the net outputs (that is, gross output minus intermediate demand) in view of (8), and for these to be positive, Q must appear in this first quadrant. For this to occur, the absolute value of the slope of $\mathbf{A}^1$ with respect to the horizontal axis, that is, $a_{21}/(1 - a_{11})$, must be greater than that of $\mathbf{A}^2$, that is, $(1 - a_{22})/a_{12}$. That is,

$$\frac{a_{21}}{1 - a_{11}} > \frac{1 - a_{22}}{a_{12}}$$

which is true if

$$1 - a_{11} > 0$$

and $(1 - a_{11})(1 - a_{22}) > a_{12} a_{21}$, that is,

$$\begin{vmatrix} 1 - a_{11} & -a_{12} \\ -a_{21} & 1 - a_{22} \end{vmatrix} > 0$$

SOLOW CONDITION

The necessary and sufficient condition given by Hawkins and Simon is difficult to use. A sufficient condition that is more stringent but easier to use has been given by Solow. The condition is that the column sum of $\mathbf{L}$ does not exceed one for all columns, and at least one column sum is less than one.

The matrix $\overline{\mathbf{A}}$ introduced in the following section has the property

$$\sum_{i=1}^{n} a_{ij} < 1 \qquad j = 1, \ldots, n$$

satisfying the Solow condition. It also satisfies the Hawkins-Simon condition.

FEASIBLE OUTPUTS

The output of the economy is restricted by the available primary factor. For an output vector $\mathbf{X}$, the total labor needed is

$$x_0 = \sum_{j=1}^{n} x_{0j} = \sum_{j=1}^{n} a_{0j} X_j = \mathbf{a}_0'(\mathbf{I} - \mathbf{A})^{-1}\mathbf{x} \tag{10}$$

where

$\mathbf{a}_0$ = column vector of $a_{0j}, j = 1, \ldots, n$

This labor requirement cannot exceed the total available labor. Thus the available labor force limits feasible outputs.

PRICES IN THE LEONTIEF SYSTEM

Substituting (4) and (5) in (2),

$$\sum_{i=1}^{n} p_i a_{ij} X_j + w a_{0j} X_j = p_j X_j \qquad j = 1, \ldots, n \tag{11}$$

Therefore

$$\sum_{i=1}^{n} p_i a_{ij} + w a_{0j} = p_j \qquad j = 1, \ldots, n \tag{12}$$

Let:

$\mathbf{p}$ = column vector of p_i, $i = 1, \ldots, n$

Then, in matrix notation, (12) is equivalent to

$$\mathbf{p}'\mathbf{A} + w\mathbf{a}_0' = \mathbf{p}' \tag{13}$$

that is,

$$\mathbf{p}'(\mathbf{I} - \mathbf{A}) = w\mathbf{a}_0' \tag{14}$$

$$\mathbf{p}' = w\mathbf{a}_0'(\mathbf{I} - \mathbf{A})^{-1} \tag{15}$$

Thus given the wage rate, the prices of the commodities are determined by the input coefficients.

Postmultiply (14) through by $\mathbf{X}$, obtaining

$$w\mathbf{a}_0'\mathbf{X} = \mathbf{p}'(\mathbf{I} - \mathbf{A})\mathbf{X} \tag{16}$$

and premultiply (8) through by $\mathbf{p}'$, obtaining

$$\mathbf{p}'(\mathbf{I} - \mathbf{A})\mathbf{X} = \mathbf{p}'\mathbf{x} \tag{17}$$

Expressions (16) and (17) imply that

$$w\mathbf{a}_0'\mathbf{X} = \mathbf{p}'\mathbf{x} \tag{18}$$

Expression (18) states that income of the factor, labor, equals expenditures on final goods.

It should be noted that the relative prices of the commodities are determined by the technological condition represented by $\mathbf{A}$, independently of output levels of these commodities.[1]

8.3 INPUT-OUTPUT ACCOUNTING IN MONEY-VALUE TERMS

The *value transactions matrix* is

$$\mathbf{V} = (v_{ij}) \qquad i = 1, \ldots, n; \quad j = 1, \ldots, n \tag{1}$$

[1] On input-output models, see Leontief (1941, 1951), and Dorfman *et al.* (1958).

With respect to each row of the matrix,

$$\sum_{j=1}^{n} v_{ij} + v_i = V_i \qquad (2)$$

where

v_{ij} = value of intermediate output from industry i to industry j; $i = 1, \ldots, n$; $j = 1, \ldots, n$
v_i = value of final demand for industry i; $i = 1, \ldots, n$
V_i = value of gross output of industry i; $i = 1, \ldots, n$

Note that all these magnitudes represent not physical quantities, but values (reflecting not only quantities but also prices).

With respect to each column of the matrix, the following equality holds:

$$\sum_{i=1}^{n} v_{ij} + v_{0j} = V_j \qquad (3)$$

where

v_{0j} = value of primary input in industry j

The input coefficients in value terms are

$$\bar{a}_{ij} = \frac{v_{ij}}{V_j} \left(= \frac{p_i x_j}{p_j X_j} = \frac{p_i}{p_j} a_{ij} \right) \qquad \begin{aligned} i &= 1, \ldots, n \\ j &= 1, \ldots, n \end{aligned} \qquad (4)$$

$$\bar{a}_{0j} = \frac{v_{0j}}{V_j} \left(= \frac{w x_{0j}}{p_j X_j} = \frac{w}{p_j} a_{0j} \right) \qquad j = 1, \ldots, n \qquad (5)$$

where a_{ij} and a_{0j} are those defined in Section 8.2.

With respect to each row of the transactions matrix, using (4) in (2) yields

$$\sum_{j=1}^{n} \bar{a}_{ij} V_j + v_i = V_i \qquad i = 1, \ldots, n \qquad (6)$$

Using (4) and (5) in (3) shows, with respect to each column,

$$\sum_{i=1}^{n} \bar{a}_{ij} V_j + \bar{a}_{0j} V_j = V_j \qquad j = 1, \ldots, n \qquad (7)$$

Thus

$$\sum_{i=1}^{n} \bar{a}_{ij} + \bar{a}_{0j} = 1 \qquad (8)$$

Each column of input and employment coefficients adds up to one.

Using the matrix notation

$$\mathbf{\bar{A}} = (\bar{a}_{ij}) \qquad i = 1, \ldots, n_j; \quad j = 1, \ldots, n \qquad (9)$$

$$\mathbf{V} = (V_j) \qquad \mathbf{v} = (v_j)$$

(6) becomes

$$\overline{\mathbf{A}}\mathbf{V} + \mathbf{v} = \mathbf{V} \tag{10}$$

Therefore

$$\mathbf{V} = (\mathbf{I} - \overline{\mathbf{A}})^{-1}\mathbf{v} \tag{11}$$

That is, gross output can be obtained by premultiplying final demand by the Leontief inverse matrix.[2]

8.4 THE CLOSED LEONTIEF SYSTEM

The preceding Leontief model has been called *open*, since the final demand sector or the consuming sector is regarded as exogenous. Consider the final demand sector as another industry which requires various commodities as inputs and produces labor as output for use by other commodity-producing industries as input. Then the final demand and primary input disappear, and all goods become intermediate goods, since all outputs are produced to be used only as inputs and never as final output. Such a Leontief model is said to be *closed*.

Its value transactions matrix can be written

$$\overline{\mathbf{A}} = (\bar{a}_{ij}) \qquad i = 1, \ldots, n+1; j = 1, \ldots, n+1 \tag{1}$$

where

$\bar{a}_{ij}$ = input of industry i required per unit output of industry j

Then the equilibrium condition is

$$\overline{\mathbf{A}}\mathbf{X} = \mathbf{X} \tag{2}$$

where

$\mathbf{X}$ = column vector of activity levels X_i, $i = 1, \ldots, n+1$

Equation (2) is a homogeneous equation system

$$(\mathbf{I} - \overline{\mathbf{A}})\mathbf{X} = 0 \tag{3}$$

The relative activity levels of all the industries can be determined from (3). Since $\overline{\mathbf{A}}$ is a value transactions matrix, the elements of each column add up to one, that is,

$$\sum_{i=1}^{n+1} \bar{a}_{ij} = 1 \tag{4}$$

Consider the first column of the Leontief matrix $\mathbf{I} - \overline{\mathbf{A}}$. Its first element is

$$1 - \bar{a}_{11} \tag{5}$$

[2] For an application see Leontief *et al.* (1965).

while the sum of the remaining elements of the column is

$$-\sum_{i=2}^{n+1} \bar{a}_{i1} \qquad (6)$$

In view of the column-sum property (4), (5) equals the negative of (6). This holds for every column. Since the first element is the negative of the sum of all other elements, the rows of the matrix $I - \bar{A}$ are linearly dependent. From the theory of equations, there exists nontrivial solutions to the homogeneous equation system (3) determining the proportions of the $(n + 1)$ activity levels.

8.5 THE SUBSTITUTION THEOREM

The substitution theorem states that although the Leontief input-output system assumes input coefficients to be fixed, it need not rule out substitution of inputs in response to changes in relative prices.

The theorem, as summarized by Morishima (1964), is as follows: Assume a perfectly competitive economy. Then a system of equations expressing the equality of the prices of goods to their unit costs determines a unique set of equilibrium prices. Further, assume constant returns-to-scale. Then the final demand or the scale of production does not affect the unit cost of each good. Hence no change in prices, and therefore input ratios remain constant. Thus the economy will behave as if each industry had only one set of input ratios.[3] Morishima (1964) and Samuelson (1961) discuss substitution theorems in dynamic contexts.

[3] Cf. Koopmans (1951), chaps. 7–10.

9
GENERAL EQUILIBRIUM
IN LINEAR
MICROECONOMIC MODELS

9.1 INTRODUCTION

Part I considered the possibility of competitive general equilibrium under neo-classical assumptions of twice-differentiable production functions. Counting equations and variables alone, however, could not prove existence of such equilibrium. Here general equilibrium is considered under linearity assumptions. It was in this linear production model that Wald first proved the existence of competitive equilibrium.

9.2 COMPETITIVE EQUILIBRIUM

Dorfman, Samuelson, and Solow (1958) have worked out an existence proof for competitive equilibrium in a linear model of production with ordinary demand functions. Their proof can be presented using the following notation:

n = the number of products
m = the number of factors
$\mathbf{v} = (v_i)$ m-dimensional vector of quantities of factors supplied; $\mathbf{v} > \mathbf{0}$

$\mathbf{y} = (y_j)$ n-dimensional vector of quantities of products produced; $\mathbf{y} \geq \mathbf{0}$

$\mathbf{A} = (a_{ij})$ m by n matrix of input coefficients, a_{ij} being the amount of the ith factor needed in producing one unit of product j. These coefficients are the same as in the Leontief input-output models; there is no joint production. Further, $a_{ij} \geq 0$; and for each j, at least one a_{ij} is positive.

$\mathbf{r} = (r_i)$ m-dimensional vector of prices of factors; $\mathbf{n} \geq \mathbf{0}$

$\mathbf{p} = (p_j)$ n-dimensional vector of prices of products; $\mathbf{p} \geq \mathbf{0}$

THE PRODUCING SECTOR

The demand for factor i is $\sum_j a_{ij} y_j$, which must not exceed the available supply of the factor, that is,

$$\sum_{j=1}^{n} a_{ij} y_j \leq v_i \qquad i = 1, \ldots, m$$

or

$$\mathbf{A}\mathbf{y} \leq \mathbf{v} \tag{1}$$

In the long-run competitive equilibrium, the price of each product must not exceed its unit costs. Therefore

$$\sum_{i=1}^{m} a_{ij} r_i \geq p_j \qquad j = 1, \ldots, n$$

or

$$\mathbf{A}'\mathbf{r} \geq \mathbf{p} \tag{2}$$

THE HOUSEHOLD SECTOR

The product-demand equations are

$$y_j = f^j(p_1, \ldots, p_n; r_1, \ldots, r_m) \geq 0 \qquad j = 1, \ldots, n$$

In matrix notation

$$\mathbf{y} = \mathbf{F}(\mathbf{p}, \mathbf{r}) \geq \mathbf{0} \tag{3}$$

where $\mathbf{F}$ is the vector function made up of $f^j, j = 1, \ldots, n$

$$\mathbf{F} = (f^j)$$

The factor-supply equations are

$$v_i = g^i(p_1, \ldots, p_n; r_1, \ldots, r_m) > 0 \qquad i = 1, \ldots, m$$

In matrix notation

$$\mathbf{v} = \mathbf{G}(\mathbf{p}, \mathbf{r}) \tag{4}$$

where $\mathbf{G}$ is the vector function made up of g^i, $i = 1, \ldots, m$

$$\mathbf{G} = (g^i)$$

It is assumed that these demand and supply functions are defined for all $\mathbf{p}, \mathbf{r} \geq \mathbf{0}$, twice-differentiable, and homogeneous of degree zero in $\mathbf{p}$ and $\mathbf{r}$.

Note that the market demand and supply equations are not independent, since they must satisfy Walras' law.

If $\mathbf{p}^*$ is the equilibrium price vector, then the equilibrium output and factor-price vectors, $\mathbf{y}^*$ and $\mathbf{r}^*$, are optimal in the following linear programming problem.

$$\text{Max } \mathbf{p}^{*\prime}\mathbf{y} \tag{5}$$

subject to

$$\mathbf{Ay} \leq \mathbf{v} \tag{6}$$

and its dual,

$$\text{Min } \mathbf{v}'\mathbf{r} \tag{7}$$

subject to

$$\mathbf{A}'\mathbf{r} \geq \mathbf{p}^* \tag{8}$$

For if $\mathbf{y}^*$ and $\mathbf{r}^*$ are the equilibrium vectors, they must satisfy (6) and (8), respectively. From (1), $\mathbf{y}^*$ satisfies (6), and is feasible. But (2) is not sufficient for (8), and $\mathbf{r}^*$ may not be feasible. However, $k\mathbf{r}^*$ will be feasible if k is large enough. Since $\mathbf{y}^*$ and $k\mathbf{r}^*$ are feasible in (5)–(6) and (7)–(8), respectively,

$$\mathbf{p}^{*\prime}\mathbf{y}^* \leq (k\mathbf{r}^*)'\mathbf{v}$$

But by the budget constraint

$$\mathbf{p}^{*\prime}\mathbf{y}^* = \mathbf{r}^{*\prime}\mathbf{v}$$

Therefore k must be equal to 1. Therefore $\mathbf{y}^*$ and $\mathbf{r}^*$ are feasible, and from the duality theorem they are optimal, proving the proposition of the preceding paragraph.

The existence of equilibrium is equivalent to the existence of $\mathbf{p}, \mathbf{r}, \mathbf{v}$, and $\mathbf{y}$, such that (1)–(4) are satisfied.

Normalize prices so that

$$\sum p_j + \sum r_i = 1 \qquad p_j, r_i \geq 0$$

The normalized prices can be represented by a point in the simplex in the $m + n$-dimensional euclidean space. The set is nonempty, compact, and convex. One can construct a correspondence from points of this set into subsets of this set, which is upper semicontinuous and therefore has a fixed point. And this fixed point represents the equilibrium prices, as the following steps will show.

Step 1: $(\mathbf{p}, \mathbf{r}) \rightarrow (\mathbf{y}, \mathbf{v})$

Given an initial set of price vectors $\mathbf{p}$ and $\mathbf{r}$, (3) and (4) give the output-demand vector $\mathbf{y}$ and factor-supply vector $\mathbf{v}$.

Step 2: $\mathbf{y} \rightarrow k\mathbf{y}$

But this $\mathbf{y}$ might not be feasible (not satisfying (1)), or efficient (not using up at least one factor).

If so, scale $\mathbf{y}$ down or up to $k\mathbf{y}$ so that $\mathbf{y}$ is producible (that is, satisfies (1)) and efficient in the sense that at least one factor is fully used up (that is, at least one expression in (1) holds with equality). $k\mathbf{y}$ lies on the production-possibility frontier.

Step 3: $k\mathbf{y} \rightarrow P$

Corresponding to this efficient $k\mathbf{y}$ on the production-possibility frontier, there exists a set of prices $\mathbf{p}$ such that $k\mathbf{y}$ is a solution to the linear programming problem (5)–(6). This set of prices $\mathbf{p}$ need not be unique as at A in Figure MR 11.2. Denote the set of all such price vectors by P.

Step 4: $P \rightarrow R$

A given price vector $\mathbf{p}$ in P determines the constraints for the linear programming problem (7)–(8). Corresponding to this $\mathbf{p}$ there exists a factor-price vector $\mathbf{r}$. The set of all such factor-price vectors as $\mathbf{p}$ ranges over P is denoted by R. Thus the set (P, R) has been constructed.

There exists the mapping now

$$(\mathbf{p}, \mathbf{r}) \rightarrow \mathbf{y} \rightarrow k\mathbf{y} \rightarrow (P, R)$$

The mapping of step 1 (demand functions) is assumed to be continuous. The mapping of step 2 is also continuous since it is only the scalar multiplication operation. The mappings of steps 3 and 4 are upper semicontinuous. Thus the mapping satisfies the conditions of the Kakutani Fixed-Point Theorem. Therefore there exist equilibrium prices $\mathbf{p}^*$, $\mathbf{r}^*$, and corresponding $\mathbf{y}^*$ and $\mathbf{v}^*$.(See also Morishima (1964), Sec. 2.2; Karlin (1959), Sec. 8.7.)

9.3 EFFICIENCY AND COMPETITIVE EQUILIBRIUM

DEFINITION OF EFFICIENCY

The output vector $\mathbf{y}^*$ is *technologically efficient* if, first, it is feasible, that is, it satisfies (9.2.1); and, second, there is no other feasible $\mathbf{y}$ such that $\mathbf{y} \geq \mathbf{y}^*$ (with the strict inequality holding for at least one component).

Assuming more generally that factors are not fixed in supply, the output vector $\mathbf{y}^*$ and the input vector $\mathbf{v}^*$ are *technologically efficient* if, first, they are feasible, that is, they satisfy (9.2.1); and, second, if there is no other feasible input-output combination $(\mathbf{y}, \mathbf{v})$ such that $\mathbf{y} \geq \mathbf{y}^*$ (with the strict inequality holding at least once), and $\mathbf{v} \leq \mathbf{v}^*$.

DEFINITION OF COMPETITIVE EQUILIBRIUM

A *competitive equilibrium* is the set of $\mathbf{p}$, $\mathbf{r}$, $\mathbf{y}$, and $\mathbf{v}$ that satisfies (1), (2), (3), and (4) of Section 9.2. It was shown that any competitive equilibrium solution maximized $\mathbf{p}'\mathbf{y}$ and minimized $\mathbf{r}'\mathbf{v}$ subject to the resource and cost constraints (1) and (2), respectively. It was also shown that any solution of this pair of linear programming problems that satisfied the demand functions (3) and (4) was a competitive equilibrium.

COMPETITIVE EQUILIBRIUM IS EFFICIENT

Consider a competitive equilibrium, that is, a set of $\mathbf{p}$, $\mathbf{r}$, $\mathbf{y}$, and $\mathbf{v}$ such that aggregate profits $\mathbf{p}'\mathbf{y} - \mathbf{r}'\mathbf{v}$ are maximized by firms assuming $\mathbf{p}$ and $\mathbf{r}$ are given, and $\mathbf{y}$ and $\mathbf{v}$ are constrained by the technological constraint

$$\mathbf{Ay} \leq \mathbf{v}$$

Then such $\mathbf{y}$ and $\mathbf{v}$ can be shown to be efficient. The proof is by contradiction. Suppose $\mathbf{y}$ and $\mathbf{v}$ are not efficient. Then one can increase some component of $\mathbf{y}$ and may decrease some components of $\mathbf{v}$. But this increases $\mathbf{p}'\mathbf{y} - \mathbf{r}'\mathbf{v}$. Such a possibility contradicts the assumption that profits were already at a maximum. Therefore $\mathbf{y}$ and $\mathbf{v}$ are efficient.

EFFICIENT INPUTS AND OUTPUTS REPRESENT A COMPETITIVE EQUILIBRIUM

If a pair of output and input vectors $\bar{\mathbf{y}}$ and $\bar{\mathbf{v}}$ is efficient, then there exists a set of product and factor prices $\mathbf{p}$ and $\mathbf{r}$ for which $\bar{\mathbf{y}}$ and $\bar{\mathbf{v}}$ form a competitive equilibrium, that is, profits are maximized.

It has been shown that if $\bar{\mathbf{y}}$ is efficient, there certainly exists at least one price vector $\bar{\mathbf{p}}$ such that $\bar{\mathbf{p}} \cdot \mathbf{y}$ is maximized at $\bar{\mathbf{y}}$ among all feasible outputs $\mathbf{y}$ satisfying (9.2.1). On the other hand the factor prices $\mathbf{r}$ must satisfy (9.2.2).

$$\mathbf{A}'\mathbf{r} \geq \bar{\mathbf{p}}$$

Take $\mathbf{r}$ which solves the dual linear programming problem of minimizing $\mathbf{r}\bar{\mathbf{v}}$ subject to the above price-cost inequalities, and call this $\bar{\mathbf{r}}$. Then these $\bar{\mathbf{p}}$ and $\bar{\mathbf{r}}$ will maximize profits (zero) and satisfy the competitive price-cost relationships. Thus $\bar{\mathbf{p}}$ and $\bar{\mathbf{r}}$ are competitive equilibrium prices.[1]

---

[1] *Cf.* Dorfman *et al.* (1958), chap. 14.

10
VON NEUMANN'S DYNAMIC GENERAL EQUILIBRIUM MODEL

10.1 INTRODUCTION

Most of the preceding microeconomic models have analyzed outputs and prices in static equilibrium. Dynamic models here examine the changes in equilibrium positions over time. Static models can be regarded as special cases of the more general dynamic models.

Two representative linear dynamic models are the von Neumann model and the dynamic Leontief model. The former is considered here to examine the role played by the price system in it.

The von Neumann model of dynamic general equilibrium of a multisector economy gives some specific results. The model is based on a stock-input, stock-output system concentrating on the accumulation of stocks. In the state of "dynamic equilibrium" it shows that there exist some unique output and price configurations; it gives the equilibrium growth rate of the outputs and the equilibrium interest rate. This chapter brings up a number of new notions which von Neumann introduced into economic analysis, among them the theory of games and the axiomatic formulation.

10.2 THE VON NEUMANN MODEL

Consider all goods in the economy to be producible. There are no scarce limitational factors of production such as land. Hence there is no reason that the law of diminishing returns is inevitable, and the law of constant returns to scale is assumed.

Such a situation is not totally hypothetical. For example, the industrial sector of a developing economy may be able to get an unlimited supply of labor from the rural sector; it may need little land. Capital goods can be produced, and needed foreign products can be imported.

The economy is described by a constant-returns-to-scale input-output system in terms of stocks. Each activity uses stocks of produced goods at the beginning of the period as inputs and produces stocks of goods at the end of the period as outputs. The von Neumann model is a closed system, in the sense that no inputs are brought into the system, and no outputs are taken out of the system. All the outputs are plowed back into further production of the goods of the economy. The input-output system in the von Neumann model allows for joint production. That is, more than one good can be produced by an activity.

The input-output system is described using an input matrix and an output matrix, rather than a simple net-output matrix. Let there be m goods and n activities in the economy. Assume that the jth activity when operated at unit intensity requires a_{ij} units of the ith good as an input. Similarly assume that the jth activity when operated at unit itensity produces b_{ij} units of the ith good as an output. Define $\mathbf{A}$ to be the $m \times n$ matrix with components a_{ij} and $\mathbf{B}$ to be the $m \times n$ matrix with components b_{ij}. Then the entire economy is described by these two matrices.

It should be noted that the notation differs from that of the theory of the firm (Section 7.3) allowing for joint production where the element of the linear activity vector represented the net output of the good involved. For example, a_{ij} represented the amount of the net output of good i if a_{ij} is positive, and the amount of the net input if a_{ij} is negative, when the activity is operated at unit intensity. In this section, a_{ij} represents the nonnegative amount of good i used up as input, and b_{ij} represents the nonnegative amount of good i produced as output, when activity j is operated at unit intensity. Therefore, the net increase in the stock of good i is $b_{ij}-a_{ij}$. If this quantity is positive, good i is net output, and if this quantity is negative, good i is net input, in activity j. Further, the input-output system of Section 8.2 had one activity vector for each good, but the von Neumann model has more than one activity producing the same good.

The intensities of the activities in the von Neumann model are represented by a column vector $\mathbf{y}$ whose j^{th} component y_j denotes the nonnegative intensity of operation of the jth activity. The prices of the goods are denoted by a column vector $\mathbf{p}$, whose i^{th} component p_i denotes the nonnegative price of a unit of the ith good.

Hence

  $\mathbf{Ay}$ = column vector of *inputs* of each good used up
  $\mathbf{By}$ = column vector of *outputs* of each good produced
  $\mathbf{p'A}$ = row vector of the *costs of inputs* for a unit-intensity operation of each activity
  $\mathbf{p'B}$ = row vector of the *values of outputs* of each activity
  $\mathbf{p'Ay}$ = *total cost* (scalar) of inputs when the economy is operated at intensity $\mathbf{y}$
  $\mathbf{p'By}$ = *total value* (scalar) of all outputs produced when the economy is operated at intensity $\mathbf{y}$

Example 1

Let the goods be wheat and workers. It takes one unit of wheat (seed) and one worker to produce three units of wheat and it requires one unit of wheat (food) to have 1.5 workers for the next year. Assume that land is unlimited in supply.

Then the two activities are producing wheat with wheat and labor, and producing labor with wheat, and the $\mathbf{A}$ and $\mathbf{B}$ matrices are

$$\begin{array}{cc} & \begin{matrix} \text{Producing} & \text{Producing} \\ \text{wheat} & \text{labor} \end{matrix} \end{array}$$

$$\mathbf{A} = \begin{matrix} \text{wheat} \\ \text{labor} \end{matrix}\begin{bmatrix} 1 & 1 \\ 1 & 0 \end{bmatrix} \qquad \mathbf{B} = \begin{bmatrix} 3 & 0 \\ 0 & 1.5 \end{bmatrix}$$

Suppose that this economy starts out with 100 units of wheat and 50 workers. The economy can use the intensity

$$\mathbf{y} = \begin{bmatrix} 50 \\ 50 \end{bmatrix}$$

Then

$$\mathbf{Ay} = \begin{bmatrix} 100 \\ 50 \end{bmatrix}$$

that is, the input requirements are satisfied. Also

$$\mathbf{By} = \begin{bmatrix} 150 \\ 75 \end{bmatrix}$$

that is, there will be 150 units of wheat and 75 workers at the end of the year. The next year the economy can use the intensity

$$\mathbf{y} = \begin{bmatrix} 75 \\ 75 \end{bmatrix}$$

so that

$$\mathbf{Ay} = \begin{bmatrix} 150 \\ 75 \end{bmatrix} \qquad \mathbf{By} = \begin{bmatrix} 225 \\ 112.5 \end{bmatrix}$$

Wheat has increased by 50 percent. This economy can continue to operate in equilibrium; if the beginning wheat supply is 100, and intensities 50 and 50, the economy expands at the fixed rate $\alpha = 1.5$.

Example 2

$$A = \begin{pmatrix} 3 & 1 \\ 1 & 2 \end{pmatrix} \qquad B = \begin{pmatrix} 2 & 3 \\ 2 & 1 \end{pmatrix}$$

Let activities be operated at $\mathbf{y}$. Then the input vector is

$$A\mathbf{y} = \begin{pmatrix} 3y_1 + y_2 \\ y_1 + 2y_2 \end{pmatrix}$$

and the output vector is

$$B\mathbf{y} = \begin{pmatrix} 2y_1 + 3y_2 \\ 2y_1 + y_2 \end{pmatrix}$$

The value of inputs is

$$\mathbf{p}'A\mathbf{y} = p_1(3y_1 + y_2) + p_2(y_1 + 2y_2)$$

while the value of outputs is

$$\mathbf{p}'B\mathbf{y} = p_1(2y_1 + 3y_2) + p_2(2y_1 + y_2)$$

The rate of return $f(\mathbf{y}, \mathbf{p})$ can be written

$$f(\mathbf{y}, \mathbf{p}) = \frac{\mathbf{p}'B\mathbf{y}}{\mathbf{p}'A\mathbf{y}} - 1$$

Assume that the producers take the commodity prices $\mathbf{p}$ as given and *determine the activity levels* $\mathbf{y}$ *so that the rate of return will be maximized*, while *the prices* $\mathbf{p}$ *are determined by the market so that the rate of return will be minimized as a result of competition*, taking activity levels $\mathbf{y}$ as given. The equilibrium output and price configurations $(\bar{\mathbf{y}}, \bar{\mathbf{p}})$ must be such that

$$f(\mathbf{y}, \bar{\mathbf{p}}) \text{ will be maximum at } (\bar{\mathbf{y}}, \bar{\mathbf{p}}) \tag{1}$$

$$f(\bar{\mathbf{y}}, \mathbf{p}) \text{ will be minimum at } (\bar{\mathbf{y}}, \bar{\mathbf{p}}) \tag{2}$$

that is, $(\bar{\mathbf{y}}, \bar{\mathbf{p}})$ is a saddle point of $f(\mathbf{y}, \mathbf{p})$:

$$f(\mathbf{y}, \bar{\mathbf{p}}) \leq f(\bar{\mathbf{y}}, \bar{\mathbf{p}}) \leq f(\bar{\mathbf{y}}, \mathbf{p}) \tag{3}$$

Normalize the prices so that

$$p_1 + p_2 = 1 \qquad p_1 \geq 0 \quad p_2 \geq 0 \tag{4}$$

Also normalize the activity levels

$$y_1 + y_2 = 1 \qquad y_1 \geq 0 \quad y_2 \geq 0 \tag{5}$$

that is, y_1, y_2 determine only the ratio between the activity levels.

The ratio between total value and total cost is

$$\gamma = \frac{p_1(2y_1 + 3y_2) + p_2(2y_1 + y_2)}{p_1(3y_1 + y_2) + p_2(y_1 + 2y_2)} \tag{6}$$

p_1 and p_2 are determined by the market so that the ratio (6) will be minimized. If

$$p_1 = 1, p_2 = 0 \qquad \text{then} \qquad \gamma = \frac{2y_1 + 3y_2}{3y_1 + y_2} \tag{7}$$

and if

$$p_1 = 0, p_2 = 1 \qquad \text{then} \qquad \gamma = \frac{2y_1 + y_2}{y_1 + 2y_2} \tag{8}$$

If the first value of γ is smaller than the second value of γ, then $p_1 = 1$, and $p_2 = 0$, and vice versa. If both values are equal, then p_1 and p_2 can be any combination as long as $p_1 + p_2 = 1$. Thus one can say p_1 and p_2 are determined so that the value-cost ratio will be equal to the smaller of the above two values.

But firms determine y_1 and y_2 so that the smaller of the above two values of γ is at maximum. Using (5), the above two values of γ can be written

$$\gamma = \frac{3 - y_1}{1 + 2y_1} \tag{9}$$

$$\gamma = \frac{1 + y_1}{2 - y_1} \tag{10}$$

In Figure 10.2.1, (9) falls while (10) rises as y_1 is increased from O to 1. At $y_1 = 0$, (10) is the smaller, and at $y_1 = 1$, (9) is the smaller. The heavy line graphs

Figure 10.2.1

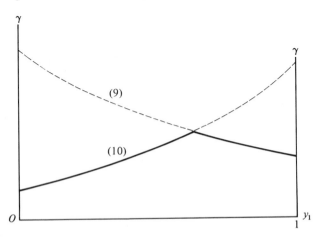

the smaller value of γ as y_1 changes. This graph reaches a peak at $y_1 = 0.58$ and hence $y_2 = 0.42$. These are the equilibrium activity levels.

Similar argument can show that the equilibrium prices will be $p_1 = 0.39$ and $p_2 = 0.61$. Hence $\gamma = 1.11$.

AXIOMATIC FORMULATION

Let the constant positive expansion factor of the economy in dynamic equilibrium be α, and the constant positive interest-rate factor on money in the same dynamic equilibrium be β. Normally $\alpha, \beta > 1$ so that there are positive growth and interest rates. One can show that if the economic system satisfies the following plausible axioms, then there exist equilibrium output proportions **y** and price proportions **p** together with the growth factor α and interest factor β.

1. *Sufficient Outputs*

$$\mathbf{By} \geqq \alpha \mathbf{Ay}$$

The current period's outputs are at least as large as the next period's inputs.

2. *Maximum Profit Rate*

$$\mathbf{p'B} \leqq \beta \mathbf{p'A}$$

But no activity yields a rate of profit greater than the rate of interest. If this is not true and some activity's outputs are worth more than β times its inputs, then the activity can afford to pay an interest rate higher than β to the investors in this activity, and the rate of interest will rise. This is in violation of the definition of the equilibrium interest factor β.

3. *Zero Prices for Overproduced Goods*

$$\mathbf{p'(B} - \alpha \mathbf{A)y} = 0$$

All goods whose current period outputs are in excess of the next period's inputs have zero prices. $\mathbf{By} - \alpha \mathbf{Ay}$ represents a vector of excess supply which is zero or positive by axiom 1. Assigning zero price to positive excess supply yields the above equality.

4. *Zero Activity Levels for Unprofitable Activities*

$$\mathbf{p'(B} - \beta \mathbf{A)y} = 0$$

Axiom 2 set the upper limit to the profit rate of any activity, which was the rate of interest. This axiom sets the lower limit to the profit rate, which is also the rate of interest. If an activity's profit rate is less than the rate of interest, it will not be operated since investments in money will be preferable. $\mathbf{p'(B} - \beta \mathbf{A)}$ represents a vector of losses, which is nonpositive. Assigning zero activity levels to the activities with negative profits yields the above equation.

5. *Positive Output Value*

$$\mathbf{p'By} > 0$$

Prices and activity levels are such that something of value is being produced.

The intrinsic properties of technology are as follows: Outputs cannot be obtained without inputs. Hence every activity must require at least one good as input. Therefore every column of $\mathbf{A}$ must have at least one positive component. Furthermore, the goods must somehow be produced. Hence every good must have at least one activity that produces it. Therefore every row of $\mathbf{B}$ must have at least one positive component. Kemeny *et al.* (1956) prove the existence of the equilibrium $\mathbf{y}$, $\mathbf{p}$, α and β, and the equality of α and β. They also show that there is at least one and at most a finite number of expansion factors representing equilibrium. A partial sketch of the proof is as follows:[1] From axioms 3 and 4

$$\alpha \mathbf{p'Ay} = \beta \mathbf{p'Ay}$$

From axiom 5, $\mathbf{p'By}$ is nonzero; hence $\mathbf{p'Ay}$ is nonzero. Therefore

$$\alpha = \beta$$

Hence the system is reduced to

$$(\mathbf{B} - \alpha\mathbf{A})\mathbf{y} \geqq 0$$
$$\mathbf{p'}(\mathbf{B} - \alpha\mathbf{A}) \leqq 0$$
$$\mathbf{p'By} > 0$$

From the first two inequalities

$$\mathbf{p'}(\mathbf{B} - \alpha\mathbf{A})\mathbf{y} \geqq 0$$

and

$$\mathbf{p'}(\mathbf{B} - \alpha\mathbf{A})\mathbf{y} \leqq 0$$

Hence

$$\mathbf{p'}(\mathbf{B} - \alpha\mathbf{A})\mathbf{y} = 0$$

One can regard $(\mathbf{B} - \alpha\mathbf{A})$ as the payoff matrix of a game, and the output-proportions vector $\mathbf{y}$ and the price-proportions vector $\mathbf{p}$ as the optimum mixed strategies. This payoff matrix may be regarded as the sum of $\mathbf{B}$ and $\alpha(-\mathbf{A})$.

Since every row of $\mathbf{B}$ has at least one positive element, when premultiplied by $\mathbf{p'}$, at least one component of $\mathbf{p'B}$ is positive. Hence the value of the game $\mathbf{B}$ is positive. Since every column of $\mathbf{A}$ has at least one positive element, when postmultiplied by $\mathbf{y}$, $\mathbf{Ay}$ has at least one positive element. Therefore the value of the game $-\mathbf{A}$ must be negative. As α is changed from 0 to infinity, the value of the

---

[1] *Cf.* von Neumann (1945); Kemeny *et al.* (1956); Morishima (1964), chap. 5.

entire game changes from positive to negative. And the game assumes value zero. Hence there exists at least one equilibrium expansion factor α.

This is a sketch of a slave economy, where production is successively expanded at the subsistence wages. There are models that incorporate consumption in this scheme.

10.3   THE TURNPIKE THEOREM

Suppose an underdeveloped economy (endowed with relatively scarce manufactured products but with relatively abundant agricultural products) plans to develop into an industrialized economy with more manufactured products relative to agricultural products compared with the initial situation. That is, the economy desires not only to increase total production as much as possible, but also to modernize its industrial structure. For example, it starts out with one unit of steel and 2 units of wheat, and plans to industrialize so that within T years the ratio of steel to wheat will be 3 to 1. Furthermore, it wishes to have as much stock as possible at the end of the fourth year.

In Figure 10.3.1 starting from the initial point $X(O)$, the economy develops so as to achieve the target ratio at the end of T years. Following path 1 the economy attains a higher productive capacity than following path 2. The path that leads the economy to the highest attainable point on the target line is the *efficient* growth path.

The Turnpike Theorem states that the long-run efficient path stays on or close to the von Neumann growth path on which all sectors grow at a uniform,

Figure 10.3.1

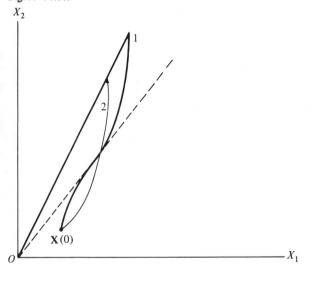

constant rate. The von Neumann path is "a fastest route between any two points, origin and end ... if origin and destination are far enough apart, it will always pay to get on to the turnpike and cover distance at the best rate of travel."[2]

Several different versions of the theorem have been proved using different mathematical methods. Here a numerical example is given for a simplified version of the model of Morishima (1961).

This model differs from von Neumann's in that it rules out joint production. Suppose there are only two goods, 1 and 2, and technology is described by a matrix of input coefficients, $\mathbf{A} = (a_{ij})$, $(i, j = 1, 2)$, where a_{ij} denotes the amount of commodity i needed to produce one unit of commodity j. Then the matrix of output coefficients becomes an identity matrix. Let $\mathbf{X}(0)$ = column vector $[X_1(0), X_2(0)]$ be initially given supplies of the two commodities, and $\mathbf{X}(1)$ = column vector $[X_1(1), X_2(1)]$ be the amounts to be produced in the first period. Since the inputs of the first period cannot exceed the given initial supplies,

$$\mathbf{AX}(1) \leq \mathbf{X}(0)$$

In general,

$$\mathbf{AX}(t + 1) \leq \mathbf{X}(t) \qquad \text{for } t = 0, \ldots, T - 1$$

Assume that the ratios between outputs of commodities 1 and 2 at the end of the Tth period be denoted by column vector $\mathbf{x}^*$. Then the problem becomes the following: Determine

$$\mathbf{X}(t) \text{ for } t = 1, \ldots, T$$

so as to maximize q subject to

$$\mathbf{AX}(t + 1) \leq \mathbf{X}(t) \text{ for } t = 0, \ldots, T - 1$$

and

$$q\mathbf{x}^* \leq \mathbf{X}(T)$$

where

$$\mathbf{X}(1), \ldots, \mathbf{X}(T)$$

are two-dimensional vectors, and q is a nonnegative scalar. This is a linear programming problem which can be solved easily.

Take an economy with two sectors: agriculture and manufacturing. Let its matrix of input coefficients be

$$\mathbf{A} = \begin{bmatrix} \frac{2}{5} & \frac{1}{5} \\ \frac{1}{5} & \frac{2}{5} \end{bmatrix}$$

[2] Dorfman et al. (1958), p. 331.

It can be seen that the equilibrium output proportions are (0.5 0.5). If one starts out with one unit of each good, and a is the activity level for period 1, then $(\frac{2}{5})a + (\frac{1}{5})a = 1$. Hence $a = \frac{5}{3}$, the equilibrium growth rate is $\frac{2}{3}$.

Suppose an economy starts out from the initial position $(2, 1)$ and aims to attain the $1 : 3$ ratio in the outputs of commodities 1 and 2 in T periods. Optimum paths for various values of T are

$$T = 2 \quad \mathbf{X}(1) = \begin{bmatrix} 1.316 \\ 1.842 \end{bmatrix}, \quad \mathbf{X}(2) = \begin{bmatrix} 1.315 \\ 3.947 \end{bmatrix} \quad q = 5.263$$

$$T = 3 \quad \mathbf{X}(1) = \begin{bmatrix} 1.545 \\ 1.727 \end{bmatrix}, \quad \mathbf{X}(2) = \begin{bmatrix} 2.273 \\ 3.182 \end{bmatrix}, \quad \mathbf{X}(3) = \begin{bmatrix} 2.273 \\ 6.818 \end{bmatrix} \quad q = 9.091$$

$$T = 4 \quad \mathbf{X}(1) = \begin{bmatrix} 1.625 \\ 1.687 \end{bmatrix}, \quad \mathbf{X}(2) = \begin{bmatrix} 2.607 \\ 2.914 \end{bmatrix}, \quad \mathbf{X}(3) = \begin{bmatrix} 3.803 \\ 5.368 \end{bmatrix},$$

$$\mathbf{X}(4) = \begin{bmatrix} 3.834 \\ 11.503 \end{bmatrix} \quad q = 15.337$$

The results are shown in Figure 10.3.2. It should be noted that as T increases the path $\mathbf{X}(t)$ comes closer to the balanced-growth path. Starting from $\mathbf{X}(0)$ the

Figure 10.3.2

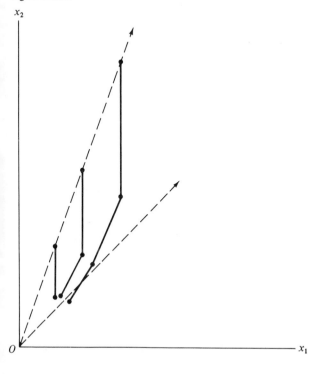

economy jumps to a point near the balanced growth, begins to move along the path, and then gradually departs from it to reach the target line.[3]

CONCLUDING REMARK FOR PART II

Part II concentrated on the linear aspects of microeconomic theory. These were examined in the models of linear programming, input-output analysis, and von Neumann's dynamic equilibrium. The essential mathematical concept that characterizes these models is that of linear inequalities. The connection with the marginalist models was maintained through the theory of nonlinear programming. The theory of convex sets (or, more particularly, the theory of convex polyhedral cones) was largely bypassed. Part III covers both marginal and linear models in terms of convex sets in euclidean spaces.

[3] *Cf.* Dorfman *et al.* (1958), pp. 335–345; Morishima (1961). For an application, see Kogiku (1967b).

PART III
SET-THEORETIC MICROECONOMIC MODELS

The models of Part I were particularized in Part II by linearization of the production relationships; they are to be generalized in Part III by concepts and models that encompass both nonlinear and linear models.

Part I analyzed the working of an economic system under the marginalist assumptions, using calculus as the tool. Consumer behavior was summarized by differentiable utility and demand functions whose properties were analyzed largely by calculus. Producer behavior was analyzed using the differentiable production function which gives the maximum outputs that can be produced from given inputs. The production function introduced such other concepts as cost, profit, and supply functions, which were analyzed mainly in terms of derivatives of these functions.

When resource allocation and the price system were analyzed by these concepts and tools, there remained many fundamental details that could not be satisfactorily explained. Models that account for such details call for more general concepts and tools. Part III considers such models which pertain to fundamental theoretical problems in economics.

In the set-theoretic models of this part, the consumer's or firm's choice is represented by a point or set of points in a euclidean space. The same is true with the aggregate choice of all the consumers and all the firms. A price configuration can also be represented by a point in a euclidean space. The models utilize this approach to study equilibrium quantities and prices.

Changes from Part I are as follows:

• In the marginalist models technical conditions of production were described by the production function. In set-theoretic models technical conditions of production are described by the mathematical notion called a *set*. The set replacing the production function usually contains an infinite number of elements, each of which represents a feasible combination of inputs and outputs.

Similarly, the condition of consumption is described in terms of such set-theoretic concepts as the consumption set and the preference preordering.

• In marginalist models goods were classified into products and factors. Set-theoretic models consider simultaneously final goods for consumption, intermediate goods used in the production of other goods, and primary factors of production.

• Set-theoretic models can handle the cases where, for example, the optimum demand or supply is a set of points rather than a point. And the relationship between the prices and the optimum quantities demanded or supplied is therefore a correspondence rather than a function.

• The typical marginalist model assumes variable proportions in production. The set-theoretic models can more rigorously consider all possibilities, including both fixed and variable proportions.

• Equilibrium in marginalist models postulated the strict equality of demand and supply. The set-theoretic models can allow for the possibility that for some commodities supply could exceed demand.

Although there are these differences, Part III follows the same pattern of presentation as used in Part I. Here consumers own initial endowments of goods (and receive the profits of firms) and these make up their income. They choose consumption bundles so as to maximize satisfaction under the given set of prices. Firms choose production bundles that maximize profits at the same given set of prices. The selected consumption and production bundles must balance, in the sense that aggregate consumption does not exceed aggregate production plus the initial aggregate endowments. Under perfect competition each consumer or producer takes the prices as given, and these prices are the same for all consumers and producers.

11
A SET-THEORETIC
MODEL OF COMPETITIVE
EQUILIBRIUM

11.1 INTRODUCTION

The consumer's optimum is described by a set of points in the commodity space. The consumer's choice is considered within this framework. Similarly, the firm's optimum production is represented by a set of points denoting all possible combinations of outputs and inputs, and the firm's choice is considered in this context. For a rigorous theory there is no substitute for rigorous mathematics. The following only sketches the outline of the set-theoretic models.

11.2 REVEALED PREFERENCE

The theory of consumer behavior discussed in Part I assumed that the consumer behaves rationally so as to maximize his differentiable utility index. That is, the consumer was assumed to base his behavior upon his indifference surface, implying his introspection. Once the viewpoint is shifted to the objective observation of actual behavior, the consumer's utility index or indifference surface cannot be observed directly. What one can observe is the quantity that the consumer demands under a given set of prices and a given income. That is, the consumer's preferences are only revealed. Samuelson (1938) derived various properties of demand from the assumption that the consumer behaves consistently in some sense involving the price-quantity relationship that can be directly revealed.

Let the m-dimensional vector $\mathbf{x}^1 = (x_1^1, \ldots, x_m^1)$ denote the commodity bundle chosen by a consumer when the prices of these commodities were given by the m-dimensional vector $\mathbf{p}^1 = (p_1^1, \ldots, p_m^1)$.

Suppose

$$\mathbf{p}^1 \cdot \mathbf{x}^2 \leq \mathbf{p}^1 \cdot \mathbf{x}^1 = M^1 \tag{1}$$

That is, the commodity bundle $\mathbf{x}^2$ could have been bought as well as $\mathbf{x}^1$ at the price configuration $\mathbf{p}^1$. Since $\mathbf{x}^1$ was chosen nevertheless, $\mathbf{x}^1$ is said to be *revealed preferred* to $\mathbf{x}^2$.

An assumption is introduced here which replaces the assumption of the existence of the indifference map, namely: *If under the price $\mathbf{p}^1$ and M^1 a commodity bundle $\mathbf{x}^1$ is revealed preferred to a commodity bundle $\mathbf{x}^2$, then under any combination of the prices and income where both $\mathbf{x}^1$ and $\mathbf{x}^2$ can be bought, the commodity bundle $\mathbf{x}^2$ will never be revealed preferred to $\mathbf{x}^1$.* This assumption is called the *Weak Axiom of Revealed Preference*. From this assumption a model of consumer choice can be derived.

Assume that $\mathbf{x}^1$ and $\mathbf{x}^2$ are chosen at $\mathbf{p}^1$ and $\mathbf{p}^2$, respectively. Suppose (1) is true; then $\mathbf{x}^1$ is revealed preferred to $\mathbf{x}^2$. If

$$\mathbf{p}^2 \cdot \mathbf{x}^1 \leq \mathbf{p}^2 \cdot \mathbf{x}^2 = M^2 \tag{2}$$

then according to the Weak Axiom of Revealed Preference $\mathbf{x}^1$ should be chosen at $\mathbf{p}^2$. But $\mathbf{x}^2$ was chosen at $\mathbf{p}^2$. Therefore, expression (2) is not true and

$$\mathbf{p}^2 \cdot \mathbf{x}^1 > \mathbf{p}^2 \cdot \mathbf{x}^2 = M^2 \tag{3}$$

That is, $\mathbf{x}^1$ exceeds the budget constraint. Therefore, under the Weak Axiom of Revealed Preference, (1) implies (3).

Write

$$\mathbf{x}' \, R \, \mathbf{x}'' \tag{4}$$

which is to be read, $\mathbf{x}'$ is revealed preferred to $\mathbf{x}''$. Then the Weak Axiom of Revealed Preference is

$$\mathbf{x}' \, \cancel{R} \, \mathbf{x}'' \text{ implies } \mathbf{x}'' \, \cancel{R} \, \mathbf{x}' \tag{5}$$

where $\cancel{R}$ means the negation of R. That is, R is antisymmetric.

The Weak Axiom can lead to the law of demand for the consumer, that is, when the price of a good increases, the quantity demanded decreases.

Assume that $\mathbf{x}^1$ and $\mathbf{x}^2$ are chosen at $\mathbf{p}^1$ and $\mathbf{p}^2$, respectively. If (1) is true then $\mathbf{x}^1$ is revealed preferred to $\mathbf{x}^2$. This implies (3). That is,

$$\mathbf{p}^2 \cdot (\mathbf{x}^2 - \mathbf{x}^1) < 0 \tag{6}$$

Suppose when $\mathbf{p}^1$ changes to $\mathbf{p}^2$, income is adjusted from M^1 to M^2 and quantity $\mathbf{x}^1$ to $\mathbf{x}^2$ so as to have $\mathbf{p}^1 \cdot \mathbf{x}^2 = \mathbf{p}^1 \cdot \mathbf{x}^1$. That is,

$$\mathbf{p}^1 \cdot (\mathbf{x}^2 - \mathbf{x}^1) = 0 \tag{7}$$

Subtracting (7) from (6),

$$(\mathbf{p}^2 - \mathbf{p}^1) \cdot (\mathbf{x}^2 - \mathbf{x}^1) < 0 \tag{8}$$

That is, if the price of the ith good only changes so that

$$p_i^2 - p_i^1 > 0 \qquad \text{then} \qquad x_i^2 - x_i^1 < 0$$

In other words, if

$$p_i^2 > p_i^1 \qquad \text{then} \qquad x_i^2 < x_i^1$$

showing that a rise in the price of a good results in a fall in the demand for it. This proves the *law of demand*.[1]

11.3   THE CONSUMPTION SET

The ith consumer's choice of a commodity bundle for consumption can be represented by a vector in the m-dimensional euclidean space

$$\mathbf{x}_i = (x_{ij}) \qquad j = 1, \ldots, m \tag{1}$$

where x_{ij} denotes a good consumed if it is positive, and a good supplied (like a factor of production) if it is negative.

Consider one consumer and two goods: labor x_1 and food x_2. When he supplies labor and demands food, the consumer makes a choice of a commodity bundle (x_1, x_2) which can be represented by the point in Figure 11.3.1. According

Figure 11.3.1

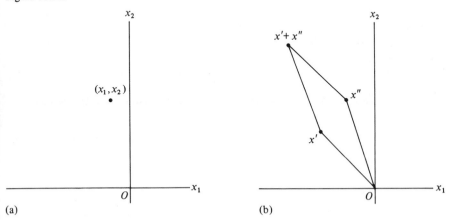

(a)   (b)

[1] *Cf.* Samuelson (1938), Samuelson (1947), pp. 107–117. For further uses and evaluation of the revealed preference approach, *cf.* Houtthaakker (1961), especially sec. 1.6. Also *cf.* Uzawa (1960b).

to the convention of the preceding paragraph, the supply of labor x_1 is negative, so that the commodity bundle appears in the second quadrant. Thus each consumer chooses a point from the set of commodity bundles whose supply components have negative values and demand components have positive values. The set of all physically feasible $\mathbf{x}_i$, denoted by X_i, is called the *consumption set*.

$$X_i = \{\mathbf{x}_i\} \tag{2}$$

It is a nonempty subset of the m-dimensional euclidean space.

Regarding the consumption set the following assumptions are made:

• Continuity: A converging sequence of points of the consumption set converges to a point of the consumption set. This assumption can be represented by the following statement regarding the consumption set:

$$X_i \text{ is closed for all } i \tag{3}$$

• Boundedness: There is a lower limit to the amount of a consumer good which enables the consumer to survive, and an upper limit to the amount of a factor of production which the consumer can physically supply. Therefore

$$X_i \text{ is bounded from below} \tag{4}$$

The set-theoretic models looking toward the question of the competitive equilibrium state these assumptions explicitly.

• Convexity: The model assumes that if two commodity bundles $\mathbf{x}'$ and $\mathbf{x}''$ are possible for the ith consumer, then the positive weighted average of these two consumptions is also possible. The consumer generally does not consume some goods; therefore the consumption set is usually contained in a subspace. The consumption set is defined in terms of the amounts of goods *available* to the consumer, assuming that he can dispose of the goods freely. The consumption set so defined is always convex, making later theorems possible.[2] Thus

$$X_i \text{ is convex for all } i \tag{5}$$

The total consumption set X, where there are n consumers in the economy, is defined by

$$X = \sum_{i=1}^{n} X_i \tag{6}$$

X is closed and convex.

PREFERENCES

The preference preordering R of Section 1.2 is refined somewhat. *The binary relation* R defined there was *reflexive* and *transitive*. Therefore it is a preordering.

---

[2] *Cf.* Debreu (1959), p. 51f.

Assuming that any two commodity bundles can be compared makes the relation a *complete* preordering.

The binary relation I was defined in Section 1.2 as follows: if $\mathbf{x}''$ R $\mathbf{x}'$ and $\mathbf{x}'$ R $\mathbf{x}''$, then $\mathbf{x}''$ I $\mathbf{x}'$. This binary relation is reflexive, symmetric, and transitive. If $\mathbf{x}''$ R $\mathbf{x}'$ and not $\mathbf{x}'$ R $\mathbf{x}''$, then one can write $\mathbf{x}''$ P $\mathbf{x}'$.

Several assumptions regarding the preference preordering R are made:

• The preference preordering is continuous. (For every $\mathbf{x}' \in X$, the sets $\{\mathbf{x} | \mathbf{x}$ R $\mathbf{x}'\}$ and $\{\mathbf{x} | \mathbf{x}'$ R $\mathbf{x}\}$ are closed.) The assumptions regarding preferences imply the existence of a continuous utility function.[3]
• The preference preordering is convex. (If $\mathbf{x}''$ P $\mathbf{x}'$, then $\theta\mathbf{x}' + (1 - \theta)\mathbf{x}''$ P $\mathbf{x}'$, $0 < \theta < 1$.) For example, the indifference curve in two dimensions can have a straight segment. This is weaker than the assumption of strong convexity made in marginalist models, that is, the utility function is strictly quasi-concave and the indifference curve is strictly convex to the origin.
• The consumer is nonsatiated. That is, there are always some commodities that are desirable (and the consumer will spend all his income in order to maximize utility). This corresponds to the assumption of positive marginal utility in the marginalist model. In terms of the preference preordering nonsatiety can be expressed by saying that, for any $\mathbf{x}'$ in X_i, there is an $\mathbf{x}''$ in X_i such that $\mathbf{x}''$ P $\mathbf{x}'$.

OPTIMUM CONSUMPTION SET

Let the ith consumer's initial endowments of goods be represented by $\mathbf{v}_i$. Then his wealth W_i is given by

$$W_i = \mathbf{p} \cdot \mathbf{v}_i$$

where prices are given by $\mathbf{p}$. His budget hyperplane then is

$$\mathbf{p} \cdot \mathbf{x}_i = W_i \tag{7}$$

and he chooses the point of the budget hyperplane which is the greatest with respect to the preference preordering. There may be more than one such point. Given his initial endowments of goods, this set of all the optimum consumptions depends only on the price vector $\mathbf{p}$ and is called the *demand set*. This set of demands for the goods (demands for some goods and supplies of some other goods) defines the *demand correspondence* from the set of all $\mathbf{p}$ to the commodity space. This is a more inclusive concept than the demand function of Part I.

More formally, let $X_i(\mathbf{p})$ be the set of all vectors $\mathbf{x}_i$ which are maximum with respect to consumer's preference preordering and subject to the wealth constraint when prices are $\mathbf{p}$. Then $X_i(\mathbf{p})$ is the consumer's demand set for prices $\mathbf{p}$.

---

[3] Debreu (1959), sec. 4.6; Debreu (1964).

The sum of these demand sets over all consumers, $X(\mathbf{p})$, represents the *total demand set* of the economy for all goods. The total demand set defines the *total demand correspondence* from the price vector $\mathbf{p}$.[4]

Example

For the consumer of the two-commodity economy a consumption set could be represented by Figure 11.3.2. In this case his preference map could be represented by the indifference curves some of which have been drawn in the same figure, and his utility function would take the form

$$U = x_2 - x_1^2$$

The consumer's wealth W_i may be represented by a quantity of good 2, and the relative prices of the two goods by the slope of the wealth constraint line

Figure 11.3.2

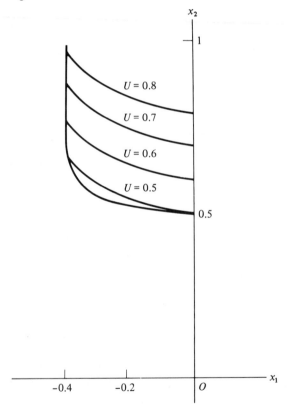

[4] On the consumption theory in set-theoretic terms, see Debreu (1959), chap. 4.

through W_i. Then the consumer's demand set is a single point $x_i(\mathbf{p})$. The convex preference preordering may have straight segments in the indifference curves, and the demand set may contain more than one element. The sum of the demand sets of all the consumers represents the total demand set.

EXISTENCE OF COMPETITIVE EXCHANGE EQUILIBRIUM

The existence of competitive equilibrium in an *exchange economy* has been proved by Nikaido (1956) and others.

Let all goods be consumer goods whose demands are nonnegative, and let:

$\mathbf{x}_i$ = the ith consumer's demand vector, $\mathbf{x}_i \in R_+^m$ (nonnegative orthant of R^m)
$\mathbf{v}_i$ = the ith consumer's initial endowments vector, $\mathbf{v}_i \in R_+^m$, $\mathbf{v}_i > 0$
n = the number of consumers
$\mathbf{x} = \sum \mathbf{x}_i$, the total demand vector
$\mathbf{v} = \sum \mathbf{v}_i$, the total endowments vector
$X_i = \{\mathbf{x}_i\}$, the ith consumer's demand set
$X = \{\mathbf{x}\}$, the total demand set
$P = \{\mathbf{p} \mid \sum p_i = 1, p_i \geq 0\}$, the price set

Figure 11.3.3

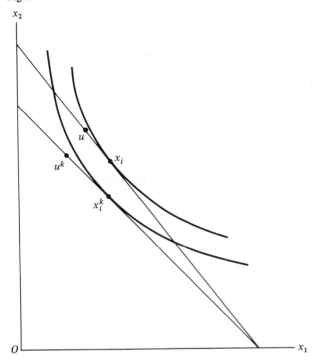

Assume that the consumer's preference preordering is continuous, convex, and not satiated for any commodity. Then *competitive equilibrium* is an allocation and a price system, $\{(\mathbf{x}_i^*), \mathbf{p}^*\}$, such that

(a) $\mathbf{x}^* = \mathbf{v}$ where $\mathbf{x}^* = \sum \mathbf{x}_i^*$

(b) $\mathbf{x}_i^*$ is the greatest element for R_i of the demand set $\{\mathbf{x}_i \in R_+^m \mid \mathbf{px}_i \leq \mathbf{pv}_i\}$
      for all i

It can be shown that $\mathbf{p}^* > 0$, and $\mathbf{x}_i^*$ will be in a bounded set containing $\mathbf{v}$:

$$E = \{\mathbf{e} \mid 0 \leq \mathbf{e} \leq \mathbf{c}, \mathbf{v} < \mathbf{c} \, (= \text{an arbitrary commodity bundle})\}$$

Assume that an auctioneer set an initial price $\mathbf{p}$ and that the ith consumer chooses a consumption $\mathbf{x}_i$. Denote his demand set at price $\mathbf{p}$ by $X_i(\mathbf{p})$, which defines a demand correspondence. It can be shown that

(a) $X_i(\mathbf{p})$ is nonempty, compact, and convex
(b) it is upper semicontinuous (*cf.* Figure 11.3.3) ·
(c) $X(\mathbf{p})$ is nonempty, compact, and convex
(d) it is also upper semicontinuous
(e) $\mathbf{x}$ of $X(\mathbf{p})$ satisfies Walras' law $\mathbf{p}(\mathbf{x} - \mathbf{v}) \leq 0$[5]

These results suggest the assumptions of the following general theorem: Let X be

(a) a subset of R^m
(b) compact

and let $X(\mathbf{p})$ be the correspondence from P to X such that it is

(c) nonempty for all $\mathbf{p}$ in P
(d) convex for all $\mathbf{p}$ in P
(e) upper semicontinuous

---

[5] *A proof of the propositions*

(a) $X_i(\mathbf{p})$ is nonempty, compact, and convex. (This follows from convexity and continuity of R_i.)

(b) $X_i(\mathbf{p})$ is upper semicontinuous. (*Cf.* Gale (1955), p. 168; Nikaido (1956), p. 140; Debreu (1959), p. 72; Nikaido's version may be seen more easily by Figure 11.3.3.)

Let $\mathbf{x}_i^k \to \mathbf{x}_i$ in E, $\mathbf{p}^k \to \mathbf{p}$, and $\mathbf{x}_i^k \in X_i(\mathbf{p}^k)$. Let $\mathbf{u}$ be another commodity bundle such that $\mathbf{pu} = \mathbf{pv}_i$ and $\mathbf{u} \in E$ and let $\mathbf{u}^k$ be another commodity bundle such that $\mathbf{p}^k \mathbf{u}^k = \mathbf{p}^k \mathbf{v}_i$ and $\mathbf{u}^k \in E$, $\mathbf{u}^k$ is the nearest to $\mathbf{u}$.

Since $\mathbf{p}^k \to \mathbf{p}$, $\mathbf{u}^k \to \mathbf{u}$. Also $\mathbf{x}_i^k \in X_i(\mathbf{p}^k)$ implies $\mathbf{x}_i^k R_i \mathbf{u}^k$. Let $k \to \infty$, then from the continuity $\mathbf{x}_i R_i \mathbf{u}$. Therefore $\mathbf{x}_i \in X_i(\mathbf{p})$.

(c) $X(\mathbf{p})$ is nonempty, compact, and convex, since the $X_i(\mathbf{p})$ are.

(d) $X(\mathbf{p})$ is upper semicontinuous, since the $X_i(\mathbf{p})$ are.

(e) $\mathbf{x}$ or $X(\mathbf{p})$ satisfies the constraint $\mathbf{px} \leq \mathbf{pv}$.

For each consumer, $\mathbf{px}_i \leq \mathbf{pv}_i$. Summing over all consumers, $\mathbf{px} \leq \mathbf{pv}$ or $\mathbf{p}(\mathbf{x} - \mathbf{v}) \leq 0$.

and

(f) all elements of $X(\mathbf{p})$ satisfy the constraint $\mathbf{px} \leqq \mathbf{pv}$

Then there is a $\mathbf{p}$ in P such that the excess demand $X(\mathbf{p}) - \mathbf{v}$ intersects with the nonpositive orthant of R^m, that is,

$$(X(\mathbf{p}) - \mathbf{v}) \cap R^m_- \neq \emptyset$$

This theorem establishes the existence of competitive exchange equilibrium.[6]

[6] *A proof of the theorem* (*Cf.* Gale (1955), p. 159; Nikaido (1956), p. 138; Debreu (1959), p. 82.)

1. *P is nonempty, closed, bounded, and convex*—nonempty since any unit vector is an element of P; closed, bounded, and convex since P is the set of all weighted averages of the unit vectors.
2. *Replace X with X′ containing X*, which has not only the properties (a) and (b) but also the property (g): $X′$ is convex.
3. Define the *price-response correspondence* by the set

$$Q(\mathbf{x}) = \{\mathbf{p} \mid \mathbf{p}(\mathbf{x} - \mathbf{v}) \text{ is maximum, for } \mathbf{x} \text{ in } X′ \text{ and } \mathbf{p} \text{ in } P\}$$

If $\mathbf{x}$ does not match $\mathbf{v}$, the auctioneer sets up a new price configuration so as to induce individuals to adjust their demands so that the excess demand and supply will be reduced. This is most effectively accomplished by choosing $\mathbf{p}$ such that $\mathbf{p}(\mathbf{x} - \mathbf{v}) = \max$ for $\mathbf{p}$ in P, that is, the price of the good with positive (negative) excess demand is raised (lowered). Let the set of such $\mathbf{p}$ be $Q(\mathbf{x})$.

Since $\mathbf{p}(\mathbf{x} - \mathbf{v})$ is a continuous real-valued function defined on a nonempty compact set P and concave in $\mathbf{p}$, it assumes its maximum value on P. That is, choose an arbitrary demand vector $\mathbf{x}$ from the set of all demand vectors $X(\mathbf{p})$ which are attainable at some prices $\mathbf{p}$, then find price vectors for which the value of this demand $\mathbf{p}(\mathbf{x} - \mathbf{v})$ is maximized. Thus, for a given price vector $\mathbf{p}$ and demand vector $\mathbf{x}$, the price-response correspondence Q gives new price vectors. The price-response correspondence is a correspondence from $X′$ into a subset of P, which is closed and bounded.
4. *The price-response correspondence Q(x) is upper semicontinuous:* $Q(\mathbf{x})$ is upper semicontinuous if $\mathbf{p}^k \to \mathbf{p}$ in P, $\mathbf{x}^k \to \mathbf{x}$ in $X′$ and $\mathbf{p}^k \in Q(\mathbf{x}^k)$ imply $\mathbf{p} \in Q(\mathbf{x})$. Let $\mathbf{q}$ be any price configuration, then since $\mathbf{p}^k \in Q(\mathbf{x}^k)$,

$$\mathbf{p}^k(\mathbf{x}^k - \mathbf{v}) \geqq \mathbf{q}(\mathbf{x}^k - \mathbf{v})$$

Let $k \to \infty$, then one obtains $\mathbf{p}(\mathbf{x} - \mathbf{v}) \geqq \mathbf{q}(\mathbf{x} - \mathbf{v})$. Therefore $\mathbf{p} \in Q(\mathbf{x})$.
5. *Q(x) is convex:* If $\mathbf{x} = 0$, then $Q(\mathbf{x}) = P$, since $0 \cdot P = 0$ for all $\mathbf{p}$ in P. $Q(\mathbf{x})$ is convex since it is the intersection of the hyperplane $\{\mathbf{p} \mid \mathbf{p}(\mathbf{x} - \mathbf{v}) = \max P(\mathbf{x} - \mathbf{v})\}$ with P.
6. *Define* $(\mathbf{p}, \mathbf{x}) \to \{Q(\mathbf{x}), X(\mathbf{p})\}$: Consider the Cartesian product $P \times X′$, that is, the set of normalized price vectors paired with the set of demand vectors. For some vector $(\mathbf{p}, \mathbf{x})$ in $P \times X′$, $X(\mathbf{p})$ associates with $\mathbf{p}$ a set of excess-demand vectors, and $Q(\mathbf{x})$ associates with $\mathbf{x}$ a set of price vectors; the correspondence $(\mathbf{p}, \mathbf{x}) \to [Q(\mathbf{x}), X(\mathbf{p})]$ maps a point of $P \times X′$ into a subset of $P \times X′$.
7. *P × X′ and the correspondence* $(\mathbf{p}, \mathbf{x}) \to [Q(\mathbf{x}), X(\mathbf{p})]$ *satisfy the condition of the Kakutani Fixed-Point Theorem:* Both P and $X′$ are nonempty, closed, bounded, and convex. $X(\mathbf{p})$ and $Q(\mathbf{x})$ are both upper semicontinuous, and their image sets are convex. Therefore the hypothesis of the Kakutani Fixed-Point Theorem is satisfied. There exists some $\mathbf{p}^* \in P$, $\mathbf{x}^* \in X′$ which is a fixed point, that is, for which $\mathbf{p}^* \in Q(\mathbf{x}^*)$, $\mathbf{x}^* \in X(\mathbf{p}^*)$. Since $\mathbf{p}(\mathbf{x}^* - \mathbf{v}) \leqq \mathbf{p}^*(\mathbf{x}^* - \mathbf{v})$ by step 3 above and $\mathbf{p}^*(\mathbf{x}^* - \mathbf{v}) \leqq 0$ by assumption (f), $\mathbf{p}(\mathbf{x}^* - \mathbf{v}) \leqq 0$. Hence $x_j^* - v_j \leqq 0$.

Figure 11.3.4

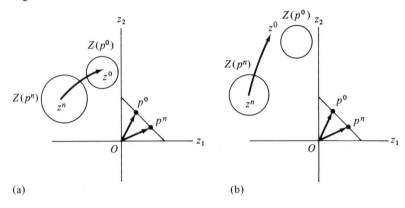

(a)

(b)

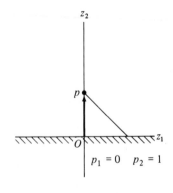

(c)

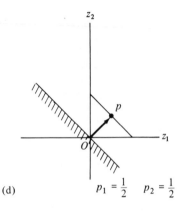

(d)

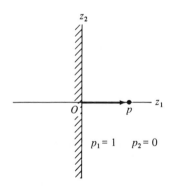

(e)

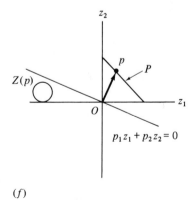

(f)

Example

Let $Z(\mathbf{p}) = X(\mathbf{p}) - \mathbf{v}$ be a bounded, upper semicontinuous correspondence, from the set

$$P = \{\mathbf{p} \mid p_1 \geq 0, p_2 \geq 0, p_1 + p_2 = 1\}$$

to the two-dimensional commodity space R^2. The upper semicontinuity of $Z(\mathbf{p})$ means that Figure 11.3.4a is true, and not Figure 11.3.4b.

Let this correspondence be such that

(a) $Z(\mathbf{p})$ is a nonvoid convex set for all $\mathbf{p} \in P$
(b) If $\mathbf{z} = (z_1, z_2)$ is in $Z(\mathbf{p})$, then $p_1 z_1 + p_2 z_2 \leq 0$

That is,

$$p_1 z_1 + (1 - p_1)z_2 \leq 0 \qquad 0 \leq p_1 \leq 1$$

Therefore, for $p_1 = 0, 1/2, 1$, the range of $\mathbf{z}$ is as shown in Figure 11.3.4c, d, and e. Thus z_1 and z_2 cannot both be positive.

Then there exist $\mathbf{p}$ in P and $\mathbf{z}$ in $Z(\mathbf{p})$ such that $\mathbf{z} \leq 0$. That is, $\mathbf{z}$ must be in the shaded area of Figure 11.3.4f. The theorem holds, since as $\mathbf{p}$ moves from one end of P to the other, the nonempty set $Z(\mathbf{p})$ will eventually intersect with the nonpositive orthant of the commodity plane.

11.4 THE PRODUCTION SET

Just as the consumer, the firm also makes a choice of a commodity bundle. The technically feasible *production* of the kth firm is described by a *vector* in the m-dimensional euclidean space

$$\mathbf{y}_k = (y_{kj}) \qquad j = 1, \ldots, m \tag{1}$$

where y_{kj} is the quantity of the jth good involved; it represents an output if positive, and input if negative. More than one element of the production vector can be positive; that is, joint production is allowed. In the economy of two goods: labor y_1 and food y_2, the producer chooses a commodity bundle (y_1, y_2), where y_1 represents his input of labor and y_2 his output of food.

There can be any number of production vectors for each firm. The set Y_k of all production vectors $\mathbf{y}_k$ of the kth firm is called his *production set*. That is,

$$Y_k = \{\mathbf{y}_k\} \tag{2}$$

A production set denotes the collection of all commodity bundles (inputs and outputs) that are technically feasible with the firm's given technology. In contrast, marginalist models of production in Part I described the technical aspect of production by the production function, which expresses the maximum amount of output producible from given inputs using the most efficient technique. The marginalist models also described the technical aspect of production by the transformation function, which expresses the maximum amounts of products obtainable at various levels of inputs assuming that the most efficient technique has been chosen.

Several assumptions made regarding the production set follow:

• Continuity: That is, any sequence of points in Y_k converges to a point in Y_k. Thus the boundary of the production set is included. This assumption is mathematically stated as

$$Y_k \text{ is closed} \tag{3}$$

Thus Y_k includes the heavy line in Figure 11.4.1.

• Possibility of Inaction: It is possible to do nothing, that is, use no inputs and produce no outputs. This fact can be expressed by saying that the origin of the vector space belongs to the production set, that is,

$$\mathbf{0} \in Y_k \tag{4}$$

This rules out the situation in Figure 11.4.2a.

• Impossibility of "Free" Production: Normally there can be no positive outputs without at least one nonzero (negative) input, that is, any production vector $\mathbf{y}$ other than inaction must contain at least one negative element. If $\mathbf{y} \geq 0$,

Figure 11.4.1

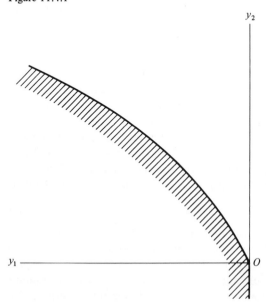

Figure 11.4.2

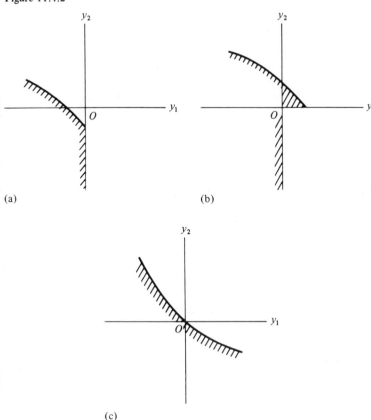

(a)   (b)

(c)

that is, if all elements of **y** are nonnegative and at least one element of **y** is positive, this implies that in the production process at least one good can be produced without any inputs. The impossibility of this occurring can be expressed by saying that the only point common to the prodution set and the nonnegative orthant is the origin, that is,

$$Y_k \cap R_+^m = 0 \tag{5}$$

This assumption rules out the situation in Figure 11.4.2b, where the production set includes part of the first quadrant.

- Irreversibility of Production: Consider a production activity **y** which is an element of the production set Y. Then $-\mathbf{y}$ represents the production activity with the inputs and outputs reversed, that is, the activity with the inputs of **y** used as outputs and the outputs of **y** used as the inputs. Therefore, **y** is technologically *reversible*. It is possible to produce according to **y**, and then, using the resulting outputs as inputs, to produce according to $-\mathbf{y}$. But there do exist such inputs as land and natural resources which cannot be produced. It is unreasonable to assume it possible to first use land, natural resources, and other goods as inputs to produce some products, and then use them as inputs to produce the original inputs: land, natural resources, and other goods. Therefore, the reversibility of production activities is ruled out. This fact can be stated by saying that it is impossible for the production set to contain the extension of the line segment connecting a point of the production set and the origin beyond the origin, that is,

$$Y_k \cap (-Y_k) = \mathbf{0} \tag{6}$$

This assumption rules out the situation in Figure 11.4.2c.

- "Free" Disposal: It is assumed possible to dispose of any amounts of goods without producing any goods. That is, a production vector can be in the third quadrant of the two-dimensional commodity space. That can be represented by

$$Y_k \cap R^m_- = R^m_- \tag{7}$$

where R^m_- denotes the nonpositive orthant of R^m. Thus the production set in Figure 11.4.1 includes the entire third quadrant.

- Production is subject to constant or decreasing returns to scale: This can be expressed by saying that if $\mathbf{y}^1$ and $\mathbf{y}^2$ are feasible productions, then their positive weighted sum $t\mathbf{y}^1 + (1 - t)\mathbf{y}^2$, $0 \leq t \leq 1$, is also a feasible production. Because of the second assumption, $\mathbf{y}^2$ could be the origin. Thus if $\mathbf{y}^1$ is feasible, then $t\mathbf{y}^1$ is possible for $0 \leq t \leq 1$. That is, if $\mathbf{y}^1$ is feasible one can arbitrarily reduce the scale of operations as shown in Figure 11.4.3a and b. This nonincreasing-returns-to-scale assumption can be expressed mathematically by saying that

$$Y_k \text{ is convex} \tag{8}$$

The marginalist models assumed the law of variable proportions, while the linear models assumed the law of constant proportions. The notion of convexity here encompass both these conditions.

Assume there are r firms in the economy, then the *total production set Y* is defined by

$$\sum_{k=1}^{r} Y_k \tag{9}$$

THE OPTIMUM PRODUCTION OF A COMPETITIVE FIRM

The objective function of the firm is the same as in Parts I and II, that is, profits. Profits can be expressed by the inner product $\mathbf{p} \cdot \mathbf{y}$ of the price vector and the production vector (in which inputs are negative). Given the price vector

Figure 11.4.3

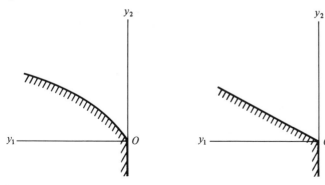

(a) Decreasing returns to scale   (b) Constant returns to scale

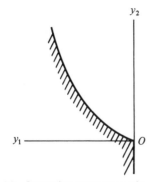

(c) Increasing returns to scale

$\mathbf{p} \geq 0$, the set of all productions $\mathbf{y}_k$ that give a certain level of profits π can be represented by the hyperplane

$$\mathbf{p} \cdot \mathbf{y}_k = \pi$$

which can be called the *isoprofit hyperplane*. It depends on the price vector $\mathbf{p}$, and should go through the interior of the nonnegative orthant of the commodity space if the firm has a positive profit.

A linear function assumes its maximum on a compact set in a point of the boundary. Thus an efficient production is on the boundary of the production set. If production follows decreasing returns to scale, that is, the production set is strictly convex, then the optimum production will be the point where the production set and an isoprofit hyperplane intersect. If production follows constant returns to scale in some range, that is, the production set is convex but

Figure 11.4.4

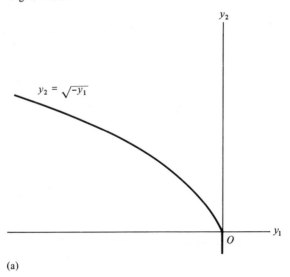

$y_2 = \sqrt{-y_1}$

(a)

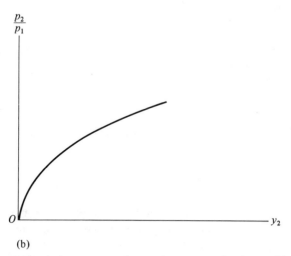

(b)

not strictly convex, the optimum production, which is the intersection of the production set and the isoprofit hyperplane, will be represented by more than one point.

Examples

The production set may be written

$$Y = \{(y_1, y_2) \mid y_1 \leq 0, y_2 \leq \sqrt{-y_1}\}$$

Figure 11.4.5

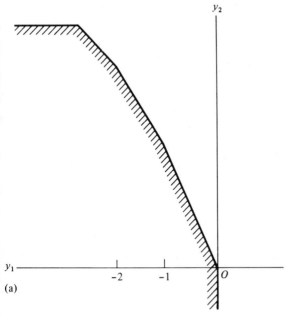

(a)

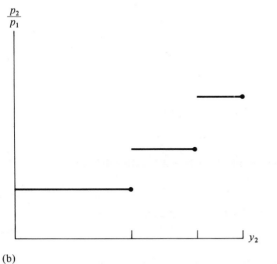

(b)

The set is as shown in Figure 11.4.4. The supply of y_2 will be a smooth, increasing function of the relative price p_2/p_1. If the production set is such that

$$Y = \{(y_1, y_2) \,|\, y_2 \leq -3y_1 \text{ for } y_1 \leq 0;\ y_2 \leq -2y_1 \text{ for } y_1 \leq -1;$$
$$y_2 \leq -y_1, \text{ for } y_1 \leq -2;\ y_2 = 6 \text{ for } y_1 \leq -3\}$$

then the set will be as shown in Figure 11.4.5 and the supply function will be a step function.[7]

11.5 COMPETITIVE EQUILIBRIUM
INDIVIDUAL BUDGET CONSTRAINTS

The following symbols are used:

v_{ij} = the ith consumer's initial endowment of the jth good; $v_{ij} \geq 0$
$\mathbf{v}_i$ = the m-dimensional vector of the ith individual's initial endowments of goods;
   $\mathbf{v}_i = (v_{ij}), j = 1, \ldots, m$
$\mathbf{v}$ = the m-dimensional vector of the total initial endowments of goods in the economy

Therefore

$$\mathbf{v} = \sum_i \mathbf{v}_i \tag{1}$$

a_{ki} = the proportion of the kth firm's profits distributed to the ith consumer;

$a_{ki} \geq 0, \sum_i a_{ki} = 1$

W_i = the ith consumer's wealth

The ith consumer's wealth consists of initial endowments of goods and profits received from the firms. Therefore

$$W_i = \mathbf{p}\mathbf{v}_i + \sum_k a_{ki}\,\mathbf{p}\mathbf{y}_k \tag{2}$$

Hence the budget constraint for each consumer is

$$\mathbf{p}\mathbf{x}_i \leq \mathbf{p}\mathbf{v}_i + \sum_k a_{ki}\,\mathbf{p}\mathbf{y}_k \tag{3}$$

AGGREGATE DEMAND, SUPPLY, AND ATTAINABILITY

The following symbols are used:

$\bar{v}_j$ = the total of the jth good initially held in the economy (scalar)
$\mathbf{v}$ = the m-dimensional vector of the total amounts of goods initially held;
   $\mathbf{v} = (\bar{v}_j), j = 1, \ldots, m$
$\mathbf{x}$ = the m-dimensional vector of total demands for goods; that is,

$$\mathbf{x} = \sum_i \mathbf{x}_i \tag{4}$$

[7] *Cf.* Debreu (1959), chap, 3 on the production theory in set-theoretic terms.

$\mathbf{y}$ = the m-dimensional vector of total supplies of goods; that is,

$$\mathbf{y} = \sum_k \mathbf{y}_k \qquad (5)$$

A state of the economy $(\mathbf{x}, \mathbf{y})$ is said to be *attainable* if

$$\mathbf{x}_i \in X_i \qquad \mathbf{y}_k \in Y_k \qquad \mathbf{x} \leqq \mathbf{v} + \mathbf{y} \qquad (6)$$

AGGREGATE EXCESS-DEMAND CORRESPONDENCE

The aggregate excess-demand correspondence is the set-valued function of the price vector

$$Z(\mathbf{p}) = X(\mathbf{p}) - Y(\mathbf{p}) - \{\mathbf{v}\} \qquad (7)$$

where $X(\mathbf{p})$ and $Y(\mathbf{p})$ are the demand and supply correspondences, respectively.

DEFINITION OF THE EXISTENCE OF COMPETITIVE EQUILIBRIUM

The existence of *competitive equilibrium* is the existence of a set of equilibrium prices (normalized nonnegative vector) $\mathbf{p}^*$ and a corresponding balancing bundle of choices, that is, a set of consumption vectors for the consumers and a set of production vectors for the firms, all of which can be denoted by

$$\{\mathbf{p}^*; \mathbf{x}_1^*, \mathbf{x}_2^*, \ldots, \mathbf{x}_n^*; \mathbf{y}_1^*, \mathbf{y}_2^*, \ldots, \mathbf{y}_r^*\}$$

such that

- Maximum Profits: The choice of each firm yields the maximum profits obtainable in its production set, that is,

$$\mathbf{p}^* \mathbf{y}_k^* = \max \mathbf{p}^* \mathbf{y}_k$$
$$\mathbf{y}_k \in Y_k$$
$$k = 1, \ldots, r$$

- Maximum Satisfaction: The choice of each consumer is considered at least as good as any other alternative choice in his consumption set which satisfies the wealth constraint

$$\mathbf{x}_i^* R_i \mathbf{x}_i$$

$$\mathbf{x}_i \in \left\{ \mathbf{x}_i \mid \mathbf{p}^* \cdot \mathbf{x}_i \leq \mathbf{p}^* \cdot \mathbf{v}_i + \sum_{k=1}^r a_{ik} \mathbf{p}^* \cdot \mathbf{y}_k^* \right\}$$

- Feasibility: For the entire economy, the demand for each good does not exceed the sum of the initial endowments and the productions of the good, and if the demand falls short of the sum of the initial holdings and the productions, then the price of the good is zero, that is, using the definitions

$$\mathbf{x}^* = \sum_{i=1}^{n} \mathbf{x}_i^* \qquad \mathbf{y}^* = \sum_{k=1}^{r} \mathbf{y}_k^* \qquad \mathbf{v} = \sum_{i=1}^{n} \mathbf{v}_i \qquad \mathbf{z}^* = \mathbf{x}^* - \mathbf{y}^* - \mathbf{v}$$

the following hold:

$$\mathbf{z}^* \leq 0 \qquad \text{and} \qquad \mathbf{p}^* \mathbf{z}^* = 0$$

For the sake of completeness, an existence theorem, one by Debreu, should be stated.

Existence Theorem

Competitive equilibrium exists under the following assumptions:

- X_i is closed, convex, and bounded from below.
- The consumer is never satiated.
- The preference preordering is continuous.
- The preference preordering is convex.
- There is a consumption $\mathbf{x}_i$ in his consumption set X_i such that $\mathbf{x}_i < \mathbf{v}_i$.
- The production set contains the origin.
- Y is closed and convex.
- $Y \cap (-Y) \supset \{0\}$
- $Y \supset R_-^m$

Debreu (1959) shows that these assumptions are sufficient to enable one to use the theorem of Section 11.3 to prove the existence of competitive equilibrium.

Under these assumptions Y_j is not closed and convex, and some of X_i and Y_j may be unbounded. Hence a closed convex hull of Y_j is used instead of Y_j. It is shown that the competitive equilibrium is an equilibrium obtained under this formulation. The proof shows that the supply correspondence is upper semicontinuous on P and the profit function is continuous on P, and that the demand correspondence is upper semicontinuous on P. Furthermore, it shows that the excess-demand correspondence is upper semicontinuous and convex, and that the excess-demand set satisfies the weak-budget constraint. Thus the conditions of the theorem of Section 11.3 are satisfied.

Thus the fixed-point theorem replaces the counting of equations and variables of Part I in proving the existence of equilibrium. The prices and quantities are again determined simultaneously. The interaction between prices and quantities, embodied in the demand, supply, excess demand, and price-response correspondences, simulates the functioning of a competitive economy. This theorem thus establishes the workability of the decentralized competitive solution to the problem of resource allocation.[8]

[8] For technical details of the existence theorem, see Arrow and Debreu (1954), and Debreu (1959), chap. 5.

12
SET-THEORETIC
WELFARE
ECONOMICS

12.1 INTRODUCTION

Optimum resource allocation was analyzed in marginalist models in terms of marginal conditions in consumption and production and was examined in the linear production models in terms of optimality conditions of linear programming. Rigorous examination of optimality requires an introduction of various set-theoretic concepts. This chapter considers the more elementary theorems in this area.

12.2 OPTIMALITY OF COMPETITIVE EQUILIBRIUM

One can prove that if no consumer is satiated and the economy is externality-free, then *competitive equilibrium is Pareto optimal.* (Externality exists in the economy if the preferences of each consumer are affected by the choices of other consumers or producers, and the production set of each producer is affected by the choices of consumers and other producers.)

In the set-theoretic context, Pareto optimality can be defined as follows: A bundle of choices is *Pareto optimum* if it is feasible, and there is no second feasible bundle which everyone considers at least as good as the first, and at least one consumer considers better.

The procedure is to show that if competitive equilibrium is not Pareto optimum, there must be a consumption vector which is greater with respect to the preference preordering than the competitive equilibrium consumption vector, but such a consumption vector violates the feasibility constraint that it be feasible relative to the amounts produced plus initial endowments.

COMPETITIVE EQUILIBRIUM IS PARETO OPTIMAL

For simplicity assume two goods, two consumers and two producers and let

$$\{x_1^*, x_2^*, y_1^*, y_2^*, p\}$$

represent competitive equilibrium; that is, by definition

(a) x_i^* is the greatest element with respect to the ith consumer's preference preordering, subject to his wealth constraint

$$\begin{array}{cc} x_i^* \text{ is the maximum element for } R_i & (1) \\ \text{of the feasible consumption set } \{x_i | px_i \leqq W_i\} \end{array}$$

(b) y_k^* maximizes the kth firm's profits, that is,

$$py_k^* \geqq py_k \text{ for all } y_k \in Y_k \qquad (2)$$

(c) The markets are cleared

$$\sum x_i^* = \sum y_k^* + v \qquad (3)$$

where $v =$ column vector (v_1, v_2) and v_j denotes the total initial endowments of the jth good in the economy. Also assume that the preference preordering is convex and that no consumer is satiated at x^*. Then the competitive equilibrium is Pareto optimum. The proof can be sketched as follows:

If

$$\{x_1^*, x_2^*, y_1^*, y_2^*\}$$

is not Pareto optimum, then there exists

$$\{x_1', x_2', y_1', y_2'\}$$

such that

(d) At least one consumer is better off without anybody being worse off; for example, using P defined in Sec. 11.3,

$$x_1' P_1 x_1^* \qquad (4)$$

$$x_2' R_2 x_2^* \qquad (5)$$

(e) Productions belong to the production sets

$$y_k' \in Y_k \qquad k = 1, 2 \qquad (6)$$

(f) Feasibility

$$\sum x'_i \leq \sum y'_k + v \tag{7}$$

Conditions (1) and (4) imply that the cost of x'_1 is greater than that of x^*_1, that is

$$px'_1 > px^*_1 \tag{8}$$

Also, according to the proof below,[1] (5) implies

$$px'_2 \geq px^*_2 \tag{9}$$

Adding (8) and (9),

$$\sum px'_i > \sum px^*_i \tag{10}$$

But from the market equilibrium condition (3)

$$\sum px^*_i = \sum py^*_k + pv \tag{11}$$

and from the maximum-profits condition (2)

$$\sum py^*_k \geq \sum py'_k \tag{12}$$

Therefore from (10)–(12),

$$\sum px'_i > \sum py'_k + pv$$

contradicting the feasibility condition (7). Therefore, there is no

$$\{x'_1, \quad x'_2, \quad y'_1, \quad y'_2\}$$

which satisfies (4) and (5), and

$$\{x^*_1, \quad x^*_2, \quad y^*_1, \quad y^*_2\}$$

is Pareto optimum.

A PARETO OPTIMUM IS A COMPETITIVE EQUILIBRIUM

One can also show that with each Pareto-optimum allocation

$$\{x^*_1, x^*_2, y^*_1, y^*_2\}$$

[1] *Proof* (cf. Debreu (1954))

Let: $x'Ix^*$. Since x^* is not a saturation point, there is x'' such that $x''Px'$. Let: $x(t)=(1-t)x' + tx''$, where $0 < t < 1$. From the convexity assumption, $x(t)Px'$. Hence, $x(t)Px^*$. Therefore, from (1),

$$px^* < px(t) = (1-t)px' + tpx''$$

Let t approach zero, then in the limit $px^* \leq px'$. Thus, if $x'Ix^*$, then $px' \geq px^*$. Also from (1), if $x'Px^*$, $px' > px^*$. Therefore, if $x'Rx^*$,

$$px' \geq px^*$$

there exists a price vector $\mathbf{p} \geq 0$ such that

(a) expenditures are minimum for each consumer: that is,

$$\mathbf{px}_i^* \leq \mathbf{px}_i \qquad \text{for all } \mathbf{x}_i \, R_i \, \mathbf{x}_i^* \tag{13}$$

(b) profits are maximum for each firm:

$$\mathbf{py}_k^* \geq \mathbf{py}_k \qquad \text{for all } \mathbf{y}_k \in Y_k \tag{14}$$

It is assumed that the preference preordering is continuous and convex, and that at least one consumer, say the first, is not satiated.

Let X_i denote the set

$$X_i = \{\mathbf{x}_i | \mathbf{x}_i \, R_i \, \mathbf{x}_i^*\} \qquad i = 1, 2 \tag{15}$$

Assuming the first consumer to not be satiated, define X_1^*

$$X_1^* = \{\mathbf{x}_1 \,|\, \mathbf{x}_1 \, P_1 \, \mathbf{x}_1^*\} \tag{16}$$

Consider the set

$$Z = X_1^* + X_2 - (Y_1 + Y_2) \tag{17}$$

that is, the set of resources which can enable the economy to achieve the state $\{\mathbf{x}_1, \mathbf{x}_2, \mathbf{y}_1, \mathbf{y}_2\}$ such that

$$\mathbf{x}_1 \, P_1 \, \mathbf{x}_1^*$$
$$\mathbf{x}_2 \, R_2 \, \mathbf{x}_2^*$$

Note that the initial endowment $\mathbf{v}$ is not an interior point of Z, but is on the boundary of Z. This can be proved by contradiction: If $\mathbf{v}$ is an interior point then there exists $\mathbf{v}' \in Z$ such that $\mathbf{v}' < \mathbf{v}$ and the consumers are at least as well off as at $\mathbf{x}_1^*$ and $\mathbf{x}_2^*$. By distributing $\mathbf{v} - \mathbf{v}'$ between the two consumers, they can be made better off than at $\mathbf{x}_1^*$ and $\mathbf{x}_2^*$. This contradicts the assumption of Pareto optimality of $\mathbf{x}_1^*$ and $\mathbf{x}_2^*$.

Further, the set Z is a convex set since it is the sum of convex sets.

Since Z is a convex set and $\mathbf{v}$ is not interior to Z, there exists a bounding line (hyperplane with the slope $-p_1/p_2$) such that Z is above the hyperplane, that is, for any $\mathbf{z} \in Z$

$$\mathbf{pz} \geq \mathbf{pv} \tag{18}$$

From the definition of $\mathbf{z}$, (18) means

$$\mathbf{p}(\textstyle\sum \mathbf{x}_i - \sum \mathbf{y}_k) \geq \mathbf{pv} \tag{19}$$

1. *Market Equilibrium*: From feasibility

$$\textstyle\sum \mathbf{x}_i^* - \sum \mathbf{y}_k^* \leq \mathbf{v} \tag{20}$$

If the jth good is in excess supply, then the corresponding p_j of the bounding line (hyperplane) will be zero. Therefore

$$\sum \mathbf{p}\mathbf{x}_i^* - \sum \mathbf{p}\mathbf{y}_k^* = \mathbf{p}\mathbf{v} \tag{21}$$

Thus $\mathbf{p}$ provides market equilibrium prices under perfect competition.

2. *Maximum Profits*: From (19) and (21),

$$\sum \mathbf{p}\mathbf{x}_i - \sum \mathbf{p}\mathbf{x}_i^* \geqq \sum \mathbf{p}\mathbf{y}_k - \sum \mathbf{p}\mathbf{y}_k^* \tag{22}$$

Let

$$\mathbf{x}_i = \mathbf{x}_i^* \qquad i = 1, 2 \qquad \mathbf{y}_2 = \mathbf{y}_2^*$$

Then (22) becomes

$$\mathbf{p}\mathbf{y}_1 \leqq \mathbf{p}\mathbf{y}_1^* \tag{23}$$

Similarly for firm 2. Thus, $\mathbf{y}_k^*$ maximizes the kth firm's profits at $\mathbf{p}$.

3. *Minimum Costs*: Let

$$\mathbf{y}_k = \mathbf{y}_k^* \qquad k = 1, 2 \qquad \mathbf{x}_2 = \mathbf{x}_2^*$$

Then (22) becomes

$$\sum \mathbf{p}\mathbf{x}_1 \geqq \sum \mathbf{p}\mathbf{x}_1^* \tag{24}$$

Similarly for consumer 2. Thus at $\mathbf{p}$, $\mathbf{x}_i^*$ minimizes costs.[2]

12.3 INTERTEMPORAL EQUILIBRIUM

The theory of intertemporal equilibrium of Chapter 6 can be formulated in set-theoretic terms as in Malinvaud (1953). Assume two goods, but an infinite number of periods.

CONSUMPTION

A bundle of two goods over time can be expressed by a two-dimensional vector

$$\mathbf{x}^t = (x_1^t \quad x_2^t) \qquad t = 1, 2, \ldots \tag{1}$$

where the subscript denotes the two different goods. The set of all $\mathbf{x}^t$ for period t is denoted by X^t, as in Section 11.3 (see Figure 12.3.1). Denote the consumer's consumption plans over time by

$$\mathbf{x} = (\mathbf{x}^1 \quad \mathbf{x}^2 \quad \mathbf{x}^3 \ldots \mathbf{x}^t \ldots) \tag{2}$$

[2] *Cf.* Arrow (1951), Debreu (1954).

Figure 12.3.1

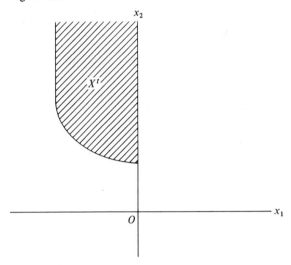

PRODUCTION

Denote the producer's stock of goods at the end of $t - 1$, available for use in production and consumption in period t, by a two-dimensional vector

$$\mathbf{b}^t = (b_1^t \quad b_2^t) \tag{3}$$

Stocks at the beginning of t and used in production in period t are denoted by a two-dimensional vector (in absolute values)

$$\mathbf{a}^t = (a_1^t \quad a_2^t) \tag{4}$$

while the flows of net outputs at the beginning of period t used for consumption can be expressed by a two-dimensional vector

$$\mathbf{y}^t = (y_1^t \quad y_2^t) \qquad t = 1, 2, \ldots \tag{5}$$

where y_i^t is positive when the good i is net output, and negative when the good i is net input.

Therefore

$$\mathbf{a}^t = \mathbf{b}^t - \mathbf{y}^t \tag{6}$$

as shown in Figure 12.3.2, or

$$\mathbf{y}^t = \mathbf{b}^t - \mathbf{a}^t \tag{7}$$

that is, the net outputs of t equals the gross outputs of $t - 1$ minus the gross inputs of t.

Figure 12.3.2

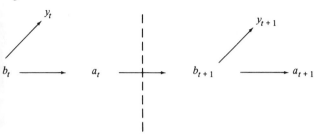

Assume as in Sections 6.3 and 11.4 that the set of efficient $\mathbf{y}^t$ is convex. Denote the production plan by

$$\mathbf{y} = (\mathbf{y}^1 \quad \mathbf{y}^2 \ldots \mathbf{y}^t \ldots) \tag{8}$$

Write the producer's feasible production plan for t as

$$\mathbf{h}^t = (-\mathbf{a}^t, \quad \mathbf{b}^{t+1}) \tag{9}$$

(as shown in Figure 12.3.3) and the feasible production plans for all periods as

$$\mathbf{h} = (\mathbf{h}^1 \quad \mathbf{h}^2 \ldots \mathbf{h}^t \ldots) \tag{10}$$

so that

$$\mathbf{h} = (-\mathbf{a}^1 \quad \mathbf{b}^2 \quad -\mathbf{a}^2 \quad \mathbf{b}^3 \ldots -\mathbf{a}^{t-1} \quad \mathbf{b}^t \ldots) \tag{11}$$

Figure 12.3.3

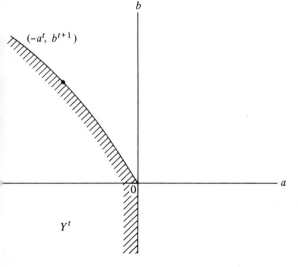

A feasible balancing bundle of consumption and production plans for many consumers-producers is

$$\sum \mathbf{x}^t = \sum \mathbf{y}^t \qquad t = 1, 2, \ldots \qquad (12)$$

where $\mathbf{x}^t$ and $\mathbf{y}^t$ belong to X^t and Y^t, respectively.

PARETO OPTIMUM

A feasible balancing bundle of consumption plan $\mathbf{x}$ and production plan $\mathbf{h}$ is Pareto optimum if no other feasible balancing bundle leaves everyone as well off and some better off. A production plan $\mathbf{h}$ is called efficient if no other plan can give net outputs algebraically at least as great as, and at least one net output greater than, $\mathbf{h}$.

COMPETITIVE EQUILIBRIUM

Competitive equilibrium is a feasible balancing bundle and a price system such that

(a) The consumer maximizes his preferences subject to the constraint of his resources.

(b) The firm maximizes the value of its net output bundle.

That is, it maximizes

$$\mathbf{p}^{t+1}\mathbf{b}^{t+1} - \mathbf{p}^t\mathbf{a}^t \qquad t = 1, 2, \ldots \qquad (13)$$

over its production set for each period and minimizes the cost (the second term of (13)) of the resulting net output bundle. Here the intertemporal price system can be written

$$\mathbf{p} = (\mathbf{p}^1 \quad \mathbf{p}^2 \ldots \mathbf{p}^t \ldots) \qquad (14)$$

where

$$\mathbf{p}^t = (p_1^t \quad p_2^t) \qquad (15)$$

The p_j^t is the price of commodity j delivered in time period t, and can be interpreted as the present value, that is, the price at time period 1, of a unit of commodity j in period t. Then the first term of (13) represents the present value of receipts, and the second term the present value of costs.

In short, in competitive equilibrium, the consumer maximizes preferences subject to the constraint on the present value of his wealth, while the producer maximizes the present value of his net output stream.

The accounting prices p_j^t are relative prices. Suppose the *numéraire* good 1 has a positive account price p_1^t in each period t. The money price of good 2 in that period is

$$p_2^{*t} = \frac{p_2^t}{p_1^t} \qquad t = 1, 2, \ldots$$

The dimension of this price is units of the *numéraire* good in period t per unit of good 2 in period t.

INTEREST RATES

The interest rate between periods 1 and 2, $r_{1,2}$, is defined as

$$r_{1,2} = \frac{\text{units of period 2 numéraire good received}}{\text{units of period 1 numéraire good loaned}} - 1$$

The creditor receives p_1^1/p_1^2 units of period 2 *numéraire* good for each unit of period 1 *numéraire* good loaned. The interest rate can also be given by

$$r_{1,2} = \frac{p_1^1}{p_1^2} - 1 \tag{16}$$

Therefore

$$p_1^1 = (1 + r_{1,2})p_1^2 \tag{17}$$

The interest rate can be defined similarly for other spans of time.

From the definition of the money price

$$p_2^2 = p_2^{*2} p_1^2$$

From (17)

$$p_1^2 = \frac{p_1^1}{1 + r_{1,2}}$$

Let

$$p_1^1 = 1$$

Then

$$p_2^2 = \frac{p_2^{*2}}{1 + r_{1,2}} \tag{18}$$

INVESTMENT

Let:

$\mathbf{b}^t$ = the amounts of the commodities available at the end of period $t - 1$
$\mathbf{a}^t$ = investments of inputs of the commodities at the beginning of period t
$\mathbf{y}^t$ = consumption of the commodities at the beginning of period t

$\mathbf{h} = (\mathbf{b}^1 \quad -\mathbf{a}^1 \quad \mathbf{b}^2 \quad -\mathbf{a}^2)$, an efficient production plan
$\mathbf{p} = (\mathbf{p}^1 \quad \mathbf{p}^2)$, a system of accounting prices
$\bar{\mathbf{h}} = (\bar{\mathbf{b}}^1 \quad -\bar{\mathbf{a}}^1 \quad \bar{\mathbf{b}}^2 \quad -\bar{\mathbf{a}}^2)$, an alternative production plan such that

$$\bar{\mathbf{b}}^1 = \mathbf{b}^1$$
$$\bar{\mathbf{a}}^2 = \mathbf{a}^2$$
$$\bar{\mathbf{y}}^1 = \bar{\mathbf{b}}^1 - \bar{\mathbf{a}}^1 < \mathbf{y}^1 = \mathbf{b}^1 - \mathbf{a}^1$$
$$\bar{\mathbf{y}}^2 = \bar{\mathbf{b}}^2 - \bar{\mathbf{a}}^2 > \mathbf{y}^2 = \mathbf{b}^2 - \mathbf{a}^2$$

Then the change in the present value of the profits of the producer when he shifts from the production plan $\mathbf{h}$ to the production plan $\bar{\mathbf{h}}$ is

$$-\mathbf{p}^1(\mathbf{y}^1 - \bar{\mathbf{y}}^1) + \mathbf{p}^2(\bar{\mathbf{y}}^2 - \mathbf{y}^2)$$

Therefore the producer will move from $\mathbf{h}$ to $\bar{\mathbf{h}}$, that is, invest, whenever the change in the present value of profits is positive.

The money prices corresponding to these accounting prices can be written

$$\mathbf{p}^{*1} = \mathbf{p}^1 \qquad \mathbf{p}^{*2} = \mathbf{p}^2(1 + r_{1,2})$$

Therefore the producer invests whenever

$$\mathbf{p}^{*1}(\mathbf{y}^1 - \bar{\mathbf{y}}^1) < \frac{\mathbf{p}^{*2}(\bar{\mathbf{y}}^2 - \mathbf{y}^2)}{1 + r_{1,2}}$$

where the left-hand side of the inequality is money cost of investment while the right-hand side is money returns from investment.

APPENDIX

MATHEMATICAL
REVIEW FOR
PART I

MR1 MATHEMATICS IN ECONOMIC MODELS

The common subject matter of economic theory is the variation in magnitude of prices and outputs. An economist cannot think clearly about them without some mathematics.

The first mathematical concept to be used in economic theory was plane geometry, using two-dimensional diagrams. This technique was followed by algebra, using equations in a few variables. Calculus was used as soon as marginal analysis in consumption and production theory was developed. This was followed in the post-World War II period by mathematical programming. The most recent development has been the extensive use of set-theoretic concepts.

In Part I the mathematics needed is essentially the ability to solve a system of equations and obtain derivatives of a function. In Part II the mathematics needed includes linear programming. In Part III the theory of vector spaces, convex sets, and topology is used.

Before proceeding further, a variety of conditional statements that are frequently used in mathematics must be clarified. The conditional statement "if p, then q" is stated in a number of different ways such as the following.

q is a necessary condition for p
if not q, then not p
p only if q
p is a sufficient condition for q
p implies q

Moreover, the conditional statement "if p, then q; and if q, then p" is stated alternatively:

q is a necessary and sufficient condition for p
q, if and only if p

MR2   MATRICES AND DETERMINANTS

Any rectangular array of numbers is called a *matrix*. A matrix whose element in the ith row and j^{th} column is a_{ij} may be written **A**, a boldface capital letter. A matrix with m rows and n columns is called a matrix of *order m* by n. If $m = n$, **A** is said to be a *square matrix* of order m. An m by 1 matrix is called a *column vector* or simply a vector, while 1 by m matrix is called a *row vector*. A vector whose i^{th} element is a_i may be written **a**, a boldface (usually) lower case letter. The *transpose* of a matrix **A** is the matrix, written **A′**, whose (i, j) element is equal to the (j, i) element of **A**.

Two matrices can be compared for equality if they have the same order. Two matrices **A** and **B** of order m by n are said to be *equal*, written **A** = **B**, if and only if $a_{ij} = b_{ij}$ for all i and j, where a_{ij} and b_{ij} are the elements in the ith row and j^{th} column of **A** and **B**, respectively. The *sum* of two comparable matrices **A** and **B** is defined as a new matrix **C** whose element c_{ij} is obtained by adding the corresponding elements of **A** and **B**, that is, $c_{ij} = a_{ij} + b_{ij}$, for all i, j. **A** is called a *zero matrix* if and only if each element of A is equal to zero. The product of a matrix **A** by a scalar k is obtained by multiplying each element of **A** by k.

The product obtained by *postmultiplication* of an m by n matrix **A** by an n by p matrix **B** (or *premultiplication* of **B** by **A**), written **AB**, is defined as the **C** matrix such that for all i, j, $c_{ij} = \sum a_{ik} b_{kj}, k = 1, 2, \ldots, n$. Note that the number of columns of **A** must equal the number of rows of **B** (hence **BA** is not generally possible), and the matrix **C** is of order m by p.

A square matrix with 1s down the principal diagonal (from the upper left to the lower right corner) and zeros elsewhere is called the *identity matrix* regardless of its order and is denoted by **I**. A square matrix **A** is said to have an *inverse matrix*, written $\mathbf{A}^{-1}$, if $\mathbf{AA}^{-1} = \mathbf{A}^{-1}\mathbf{A} = \mathbf{I}$. If **A** has an inverse, it is said to be *nonsingular*.

The *determinant* of a square matrix is a number computed from the elements of the matrix. The *determinant* of a 2×2 matrix, denoted by

$$\begin{vmatrix} a_{11} & a_{12} \\ a_{21} & a_{22} \end{vmatrix}$$

is $a_{11}a_{22} - a_{21}a_{12}$. To compute the determinant of a 3×3 matrix, denoted by

$$\begin{vmatrix} a_{11} & a_{12} & a_{13} \\ a_{21} & a_{22} & a_{23} \\ a_{31} & a_{32} & a_{33} \end{vmatrix}$$

calls for introducing the concepts of *minor* and *cofactor*. The *minor* of the element a_{ij} is the determinant obtained by removing the row and the column containing the element a_{ij}. The *cofactor* of the element a_{ij} is obtained by multiplying its minor by $(-1)^{i+j}$. Hence, the cofactor of a_{11} is $(-1)^{1+1}(a_{22}a_{33} - a_{32}a_{23})$. The determinant of the 3×3 matrix can be computed by expanding by the elements of row 1, as follows,

$$a_{11} \times (\text{cofactor of } a_{11}) + a_{12} \times (\text{cofactor of } a_{12}) + a_{13} \times (\text{cofactor of } a_{13})$$

The same result can be obtained by expanding by any row or column. Higher-order determinants can be similarly evaluated. Thus the 3×3 determinant is equal to

$$a_{11}a_{22}a_{33} + a_{21}a_{32}a_{13} + a_{31}a_{23}a_{12} - (a_{13}a_{22}a_{31} + a_{23}a_{32}a_{11} + a_{33}a_{21}a_{12})$$

In this case of third-order determinant only, the following procedure may be useful. The first term is the product of the elements of the main diagonal. The second term picks up the the two elements immediately below the main diagonal and the upper-right-corner element. The third term picks up the lower-left-corner element and the two elements immediately above the main diagonal. The three terms within the parentheses can be found by following the same procedure with respect to $a_{13} - a_{22} - a_{31}$ diagonal. (This special procedure does not apply to higher-order determinants.)

The inverse of a nonsingular square matrix $\mathbf{A}$ can be computed by dividing by the determinant of $\mathbf{A}$ the transpose of the matrix composed of cofactors of each element of $\mathbf{A}$. For example, to obtain the inverse of

$$\mathbf{A} = \begin{bmatrix} 4 & 0 & 5 \\ 0 & 1 & -6 \\ 3 & 0 & 4 \end{bmatrix}$$

we compute first the matrix of cofactors,

$$\begin{bmatrix} 4 & -18 & -3 \\ 0 & 1 & 0 \\ -5 & 24 & 4 \end{bmatrix}$$

then transpose it,

$$\begin{bmatrix} 4 & 0 & -5 \\ -18 & 1 & 24 \\ -3 & 0 & 4 \end{bmatrix}$$

and divide the resulting matrix by

$$|A| = 4 \cdot 4 - 0 \cdot 0 + 3 \cdot (-5) = 1$$

Therefore,

$$A^{-1} = \begin{bmatrix} 4 & 0 & -5 \\ -18 & 1 & 24 \\ -3 & 0 & 4 \end{bmatrix}$$

SIMULTANEOUS LINEAR EQUATIONS

The general system of n linear equations in n unknowns can be written

$$a_{11}x_1 + a_{12}x_2 + \cdots + a_{1n}x_n = b_1$$
$$a_{21}x_1 + a_{22}x_2 + \cdots + a_{2n}x_n = b_2$$
$$\cdots\cdots\cdots\cdots\cdots\cdots\cdots\cdots\cdots\cdots$$
$$a_{n1}x_1 + a_{n2}x_2 + \cdots + a_{nn}x_n = b_n$$

In matrix notation

$$Ax = b$$

where A is an n by n matrix of coefficients, $x = \text{col.} (x_1, x_2, \ldots, x_n)$ is a column vector of n variables, and $b = \text{col.} (b_1, b_2, \ldots, b_n)$ is a column vector of the given constants in the n equations. Assume A is nonsingular, and $b \neq 0$, that is, the elements of b are not all zero (when $b = 0$, that is, the elements of b are all zero, then the equations are said to be *homogeneous*). On premultiplication by A^{-1}, we obtain

$$A^{-1}Ax = A^{-1}b$$

Since $A^{-1}A = I$ and since $Ix = x$,

$$x = A^{-1}b$$

It is recalled that A^{-1} is the transpose of the matrix composed of cofactors of each element of A divided by the determinant of A. Hence the first row of A^{-1} consists of the cofactors of the first column of A divided by the determinant of A. Hence to obtain x_1, the procedure is to replace column 1 of A with vector b, evaluate the determinant of this matrix, divide it by the determinant of A. Similarly for other unknowns. This procedure has been called *Cramer's rule*. For example, given

$$\begin{cases} x_1 + 2x_2 = 200 \\ 2x_1 + 8x_2 = 560 \end{cases}$$

the application of the rule gives

$$x_1 = \frac{\begin{vmatrix} 200 & 2 \\ 560 & 8 \end{vmatrix}}{\begin{vmatrix} 1 & 2 \\ 2 & 8 \end{vmatrix}} = \frac{480}{4} = 120$$

and

$$x_2 = \frac{\begin{vmatrix} 1 & 200 \\ 2 & 560 \end{vmatrix}}{\begin{vmatrix} 1 & 2 \\ 2 & 8 \end{vmatrix}} = \frac{160}{4} = 40$$

PROPERTIES OF THE DETERMINANT

The following properties of the determinant are useful. Let $\mathbf{A}$ be a square matrix; then

(a) $|\mathbf{A}| = |\mathbf{A}'|$
(b) If $\mathbf{A}$ has a column of zeros, then $|\mathbf{A}| = 0$
(c) If $\mathbf{A}$ has two identical columns, then $|\mathbf{A}| = 0$
(d) Multiplying a column by a scalar k multiplies $|\mathbf{A}|$ by k
(e) Interchanging two columns changes the sign of $|\mathbf{A}|$
(f) Adding a multiple of a column to another leaves $|\mathbf{A}|$ unchanged
(g) Let $\mathbf{B}$ be another square matrix. Then $|\mathbf{AB}| = |\mathbf{A}| \cdot |\mathbf{B}|$
(h) Expansion by the alien cofactors: The inner product of cofactors of a column and of elements of another column is zero.

INEQUALITIES

The following conventions regarding the sign of a vector are observed:

$\mathbf{x}$ is said to be *nonnegative*, written $\mathbf{x} \geq 0$, if $x_i \geq 0$ for all i
$\mathbf{x}$ is said to be *positive*, written $\mathbf{x} > 0$ if $x_i >$ for all i
$\mathbf{x}$ is said to be *semipositive*, written $\mathbf{x} \geq 0$, if $\mathbf{x} \geq 0$ but $\mathbf{x} \neq 0$[1]

MR3 QUADRATIC FORMS

A (homogeneous) *quadratic form* in n variables $x_1, \ldots, x_n$ is a polynomial

$$\sum_{i=1}^{n} \sum_{j=1}^{n} a_{ij} x_i x_j \tag{1}$$

[1] On matrices and determinants, see Allen (1963), chaps. 11–14; Yamane (1968), chaps. 10–12.

where each term is of the second degree. It can be written in matrix notation

$$\mathbf{x}'\mathbf{A}\mathbf{x} \qquad (2)$$

where $\mathbf{x}$ = column vector $(x_1, \ldots, x_n)$ and $\mathbf{A}$ is a symmetric matrix.

The quadratic form $Q = \mathbf{x}'\mathbf{A}\mathbf{x}$ in n variables is *negative definite* when it takes a negative value for any values of the variables (not all zero). This is true if and only if its principal minors are alternatively negative and positive as follows:

$$a_{11} < 0; \qquad \begin{vmatrix} a_{11} & a_{12} \\ a_{21} & a_{22} \end{vmatrix} > 0; \qquad \begin{vmatrix} a_{11} & a_{12} & a_{13} \\ a_{21} & a_{22} & a_{23} \\ a_{31} & a_{32} & a_{33} \end{vmatrix} < 0; \ldots \qquad (3)$$

The quadratic form is *positive definite* when it takes a positive value for any values of the variables (not all zero). This is true if and only if all its principal minors are all positive as follows:

$$a_{11} > 0; \qquad \begin{vmatrix} a_{11} & a_{12} \\ a_{21} & a_{22} \end{vmatrix} > 0; \qquad \begin{vmatrix} a_{11} & a_{12} & a_{13} \\ a_{21} & a_{22} & a_{23} \\ a_{31} & a_{32} & a_{33} \end{vmatrix} > 0; \ldots \qquad (4)$$

QUADRATIC FORMS SUBJECT TO A CONSTRAINT

The quadratic form $Q = \mathbf{x}'\mathbf{A}\mathbf{x}$ in n variables is *negative definite* subject to the linear side relation,

$$\mathbf{b}'\mathbf{x} = 0 \qquad (5)$$

where $\mathbf{b}$ is a vector of coefficients, column vector $(b_1, b_2, \ldots, b_n)$, if the principal minors of the matrix $\mathbf{A}$ bordered with b_i are successively positive and negative as follows:

$$\begin{vmatrix} a_{11} & a_{12} & b_1 \\ a_{12} & a_{22} & b_2 \\ b_1 & b_2 & 0 \end{vmatrix} > 0; \qquad \begin{vmatrix} a_{11} & a_{12} & a_{13} & b_1 \\ a_{12} & a_{22} & a_{23} & b_2 \\ a_{13} & a_{23} & a_{33} & b_3 \\ b_1 & b_2 & b_3 & 0 \end{vmatrix} < 0;$$

$$\begin{vmatrix} a_{11} & a_{12} & a_{13} & a_{14} & b_1 \\ a_{12} & a_{22} & a_{23} & a_{24} & b_2 \\ a_{13} & a_{23} & a_{33} & a_{34} & b_3 \\ a_{14} & a_{24} & a_{34} & a_{44} & b_4 \\ b_1 & b_2 & b_3 & b_4 & 0 \end{vmatrix} > 0; \ldots \qquad (6)$$

The form is *positive definite* subject to the constraint if the above determinants are all negative.

A THEOREM CONCERNING QUADRATIC FORMS

Let $Q = x'Ax$ be *negative definite* subject to a side condition

$$b'x = 0 \qquad (7)$$

where A and b are the constant matrix and vector, respectively.
Let

$$B = \begin{bmatrix} A & b \\ b' & 0 \end{bmatrix} \qquad (8)$$

Then the quadratic form $z'B^{-1}z$

$$\sum_i \sum_j \frac{|B_{ij}|}{|B|} z_i z_j \qquad (9)$$

where $|B_{ij}|$ are the cofactors of the elements of B, is negative definite.

Proof

Consider the expression

$$R = x'Ax + 2\alpha b'x \qquad (10)$$

where α is a scalar constant, and hence R is a scalar. Since Q is negative definite, R is negative also. R can be written

$$R = y'By \qquad (11)$$

where

$$y = \begin{pmatrix} x \\ \alpha \end{pmatrix}, \qquad B = \begin{bmatrix} A & b \\ b' & 0 \end{bmatrix} \qquad (12)$$

Consider a new vector

$$z = By \qquad (13)$$

z is an $(n + 1)$ vector, and its last element which we denote by z_0 is

$$z_0 = (b' \quad 0)\begin{pmatrix} x \\ \alpha \end{pmatrix} = b'x \qquad (14)$$

By (7), $z_0 = 0$.
From (13)

$$y = B^{-1}z \qquad (15)$$

Therefore

$$R = z'(B^{-1})'B\,B^{-1}z = z'B^{-1}z < 0 \qquad (16)$$

Hence

$$R = \sum_i \sum_j \frac{|\mathbf{B}_{ij}|}{|\mathbf{B}|} z_i z_j < 0 \tag{17}$$

MR4   DIFFERENTIAL CALCULUS

A scalar-valued *function f* of a single variable x assigns a single number $f(x)$ to each value of x in the domain of definition. The function $f(x)$ is said to be *continuous* at a if

$$\lim_{x \to a} f(x) = f(a) \tag{1}$$

If

$$\lim_{\substack{\Delta x \to 0 \\ \Delta x < 0}} \frac{f(a + \Delta x) - f(a)}{\Delta x} \tag{2}$$

exists, it is called the *left-hand derivative* of the function at a. If in (2), $\Delta x > 0$ in the limiting process, the limit is called the *right-hand derivative*. When the two limits have the same value, the function is said to be *differentiable* at a,

Figure MR 4.1

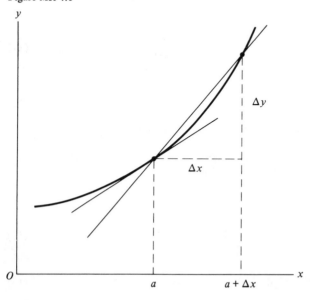

and the common limit is called simply the *derivative* at *a*. The derivative of $f(x)$ is denoted in a number of alternative ways, such as

$$\frac{df(x)}{dx} = f'(x) = \frac{dy}{dx} = y' \tag{3}$$

The derivative is the limit of the average rate of change of the function as the change in the independent variable approaches zero. Figure MR4.1 shows graphically that the derivative is the slope of the tangent to the graph of $f(x)$.

DIFFERENTIATION FORMULAS

Important formulas for differentiation are:

1. *Constant-Function Rule*

$$\frac{dc}{dx} = 0 \qquad \text{where } c \text{ is a constant}$$

2. *Constant-Multiple Rule*

$$\frac{d}{dx} cy = c\frac{dy}{dx} \qquad \text{where } c \text{ is a constant}$$

3. *Sum Rule*

$$\frac{d}{dx}(u + v) = \frac{du}{dx} + \frac{dv}{dx}$$

4. *Product Rule*

$$\frac{d}{dx}(uv) = v\frac{du}{dx} + u\frac{dv}{dx}$$

5. *Quotient Rule*

$$\frac{d}{dx}\left(\frac{u}{v}\right) = \frac{v\dfrac{du}{dx} - u\dfrac{dv}{dx}}{v^2}$$

6. *Function-of-Function Rule, Chain Rule:* If $z = f(y)$ and $y = g(x)$, then

$$\frac{dz}{dx} = \frac{dz}{dy}\frac{dy}{dx}$$

7. *Inverse-Function Rule:* If $y = f(x)$, then

$$\frac{dx}{dy} = \frac{1}{\dfrac{dy}{dx}} \qquad \text{where } f \text{ is one-to-one}$$

8. *Power-Function Rule*

$$\frac{dx^n}{dx} = nx^{n-1}$$

9. *Exponential-Function Rule*

$$\frac{d}{dx} e^x = e^x$$

10. *Logarithmic-Function Rule*

$$\frac{d}{dx} \ln x = \frac{1}{x}$$

SIGN OF THE DERIVATIVE

The sign of the derivative dy/dx indicates the direction of change of the dependent variable y relative to the independent variable x. If the sign is positive, then an increase in x results in an increase in y; if the sign is negative, an increase in x is accompanied by a decrease in y. If the derivative is neither positive nor negative, that is, the derivative is zero, then a change in x results in no change in y.

SECOND DERIVATIVES

The derivative in (1) is sometimes called a *first derivative*; the derivative of the first derivative is called a *second derivative* and is written

$$\frac{d^2}{dx^2} f(x) = f''(x) = \frac{d^2 y}{dx^2} = y''$$

MAXIMA AND MINIMA

A function $f(x)$ is said to be at a *local (proper) maximum* at a if $f(x) < f(a)$ for all values of x in the neighborhood of a, as at A and C in Figure MR4.2. It is said to be at a *local (proper) minimum* if at a, $f(x) > f(a)$ for all values of x in the neighborhood of a, as at B and D in Figure MR4.2.

The *sufficient* condition for $f(x)$ to attain local maximum (or minimum) at a is that the first derivative is zero and the second derivative negative (or positive). This can be seen intuitively from Figure MR4.2.

The necessary and sufficient condition for $f(x)$ to attain an extremum at $x = a$ is that (a) $f'(x) = 0$, (b) the first nonzero higher-order derivative is even-ordered (if the first nonzero higher-order derivative is $f^{(n)}$, n must be an even integer), (c) $f(x)$ attains a *maximum* if $f^{(n)}(x) < 0$, and a *minimum* if $f^{(n)}(x) > 0$.[2]

---

[2] On differential calculus, see Allen (1938) and Yamane (1968).

Figure MR 4.2

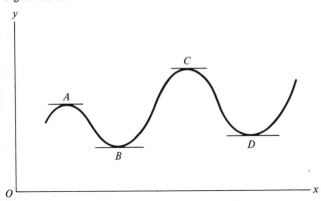

MR5   FUNCTIONS OF SEVERAL VARIABLES

PARTIAL DERIVATIVES

The *partial derivative* of a function of two variables $y = f(x_1, x_2)$ with respect to x_1 is denoted by

$$\frac{\partial y}{\partial x_1} \equiv f_{x_1} \equiv f_1 \tag{1}$$

It is defined as

$$\lim_{\Delta x_1 \to 0} \frac{f(x_1 + \Delta x_1, x_2) - f(x_1, x_2)}{\Delta x_1} \tag{2}$$

Similarly, the partial derivative of y with respect to x_2 is written

$$\frac{\partial y}{\partial x_2} \equiv f_{x_2} \equiv f_2 \tag{3}$$

and represents

$$\lim_{\Delta x_2 \to 0} \frac{f(x_1, x_2 + \Delta x_2) - f(x_1, x_2)}{\Delta x_2} \tag{4}$$

The technique of partial differentiation is similar to that of ordinary differentiation. In order to obtain the partial derivative of $f(x_1, x_2)$ with respect to x_1, one differentiates the function with respect to x_1, regarding x_2 as a constant. To obtain the partial derivative of $f(x_1, x_2)$ with respect to x_2, one differentiates the function with respect to x_2, regarding x_1 as a constant.

The definition and technique of partial differentiation given above for a function of two variables can be easily extended to a function of more than two variables.

The *second-order partial derivatives* are defined in this book as follows:

$$\frac{\partial^2 y}{\partial x_1^2} = \frac{\partial}{\partial x_1}\left(\frac{\partial y}{\partial x_1}\right) = f_{11} \tag{5}$$

$$\frac{\partial^2 y}{\partial x_2^2} = \frac{\partial}{\partial x_2}\left(\frac{\partial y}{\partial x_2}\right) = f_{22} \tag{6}$$

$$\frac{\partial^2 y}{\partial x_1\,\partial x_2} = \frac{\partial}{\partial x_2}\left(\frac{\partial y}{\partial x_1}\right) = f_{12}$$

$$\frac{\partial^2 y}{\partial x_2\,\partial x_1} = \frac{\partial}{\partial x_1}\left(\frac{\partial y}{\partial x_2}\right) = f_{21} \tag{7}$$

A continuous function $f(x_1, x_2)$ is said to be of *class C'* if the first-order partial derivatives are defined and continuous. It is said to be of *class C''* if it is of class C' and the second-order partial derivatives $f_{11}, f_{12}, f_{21}, f_{22}$ are defined and continuous. The partial derivatives f_{12} and f_{21} are equal when f is of class C''.

DIFFERENTIALS

Let y be a function of a single variable x

$$y = f(x) \tag{8}$$

The *differential* of y, denoted by dy, is defined by

$$dy = f'(x)\,dx \tag{9}$$

where dx is an arbitrarily chosen increment in x. Let y be a function of two variables x_1 and x_2, namely $y = f(x_1, x_2)$. In this case, the *total differential* (or *exact differential*, or *complete differential*) of y, written dy, is defined by

$$dy = f_1\,dx_1 + f_2\,dx_2 \tag{10}$$

where dx_1 and dx_2 are arbitrarily chosen increments in x_1 and x_2, respectively. The total differential is defined similarly for functions of three or more variables.

IMPLICIT-FUNCTION RULE

Given an implicit function of several variables, the partial derivative of one variable with respect to another may be obtained by the implicit-function rule, which follows the following steps. Let the implicit function be

$$f(x, y, z) = 0 \tag{11}$$

Take the total differential of both sides and equate them:

$$f_x\, dx + f_y\, dy + f_z\, dz = 0 \tag{12}$$

To obtain the partial derivative of z with respect to x, set $dy = 0$ in (12) and rewrite the above expression

$$dz = -\frac{f_x}{f_z}\, dx \tag{13}$$

and then divide this expression through by dx:

$$\frac{\partial z}{\partial x} = -\frac{f_x}{f_z} \tag{14}$$

To obtain the partial derivative $\partial z/\partial y$, set $dx = 0$ in (12) and follow the similar procedure to obtain

$$\frac{\partial z}{\partial y} = -\frac{f_y}{f_z} \tag{15}$$

HIGHER-ORDER DIFFERENTIALS

Higher-order differentials can be written as quadratic forms. Let

$$y = f(x_1, x_2, x_3) \tag{16}$$

Then

$$dy = \frac{\partial f}{\partial x_1}\, dx_1 + \frac{\partial f}{\partial x_2}\, dx_2 + \frac{\partial f}{\partial x_3}\, dx_3 \tag{17}$$

where dx_i are constants. Since dy is a function of x_i,

$$d^2 y = \frac{\partial(dy)}{\partial x_1}\, dx_1 + \frac{\partial(dy)}{\partial x_2}\, dx_2 + \frac{\partial(dy)}{\partial x_3}\, dx_3$$

$$= \left(\frac{\partial^2 f}{\partial x_1^2}\, dx_1 + \frac{\partial^2 f}{\partial x_1\, \partial x_2}\, dx_2 + \frac{\partial^2 f}{\partial x_1 x_3}\, dx_3 \right) dx_1$$

$$+ \left(\frac{\partial^2 f}{\partial x_1\, \partial x_2}\, dx_1 + \frac{\partial^2 f}{\partial x_2^2}\, dx_2 + \frac{\partial^2 f}{\partial x_2\, \partial x_3}\, dx_3 \right) dx_2$$

$$+ \left(\frac{\partial^2 f}{\partial x_3\, \partial x_1}\, dx_1 + \frac{\partial^2 f}{\partial x_3\, \partial x_2}\, dx_2 + \frac{\partial^2 f}{\partial x_3^2}\, dx_3 \right) dx_3$$

$$= (dx_1 \quad dx_2 \quad dx_3) \begin{pmatrix} f_{11} & f_{12} & f_{13} \\ f_{21} & f_{22} & f_{23} \\ f_{31} & f_{32} & f_{33} \end{pmatrix} \begin{pmatrix} dx_1 \\ dx_2 \\ dx_3 \end{pmatrix} \tag{18}$$

where the matrix of f_{ij} is symmetric.

MAXIMA AND MINIMA FOR FUNCTIONS OF SEVERAL VARIABLES

Consider the function of three variables

$$y = f(x_1, x_2, x_3) \tag{19}$$

For *maximum*, the first-order condition is that $dy = 0$; while the second-order condition is that d^2y be *negative definite*, that is, the matrix, called the *Hessian matrix* of f,

$$\begin{bmatrix} f_{11} & f_{12} & f_{13} \\ f_{21} & f_{22} & f_{23} \\ f_{31} & f_{32} & f_{33} \end{bmatrix} \tag{20}$$

is negative definite. This is true if and only if the principal minors of (20) are alternatively negative and positive, that is,

$$f_{11} < 0; \quad \begin{vmatrix} f_{11} & f_{12} \\ f_{21} & f_{22} \end{vmatrix} > 0; \quad \begin{vmatrix} f_{11} & f_{12} & f_{13} \\ f_{21} & f_{22} & f_{23} \\ f_{31} & f_{32} & f_{33} \end{vmatrix} < 0 \tag{21}$$

For minimum, the first-order condition is the same; while the second-order condition is that d^2y be *positive definite*, that is, the matrix (20) is positive definite. This is true if and only if the principal minors of (20) are all positive, that is,

$$f_{11} > 0; \quad \begin{vmatrix} f_{11} & f_{12} \\ f_{21} & f_{22} \end{vmatrix} > 0; \quad \begin{vmatrix} f_{11} & f_{12} & f_{13} \\ f_{21} & f_{22} & f_{23} \\ f_{31} & f_{32} & f_{33} \end{vmatrix} > 0 \tag{22}$$

LAGRANGE MULTIPLIERS

A maximization problem subject to a constraint can be solved by the use of Lagrange multipliers. Suppose we wish to choose the values of x_1, x_2, and x_3 so as to *maximize* the function

$$y = f(x_1, x_2, x_3) \tag{23}$$

subject to a constraint, say

$$g(x_1, x_2, x_3) = 0 \tag{24}$$

The Lagrangean expression is

$$L = f(x_1, x_2, x_3) + \lambda g(x_1, x_2, x_3) \tag{25}$$

This expression is a function of x_1, x_2, x_3, and λ, which is a nonzero undetermined variable called the *Lagrange multiplier*.

The first-order condition is

$$\frac{\partial L}{\partial x_1} = f_1 + \lambda g_1 = 0 \tag{26}$$

$$\frac{\partial L}{\partial x_2} = f_2 + \lambda g_2 = 0 \tag{27}$$

$$\frac{\partial L}{\partial x_3} = f_3 + \lambda g_3 = 0 \tag{28}$$

$$\frac{\partial L}{\partial \lambda} = g(x_1, x_2, x_3) = 0 \tag{29}$$

The second-order condition is that $d^2 L$ be *negative definite* subject to the constraint

$$g_1 \, dx_1 + g_2 \, dx_2 + g_3 \, dx_3 = 0 \tag{30}$$

This is true from the theorem given in MR3 if and only if

$$\begin{vmatrix} L_{11} & L_{12} & g_1 \\ L_{12} & L_{22} & g_2 \\ g_1 & g_2 & 0 \end{vmatrix} > 0; \qquad \begin{vmatrix} L_{11} & L_{12} & L_{13} & g_1 \\ L_{12} & L_{22} & L_{23} & g_2 \\ L_{13} & L_{32} & L_{33} & g_3 \\ g_1 & g_2 & g_3 & 0 \end{vmatrix} < 0 \tag{31}$$

In the case of a *minimum*, the first-order condition remains the same while the second-order condition is that $d^2 L$ be *positive definite* subject to

$$g_1 \, dx_1 + g_2 \, dx_2 + g_3 \, dx_3 = 0$$

This is true if and only if

$$\begin{vmatrix} L_{11} & L_{12} & g_1 \\ L_{21} & L_{22} & g_2 \\ g_1 & g_2 & 0 \end{vmatrix} < 0; \qquad \begin{vmatrix} L_{11} & L_{12} & L_{13} & g_1 \\ L_{21} & L_{22} & L_{23} & g_2 \\ L_{31} & L_{32} & L_{33} & g_3 \\ g_1 & g_2 & g_3 & 0 \end{vmatrix} < 0 \tag{32}$$

GENERAL CONSTRAINTS

Suppose there are more than one constraint, for example, maximize

$$y = f(x_1, x_2, x_3) \tag{33}$$

subject to

$$g^1(x_1, x_2, x_3) = 0 \tag{34}$$

and

$$g^2(x_1, x_2, x_3) = 0 \tag{35}$$

Note that the number of constraints does not exceed that of variables. Then the Lagrangean expression uses two Lagrange multipliers as follows:

$$L = f + \lambda_1 g^1 + \lambda_2 g^2 \tag{36}$$

The first-order condition is

$$\frac{\partial L}{\partial x_1} = f_1 + \lambda_1 g_1^1 + \lambda_2 g_1^2 = 0 \tag{37}$$

$$\frac{\partial L}{\partial x_2} = f_2 + \lambda_1 g_2^1 + \lambda_2 g_2^2 = 0 \tag{38}$$

$$\frac{\partial L}{\partial \lambda_1} = g^1 \qquad\qquad = 0 \tag{39}$$

$$\frac{\partial L}{\partial \lambda_2} = g^2 \qquad\qquad = 0 \tag{40}$$

INTERPRETATION OF THE LAGRANGE MULTIPLIER

Consider a three-variable case with a single constraint. Maximize

$$y = f(\mathbf{x}) \tag{41}$$

subject to

$$g(\mathbf{x}) = b \tag{42}$$

Then the Lagrangian function is

$$L(\mathbf{x}, \lambda) = f(\mathbf{x}) + \lambda[b - g(\mathbf{x})]$$

The optimum values of the variables and the Lagrange multiplier, $\mathbf{x}^*$ and λ^*, respectively, are obtained by solving

$$\begin{aligned} f_1(\mathbf{x}) - \lambda g_1(\mathbf{x}) &= 0 \\ f_2(\mathbf{x}) - \lambda g_2(\mathbf{x}) &= 0 \\ f_3(\mathbf{x}) - \lambda g_3(\mathbf{x}) &= 0 \\ b - g(\mathbf{x}) &= 0 \end{aligned} \tag{43}$$

(They can be solved for $\mathbf{x}^*$ and λ^* if the Jacobian determinant is nonzero.) Hence they are functions of b, and can be written

$$\begin{aligned} x_1^* &= h^1(b) \\ x_2^* &= h^2(b) \\ x_3^* &= h^3(b) \\ \lambda^* &= h^4(b) \end{aligned} \tag{44}$$

The corresponding value of the Lagrangean function is also a function of b, and is

$$L(\mathbf{x}^*, \lambda^*) = f(\mathbf{x}^*) + \lambda^*[b - g(\mathbf{x}^*)] \tag{45}$$

Differentiating with respect to b, and evaluating the partial derivatives at $\mathbf{x}^*$,

$$\frac{\partial L}{\partial b} = \sum_{j=1}^{3} \frac{\partial f}{\partial x_j} \frac{\partial h^j}{\partial b} + \frac{\partial h^4}{\partial b}[b - g(\mathbf{x}^*)] + h^4 \cdot \left(1 - \sum_{j=1}^{3} \frac{\partial g}{\partial x_j} \frac{\partial h^j}{\partial b}\right)$$

$$= \sum_{j=1}^{3} \left(\frac{\partial f}{\partial x_j} - h^4 \frac{\partial g}{\partial x_j}\right) \frac{\partial h^j}{\partial b} + \frac{\partial h^4}{\partial b}[b - g(\mathbf{x}^*)] + h^4$$

Because of (43), the first two terms of the right-hand side vanish. Therefore

$$\frac{\partial L}{\partial b} = h^4 = \lambda^* \tag{46}$$

Also, at x^* and λ^*,

$$L(b) = f(b) \tag{47}$$

Hence

$$\frac{\partial f}{\partial b} = \lambda^* \tag{48}$$

QUASI-CONCAVE FUNCTION

The set of points in the n-dimensional euclidean space R^n is said to be *convex* if, for $\mathbf{x}'$ and $\mathbf{x}''$ in S, the convex combination $\mathbf{x}'''$ defined by

$$\mathbf{x}''' = (1 - a)\mathbf{x}' + a\mathbf{x}'' \qquad 0 < a < 1 \tag{49}$$

also belongs to S.

A function $f(\mathbf{x})$ is said to be *quasi-concave* if, for $\mathbf{x}'$, $\mathbf{x}''$, and $\mathbf{x}'''$ defined above

$$f(\mathbf{x}''') \geqq \min[f(\mathbf{x}'), f(\mathbf{x}'')] \tag{50}$$

The function is said to be *strictly quasi-concave* if (50) holds with the strict inequality.

The *level set* of a function $f(\mathbf{x})$ for the level b, denoted by L_b, is the subset of the domain consisting of $\mathbf{x}$ such that

$$f(\mathbf{x}) \geqq b \tag{51}$$

The level set of the function is convex if and only if the function is quasi-concave. The proof can be given as follows.

Proof

1. Necessity: Let $\mathbf{x}'$ and $\mathbf{x}''$ be arbitrary points of the domain, and let

$$b = \min[f(\mathbf{x}'), f(\mathbf{x}'')] \tag{52}$$

Then $\mathbf{x}'$ and $\mathbf{x}''$ belong to L_b. Since L_b is convex, the convex combination

$$\mathbf{x}''' = (1 - a)\mathbf{x}' + a\mathbf{x}'' \qquad 0 < a < 1 \tag{53}$$

also belongs to L_b. Therefore

$$f(\mathbf{x}''') \geqq b \tag{54}$$

From (52) and (54), f is quasi-concave.

2. Sufficiency: Let L_b be the level set of $f(\mathbf{x})$ for the level b. If $\mathbf{x}'$ and $\mathbf{x}''$ belong to L_b, then

$$f(\mathbf{x}') \geqq b \qquad f(\mathbf{x}'') \geqq b$$

Since $f(\mathbf{x})$ is quasi-concave,

$$f(\mathbf{x}''') \geqq b \tag{55}$$

But this means

$$\mathbf{x}''' \in L_b \tag{56}$$

Therefore the level set is convex.

The necessary and sufficient condition can be stated as follows: If the differentiable function $f(x)$ of the n-dimensional vector $\mathbf{x}$ is quasi-concave, then

$$(-1)^k \begin{vmatrix} f_{11} & f_{12} & \cdots & f_{1k} & f_1 \\ f_{21} & f_{22} & \cdots & f_{2k} & f_2 \\ \vdots & \vdots & \vdots & \vdots & \vdots \\ f_{k1} & f_{k2} & \cdots & f_{kk} & f_k \\ f_1 & f_2 & \cdots & f_k & 0 \end{vmatrix} \geqq 0 \qquad k = 2, \ldots, n \tag{57}$$

On the other hand, if, for $\mathbf{x} \geqq 0$, the signs of the above determinants excluding the coefficient $(-1)^k$ are the same as $(-1)^k$ for all k, the function is quasi-concave.

For strictly quasi-concave functions, (57) holds with the strict inequality. It can be seen that the second-order conditions for constrained maximum (31) is satisfied if the function is strictly quasi-concave.[3]

---

[3] On quasi-concave functions, see Arrow and Enthoven (1961).

CONCAVE FUNCTIONS

A function $f(\mathbf{x})$ is said to be *concave* if and only if

$$f((1 - a)\mathbf{x}' + a\mathbf{x}'') \geq (1 - a)f(\mathbf{x}') + af(\mathbf{x}'') \tag{58}$$

for any $\mathbf{x}'$ and $\mathbf{x}''$ in the convex domain, and $0 < a < 1$. Along the straight-line segment between $\mathbf{x}'$ and $\mathbf{x}''$ a concave function cannot assume a value smaller than that of the linear function obtained by linear interpolation. In this case, the slope of the function with respect to one independent variable is never increasing as the independent variable increases, as shown in Figure MR5.1. The function is said to be *strictly concave* if and only if (58) holds for $\mathbf{x}' \neq \mathbf{x}''$ with the strict inequality. Along the straight-line segment connecting $\mathbf{x}'$ and $\mathbf{x}''$ a strictly concave function assumes a value larger than that of the linear function obtained by linear interpolation. In this case, the slope of the function is decreasing. In Figure MR5.1 the function is strictly concave if the linear segment is excluded. Thus a linear function is concave, but not strictly concave. For a concave function a local maximum is a global maximum. If a concave function has a point where the derivative is zero, then the function achieves maximum at that point, as can be seen from Figure MR5.1.

The differentiable function $f(\mathbf{x})$ is strictly concave if and only if for all $\mathbf{x}'$ and $\mathbf{x}''$ in the convex domain

$$f(\mathbf{x}'') - f(\mathbf{x}') < \sum_i f_i \cdot (x_i'' - x_i') \tag{59}$$

where the partial derivatives are evaluated at $\mathbf{x}'$.

Figure MR 5.1

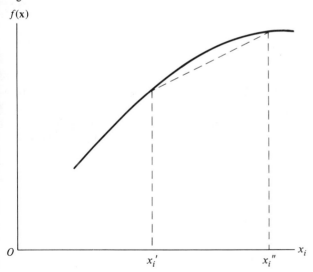

The necessity part can be proved as follows:

$$(1 - a)\mathbf{x}' + a\mathbf{x}'' = \mathbf{x}' + a(\mathbf{x}'' - \mathbf{x}') \tag{60}$$

and

$$(1 - a)f(\mathbf{x}') + af(\mathbf{x}'') = f(\mathbf{x}') + a \cdot [f(\mathbf{x}'') - f(\mathbf{x}')] \tag{61}$$

If f is strictly concave

$$f(\mathbf{x}' + a(\mathbf{x}'' - \mathbf{x}')) > f(\mathbf{x}') + a[f(\mathbf{x}'') - f(\mathbf{x}')] \tag{62}$$

Using Taylor's theorem, the left-hand side can be expanded as

$$f(\mathbf{x}') + a \sum_i f_i \cdot (x_i'' - x_i') \tag{63}$$

where the partial derivatives f_i are evaluated at a point between $\mathbf{x}''$ and $\mathbf{x}'$,

$$\mathbf{x}' + ba(\mathbf{x}'' - \mathbf{x}') \qquad 0 \leq b \leq 1$$

Substituting (63) for the left-hand side of (62) yields

$$\sum_i f_i \cdot (x_i'' - x_i') > f(\mathbf{x}'') - f(\mathbf{x}') \tag{64}$$

A twice-differentiable function $f(\mathbf{x})$ is strictly concave if and only if its Hessian is negative definite.

The necessity part of the theorem can be proved as follows: By Taylor's theorem $f(\mathbf{x})$ can be expanded around $\mathbf{x}$

$$f(\mathbf{x} + \mathbf{v}) = f(\mathbf{x}) + \sum_i f_i v_i + \frac{1}{2} \mathbf{v}' \mathbf{H} \mathbf{v} \tag{65}$$

where the partial derivatives are evaluated at $\mathbf{x}$ and the Hessian $\mathbf{H}$ of f evaluated at a point between $\mathbf{x}$ and $\mathbf{x} + \mathbf{v}$. Then

$$f(\mathbf{x} + \mathbf{v}) - f(\mathbf{x}) - \sum_i f_i v_i = \frac{1}{2} \mathbf{v}' \mathbf{H} \mathbf{v} \tag{66}$$

In view of (59) the left-hand side is negative. Hence $\mathbf{H}$ is negative definite.

It can be seen that the strictly concave function satisfies the second-order condition for unconstrained maximum.

MR6   ADDITIONAL TOPICS

HOMOGENEOUS FUNCTIONS

A function $f(x, y)$ is said to be homogeneous of the kth degree if

$$f(\lambda x, \lambda y) = \lambda^k f(x, y) \tag{1}$$

where k is a constant and λ any positive real number. Equation (1) states that, if both variables increase by the factor λ, the function increases by the factor λ^k. Hence a function $f(x, y)$ is said to be homogeneous of *degree one* if

$$f(\lambda x, \lambda y) = \lambda f(x, y) \tag{2}$$

and of *degree zero* if

$$f(\lambda x, \lambda y) = f(x, y) \tag{3}$$

EULER'S THEOREM

If $z = f(x, y)$ is homogeneous of degree k, then

$$x\frac{\partial z}{\partial x} + y\frac{\partial z}{\partial y} = kz$$

Proof

By assumption

$$f(\lambda x, \lambda y) = \lambda^k z \text{ for any positive } \lambda$$

Let $\lambda = 1/x$. Then

$$f\left(1, \frac{y}{x}\right) = x^{-k}z$$

Let us put

$$f\left(1, \frac{y}{x}\right) \equiv g\left(\frac{y}{x}\right)$$

Then

$$z = x^k g\left(\frac{y}{x}\right)$$

The partial derivatives are

$$\frac{\partial z}{\partial x} = kx^{k-1}g\left(\frac{y}{x}\right) + x^k g'\left(\frac{y}{x}\right)\frac{-y}{x^2}$$

$$= kx^{k-1}g\left(\frac{y}{x}\right) - x^{k-2}yg'\left(\frac{y}{x}\right)$$

$$\frac{\partial z}{\partial y} = x^k g'\left(\frac{y}{x}\right)\frac{1}{x}$$

$$= x^{k-1}g'\left(\frac{y}{x}\right)$$

Therefore

$$x \frac{\partial z}{\partial x} + y \frac{\partial z}{\partial y} = kx^k g - x^{k-1} yg' + x^{k-1} g'y$$

$$= kx^k g = kz$$

IMPLICIT-FUNCTION THEOREM

When is a relation defined by $f(x, y) = 0$ (where x and y are scalar variables) also a function $y = f(x)$? When can f be solved explicitly for y in terms of x, yielding a unique solution? The answer is provided by the implicit-function theorem. Given $\bar{x}$ and $\bar{y}$ such that $f(\bar{x}, \bar{y}) = 0$, if f and $\partial f/\partial y$ are continuous in some neighborhood of $(\bar{x}, \bar{y})$, and $\partial f/\partial y$ is not zero, then $f(x, y) = 0$ is also a function.

More generally, a consider a system of n equations in $(m + n)$ variables

$$f^i(x_1, x_2, \ldots, x_m; y_1, y_2, \ldots, y_n) = 0 \qquad i = 1, \ldots, n \qquad (4)$$

This system can be solved for $y_1, y_2, \ldots, y_n$ in terms of $x_1, x_2, \ldots, x_m$ if f^i are continuous and the determinant, made up of $\partial f^i/\partial y_j$:

$$\begin{vmatrix} f_1^1 & f_2^1 & \cdots & f_n^1 \\ \vdots & & & \vdots \\ f_1^n & f_2^n & \cdots & f_n^n \end{vmatrix} \qquad (5)$$

and called *Jacobian*, is not zero, in the neighborhood of $\bar{x}_1, \ldots, \bar{x}_m, \bar{y}_1 \bar{y}_2, \ldots, \bar{y}_n$ which satisfy (4).

MR7   MAXIMUM IN THE INTERIOR AND ON THE BOUNDARY

Theorem MR7.1

Let $f(\mathbf{x})$ be a scalar function of a vector[4] $\mathbf{x}$ of 3 variables

$$\mathbf{x} = (x_1, x_2, x_3)$$

For $f(\mathbf{x})$ to be local maximum (minimum) at an interior point

$$\mathbf{x}^0 = (x_1^0, x_2^0, x_3^0)$$

it is necessary that

$$\frac{\partial f}{\partial x_i} = 0 \qquad i = 1, 2, 3 \qquad (1)$$

[4] All vectors are column vectors unless specified otherwise.

Theorem MR7.2

For the function $f(\mathbf{x})$ to be local maximum (minimum) at an interior point $\mathbf{x}^0$ subject to the equality constraints

$$g^j = 0 \qquad j = 1, 2 \tag{2}$$

it is necessary that

$$\frac{\partial L}{\partial x_i} = 0 \qquad i = 1, 2, 3 \tag{3}$$

where L is the Lagrangean function defined by

$$L = f(\mathbf{x}) + \lambda_1 g^1 + \lambda_2 g^2 \tag{4}$$

and λ_j are undetermined constants called the *Lagrange multipliers*.

In these theorems we assumed that functions involved were differentiable, and maxima and minima occurred in the interior of the domain. As in Figure MR7.1, consider the domain of the function to be the *nonnegative* orthant

$$\mathbf{x} \geq 0 \tag{5}$$

Economic variables are often subject to this constraint.

Figure MR 7.1

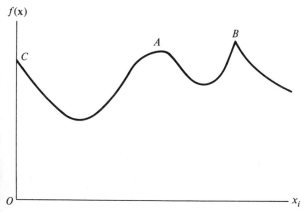

$f(\mathbf{x})$

Case A: The point A is in the interior of the domain and at that point the function is *differentiable*. In this case, the necessary condition for maximum (minimum) is

$$\frac{\partial f}{\partial x_i} = 0 \qquad i = 1, 2, 3 \tag{6}$$

Case B: The point B is also in the interior of the domain but at that point the function is not differentiable, since the right-hand derivative $\partial f^+ / \partial x_i$ and the left-hand derivative $\partial f^- / \partial x_i$ are different. In this case, the necessary condition for maximum is generally

$$\frac{\partial f^+}{\partial x_i} \leq 0 \qquad \frac{\partial f^-}{\partial x_i} \geq 0 \tag{7}$$

Case C: The point C is on the boundary of the domain, and the left-hand derivative does not exist. The necessary condition for maximum is

$$\frac{\partial f^+}{\partial x_i} \leq 0 \tag{8}$$

Cases A and C Combined: If f is differentiable (therefore B is excluded, and only points A and C are possible), then the necessary condition for maximum is

$$\frac{\partial f}{\partial x_i} = 0 \qquad \text{for } x_i > 0 \tag{9}$$

and

$$\frac{\partial f}{\partial x_i} \leq 0 \qquad \text{for } x_i = 0 \tag{10}$$

These conditions can be combined into

$$\frac{\partial f}{\partial x_i} \leq 0 \qquad x_i \frac{\partial f}{\partial x_i} = 0 \tag{11}$$

This result modifies the results of MR4 so that it can be applied to both interior and boundary maxima, which occur in economic problems that involve non-negative variables.

MR8 MAXIMIZATION UNDER INEQUALITY CONSTRAINTS

If we replace the equality constraints (MR7.2) by the more general constraints involving inequalities

$$g^j(\mathbf{x}) \geq 0 \qquad j = 1, 2 \tag{1}$$

then we will have two possibilities for each constraint:

(a) If $g^j(\mathbf{x}) = 0$, then the jth constraint is effective, that is, $\mathbf{x}$ is constrained by the jth constraint
(b) If $g^j(\mathbf{x}) > 0$, then the jth constraint is not effective, that is, $\mathbf{x}$ is not constrained by the jth constraint

In the second case, the λ_j in the Lagrangean function (MR7.4) can be considered zero. Therefore, we have either

$$g^j = 0 \qquad \text{and} \qquad \lambda_j \neq 0 \qquad\qquad (2)$$

or

$$g^j > 0 \qquad \text{and} \qquad \lambda_j = 0 \qquad\qquad (3)$$

As in (MR7.11), we can combine (2) and (3) into

$$g^j \geqq 0 \qquad \text{and} \qquad \lambda_j g^j = 0 \qquad\qquad (4)$$

MR9 NONLINEAR PROGRAMMING

The problem of finding the maximum (or minimum) of the nonlinear objective function subject to the inequality constraints involving nonlinear functions is called a *nonlinear programming* problem. The problem can be illustrated as in Figure MR9.1.

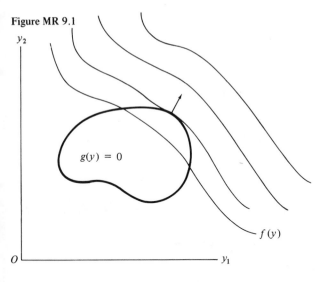

Figure MR 9.1

y_2

$g(y) = 0$

$f(y)$

O y_1

The *concave programming problem* can be stated as follows: Maximize a concave scalar function $f(\mathbf{y})$ of an m-dimensional vector variable $\mathbf{y}$, subject to n inequality constraints

$$g^j(\mathbf{y}) \geqq 0 \qquad j = 1, \ldots, n$$

where g^j is a concave function, and $\mathbf{y}$ belongs to the nonnegative orthant (a convex subset) of the m-dimensional euclidean space R^m, as shown in Figure MR9.2.

Figure MR 9.2

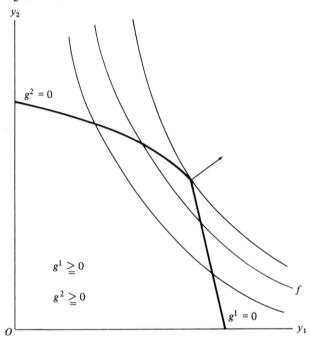

The main ideas relating to this topic may be stated in advance. The *Kuhn-Tucker theorem* of nonlinear programming states that *a particular vector* **y*** *maximizes* $f(\mathbf{y})$ *subject to the constraints*

$$g^j(\mathbf{y}) \geq 0 \qquad j = 1, \ldots, n$$

and

$$y_i \geq 0 \qquad i = 1, \ldots, m$$

if and only if there exists some m-dimensional vector **r*** *with nonnegative components*, such that

$$\pi(\mathbf{y}, \mathbf{r}^*) \leq \pi(\mathbf{y}^*, \mathbf{r}^*) \leq \pi(\mathbf{y}^*, \mathbf{r})$$

for all $\mathbf{r} \geq 0$ and $\mathbf{y} \geq 0$, where

$$\pi(\mathbf{y}, \mathbf{r}) = f(\mathbf{y}) + \sum r_j^* g^j(\mathbf{y})$$

Here, $\pi(\mathbf{y}, \mathbf{r})$ is called the *kernel* and $(\mathbf{y}^*, \mathbf{r}^*)$ the *saddle point*.

Example

Consider the producer who produces two commodities, y_1 and y_2. He is a monopolistic seller of the first commodity, with the demand function

$$p_1 = b_1 - b_2 y_1 \qquad b_1, b_2 > 0 \tag{1}$$

and a perfectly competitive seller of the second commodity. Because of the limitations on the production facilities, there are the following constraints:

$$a_{11}y_1 + a_{12}y_2 \leqq c_1 \tag{2}$$

$$a_{21}y_1 + a_{22}y_2 \leqq c_2 \tag{3}$$

$$a_{31}y_1 \qquad\quad \leqq c_3 \tag{4}$$

$$a_{42}y_2 \leqq c_4 \tag{5}$$

where a_{ij} are fixed coefficients, and c_i are constraints. Then the objective function of the firm can be written

$$\pi = (b_1 - b_2 y_1)y_1 + p_2 y_2 \tag{6}$$
$$= b_1 y_1 - b_2 y_1^2 + p_2 y_2$$

where p_2 is the given price of the second commodity. Then the producer's problem is a nonlinear programming problem of maximizing a nonlinear, concave function (6) subject to inequality constraints (2)–(5).

NONNEGATIVE SADDLE POINT

Consider a function $L(\mathbf{x}, \lambda)$ of two sets of variables

$$\mathbf{x} = (x_1, x_2, \ldots, x_m)$$
$$\lambda = (\lambda_1, \lambda_2, \ldots, \lambda_n)$$

The *saddle point* of the function in the intervals

$$\mathbf{x} \geqq 0 \qquad \lambda \geqq 0$$

is defined by the point $(\bar{\mathbf{x}}, \bar{\lambda})$ such that

$$L(\mathbf{x}, \bar{\lambda}) \leqq L(\bar{\mathbf{x}}, \bar{\lambda}) \leqq L(\bar{\mathbf{x}}, \lambda) \tag{7}$$

Alternatively the saddle point of the function $L(\mathbf{x}, \lambda)$ can be defined as the point $(\bar{\mathbf{x}}, \bar{\lambda})$ such that

$$L(\bar{\mathbf{x}}, \bar{\lambda}) = \min_{\lambda \geqq 0} \max_{\mathbf{x} \geqq 0} L(\mathbf{x}, \lambda) = \max_{\mathbf{x} \geqq 0} \min_{\lambda \geqq 0} L(\mathbf{x}, \lambda) \tag{8}$$

THE SADDLE-POINT PROBLEM

The saddle-point problem may be stated as follows: Find vectors $\bar{\mathbf{x}} \geqq 0$ and $\bar{\lambda} \geqq 0$ for the function $L(\mathbf{x}, \lambda)$ such that

$$L(\mathbf{x}, \bar{\lambda}) \leqq L(\bar{\mathbf{x}}, \bar{\lambda}) \leqq L(\bar{\mathbf{x}}, \lambda) \tag{9}$$

The following theorem gives the necessary condition for the saddle point.

Theorem MR9.1   Necessary Condition: For the pair of vectors $(\mathbf{x}, \lambda)$ to be a saddle point of a differentiable function $L(\mathbf{x}, \lambda)$ it is necessary that

$$x_i > 0 \quad \text{and} \quad \frac{\partial L}{\partial x_i} = 0$$

or

$$x_i = 0 \quad \text{and} \quad \frac{\partial L}{\partial x_i} \leq 0$$

that is,

$$\frac{\partial L}{\partial x_i} \leq 0 \quad \text{and} \quad \sum_i \frac{\partial L}{\partial x_i} x_i = 0 \tag{10}$$

and that

$$\lambda_j > 0 \quad \text{and} \quad \frac{\partial L}{\partial \lambda_j} = 0$$

or

$$\lambda_j = 0 \quad \text{and} \quad \frac{\partial L}{\partial \lambda_j} \geq 0$$

That is,

$$\frac{\partial L}{\partial \lambda_j} \geq 0 \quad \text{and} \quad \sum_j \lambda_j \frac{\partial L}{\partial \lambda_j} = 0 \tag{11}$$

The following theorem gives the sufficient condition for the saddle point.

Theorem MR9.2   Sufficient Condition: For a point $(\bar{\mathbf{x}}, \bar{\lambda})$ to be a saddle point of a differentiable function $L(\mathbf{x}, \lambda)$, it is sufficient that (10) and (11) hold and

$$L(\mathbf{x}, \bar{\lambda}) \leq L(\bar{\mathbf{x}}, \bar{\lambda}) + \sum \frac{\partial L}{\partial x_i} (x_i - \bar{x}_i) \tag{12}$$

$$L(\bar{\mathbf{x}}, \lambda) \geq L(\bar{\mathbf{x}}, \bar{\lambda}) + \sum \frac{\partial L}{\partial \lambda_j} (\lambda_j - \bar{\lambda}_j) \tag{13}$$

for all $\mathbf{x}$ and λ.

GENERAL MAXIMIZATION PROBLEM

The general maximization problem can be stated as follows: Find a vector $\mathbf{x}^*$ which maximizes

$$f(\mathbf{x}) \tag{14}$$

subject to

$$g^j(\mathbf{x}) \geq 0 \quad j = 1, 2, \ldots, n \tag{15}$$

$$x_i \geq 0 \quad i = 1, 2, 3, \ldots, m \tag{16}$$

In solving the problem one uses the Lagrangean function

$$L(\mathbf{x}, \lambda) = f(\mathbf{x}) + \lambda_1 g^1(\mathbf{x}) + \lambda_2 g^2(\mathbf{x}) + \cdots + \lambda_n g^n(\mathbf{x}) \qquad (17)$$

The following theorem gives the necessary condition, usually referred to as the *Kuhn-Tucker* condition.

Theorem MR9.3   Necessary Condition: Let f and g_j be differentiable functions of $\mathbf{x}$, and let $L(\mathbf{x}, \lambda)$ be the associated Lagrangean function. Then for vector $\mathbf{x}^*$ to be a solution to the general maximization problem, it is necessary that $\mathbf{x}^*$ and some vector λ^* satisfy (10) and (11).

The following theorem gives the sufficient condition for the general maximization problem.

Theorem MR9.4   Sufficient Condition: Let f and g^j, $j = 1, 2, \ldots, n$ be differentiable and let $L(\mathbf{x}, \lambda)$ be the related Lagrangean function. For a vector $\mathbf{x}^*$ to be a solution to the general maximization problem, it is sufficient that $\mathbf{x}^*$ and some vector λ^* satisfy the conditions (10), (11) and (12) for all possible $\mathbf{x}$, where $\partial L/\partial x_i$, $i = 1, 2, \ldots, m$, are evaluated at $\mathbf{x}^*$.

The following theorem[5] indicates the condition under which the general maximization problem is equivalent to the saddle point problem.

Theorem MR9.5:   Suppose that the functions f and g_j, $j = 1, 2, \ldots, n$ are differentiable and concave functions of $\mathbf{x}$ for $\mathbf{x} \geq 0$, and that there exists some vector $\mathbf{x}^0$ for which the following constraint qualification holds:

$$g^j(x^0) > 0 \qquad j = 1, 2, \ldots, n$$

Then $\mathbf{x}^*$ is an optimal solution to the constrained maximization problem if and only if there exists some nonnegative vector λ^* such that the pair of vectors $(\mathbf{x}^*, \lambda^*)$ is a saddle point of the Lagrangean function (17).[6]

COMPUTATIONAL ASPECTS

Example 1

Maximize

$$- 3e^{-2x_1} - 4e^{-5x_2} \qquad (18)$$

subject to

$$1 - x_1 - x_2 \geq 0 \qquad (19)$$

$$x_1, x_2 \geq 0 \qquad (20)$$

[5] Uzawa (1958).

[6] An elementary introduction to nonlinear programming can be found in Carr and Howe (1964), chap. 5. One type of nonlinear programming, quadratic programming, is applied in Markowitz (1952) to the problem of portfolio selection.

The Lagrangean function and the necessary conditions are

$$L = -3e^{-2x_1} - 4e^{-5x_2} + \lambda(1 - x_1 - x_2) \tag{21}$$

$$\frac{\partial L}{\partial x_1} = 6e^{-2x_1} - \lambda \leq 0, \qquad \text{and} = 0 \text{ if } x_1 > 0 \tag{22}$$

$$\frac{\partial L}{\partial x_2} = 20e^{-5x_2} - \lambda \leq 0, \qquad \text{and} = 0 \text{ if } x_2 > 0 \tag{23}$$

$$\frac{\partial L}{\partial \lambda} = 1 - x_1 - x_2 \geq 0, \qquad \text{and} = 0 \text{ if } \lambda > 0 \tag{24}$$

Consider four possible cases:

1. $x_1 = 0, x_2 > 0$

From (22)

$$6 - \lambda \leq 0 \tag{25}$$

From (23)

$$20e^{-5x_2} - \lambda = 0 \tag{26}$$

Hence $\lambda > 0$, and therefore, from (24)

$$1 - x_2 = 0 \qquad x_2 = 1 \tag{27}$$

Therefore, from (26)

$$\lambda = 20e^{-5} = 20 \times 0.0067 = 0.134 \tag{28}$$

thus violating (25). *Hence a solution of this type does not exist.*

2. $x_1 > 0, x_2 = 0$

From (22)

$$6e^{-2x_1} - \lambda = 0 \tag{29}$$

From (23)

$$20 - \lambda \leq 0 \tag{30}$$

Hence $\lambda > 0$, therefore from (24)

$$1 - x_1 = 0 \qquad x_1 = 1 \tag{31}$$

From (29)

$$\lambda = 6e^{-2} = 6 \times 0.1353 = 0.81$$

This violates (29). *Hence a solution of this type does not exist.*

3. $x_1 = 0, x_2 = 0$

From (22)

$$6 - \lambda \leq 0 \tag{32}$$

From (23)

$$20 - \lambda \leq 0 \tag{33}$$

(24) implies that

$$x_1 + x_2 = 1 \tag{34}$$

Hence the solution cannot exist.

4. $x_1 > 0, x_2 > 0$

From (22)

$$6e^{-2x_1} - \lambda = 0 \tag{35}$$

From (23)

$$20e^{-5x_2} - \lambda = 0 \tag{36}$$

Hence $\lambda > 0$, therefore from (24)

$$1 - x_1 - x_2 = 0 \tag{37}$$

Therefore

$$x_2 = 1 - x_1 \tag{38}$$

Substituting (38) in (36) and using (35)

$$20e^{-5(1-x_1)} = 6e^{-2x_1} \tag{39}$$

Therefore

$$\frac{20}{6} = e^{-2x_1 + 5(1-x_1)}$$

$$= e^{-2x_1 + 5 - 5x_1}$$

$$3.333 = e^{-7x_1 + 5}$$

$$-7x_1 + 5 = 1.2$$

$$-7x_1 = -3.8$$

$$x_1 = 0.54$$

$$x_2 = 0.46$$

This is the optimal solution.

Example 2

Maximize

$$-0.001e^{-2x_1} - 3e^{-4x_2} \tag{40}$$

subject to

$$1 - x_1 - x_2 \geq 0 \tag{41}$$

$$x_1 \geq 0, \ x_2 \geq 0$$

The Lagrangean function and the necessary conditions are

$$L(x_1, x_2, \lambda) = -.001e^{-2x_1} - 3e^{-4x_2} + \lambda(1 - x_1 - x_2) \tag{42}$$

$$\frac{\partial L}{\partial x_1} = 0.002e^{-2x_1} - \lambda \leq 0, \text{ and } = 0 \text{ if } x_1^* > 0 \tag{43}$$

$$\frac{\partial L}{\partial x_2} = 12e^{-4x_2} - \lambda \leq 0, \text{ and } = 0 \text{ if } x_2^* > 0 \tag{44}$$

$$\frac{\partial L}{\partial \lambda} = 1 - x_1 - x_2 \geq 0, \text{ and } = 0 \text{ if } \lambda > 0 \tag{45}$$

Consider four different possibilities:

1. $x_1^* = 0, \ x_2^* > 0$

Then

$$\frac{\partial L}{\partial x_1} = 0.002 - \lambda \leq 0 \tag{46}$$

$$\frac{\partial L}{\partial x_2} = 12e^{-4x_2} - \lambda = 0 \tag{47}$$

$$\frac{\partial L}{\partial \lambda} = 1 - x_2 \geq 0, \text{ and } = 0 \text{ if } \lambda > 0 \tag{48}$$

From (46) and (47) $\lambda > 0$. Therefore (48) must be rewritten

$$\frac{\partial L}{\partial \lambda} = 1 - x_2 = 0 \tag{49}$$

Therefore $x_2 = 1$, and (46) and (47) become

$$0.002 - \lambda < 0 \tag{50}$$

$$12e^{-4} - \lambda = 0 \tag{51}$$

From (51)

$$\lambda = 12 \times 0.018 = 0.216$$

This satisfies (50). The value of the objective function is -0.056.

2. $x_1^* > 0, x_2^* = 0$

Then

$$\frac{\partial L}{\partial x_1} = -.007e^{-2x_1} - \lambda = 0 \tag{52}$$

$$\frac{\partial L}{\partial x_2} = 12 - \lambda \leqq 0 \tag{53}$$

$$\frac{\partial L}{\partial \lambda} = 1 - x_1 \geqq 0, \text{ and } = 0 \text{ if } \lambda > 0 \tag{54}$$

(52) and (53) contradict each other.

3. $x_1^* = 0, x_2^* = 0$

In that case

$$0.002 - \lambda \leqq 0 \tag{55}$$

$$12 - \lambda \leqq 0 \tag{56}$$

$$x_1 + x_2 = 1 \tag{57}$$

Such a solution cannot exist.

4. $x_1^* > 0, x_2^* > 0$

Then

$$.002e^{-2x_1} - \lambda = 0 \tag{58}$$

$$12e^{-4x_2} - \lambda = 0 \tag{59}$$

$$1 - x_1 - x_2 = 0 \tag{60}$$

From (60) $x_2 = 1 - x_1$. Substituting in (59)

$$12e^{-4(1-x_1)} - \lambda = 0$$

Combining this equation with (58)

$$0.002e^{-2x_1} = 12e^{-4(1-x_1)}$$

$$e^{-2x_1+4(1-x_1)} = \frac{12}{.002}$$

$$e^{-2x_1+4-4x_1} = 6000$$

$$e^{4-6x_1} = 6000$$

$$4 - 6x_1 = \log_e 6000$$

$$x_1 = \frac{\log_e 6000 - 4}{-6} = -0.78$$

$$x_2 = 1 - x_1 = 1.78$$

This is not admissible. Hence the first possibility (MR9.46–MR9.51) provides the answer.

Example

Consider a firm which manufactures two products, using four inputs. The percent of each input capacity needed to produce one unit of each product is given by the following table:

Input	Product 1	Product 2
1	0.004	0.0025
2	0.003	0.005
3	0.005	0
4	0	0.006

The demand function for product 1 is given by

$$p_1 = 500 - \frac{y_1}{25}$$

while that for product 2 is

$$p_2 = 250$$

Determine the optimum outputs of products 1 and 2. See Figure MR9.3.

Solution

To solve this problem, the objective function is

$$f(y_1, y_2) = p_1 y_1 + p_2 y_2 = 500 y_1 - \frac{y_1^2}{25} + 250 y_2$$

and the linear inequality constraints are

$$g_1(y_1, y_2) = 0.004 y_1 + 0.0025 y_2 \leq 100$$
$$g_2(y_1, y_2) = 0.003 y_1 + 0.005 y_2 \leq 100$$
$$g_3(y_1, y_2) = 0.005 y_1 \qquad\qquad \leq 100$$
$$g_4(y_1, y_2) = \qquad\qquad 0.006 y_2 \leq 100$$

Consider the following five possible solutions.

1. Assume g_1 is the only effective constraint. Then the Lagrangean function is

$$L(y_1, y_2, \lambda) = 500 y_1 - \frac{y_1^2}{25} + 250 y_2 + \lambda(100 - 0.004 y_1 - 0.0025 y_2)$$

Figure MR 9.3

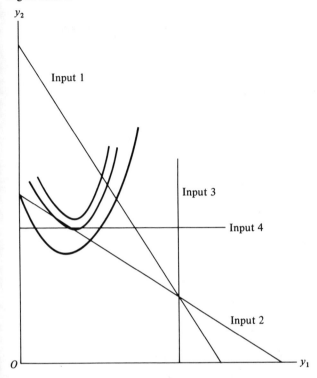

The first-order condition is

$$\frac{\partial L}{\partial y_1} = 500 - \frac{2}{25} y_1 \quad - 0.004\lambda \quad = 0$$

$$\frac{\partial L}{\partial y_2} = 250 \qquad\qquad - 0.0025\lambda \quad = 0$$

$$\frac{\partial L}{\partial \lambda} = 100 - 0.004y_1 - 0.0025y_2 = 0$$

Solving for the unknowns

$$y_1 = 1{,}250$$
$$y_2 = 38{,}000$$

The solution is not feasible, because

$$g_2 = 193.75 > 100$$

2. Assume g_2 is the only effective constraint. Then the Lagrangean expression is

$$L(y_1, y_2, \lambda) = 500y_1 - \frac{y_1^2}{25} + 250y_2 + \lambda(100 - 0.003y_1 - 0.005y_2)$$

The first-order condition is

$$\frac{\partial L}{\partial y_1} = 500 - 0.08y_1 \quad - 0.003\lambda = 0$$

$$\frac{\partial L}{\partial y_2} = 250 \quad\quad\quad - 0.005\lambda = 0$$

$$\frac{\partial L}{\partial \lambda} = 100 - 0.003y_1 - 0.005y_2 = 0$$

Solving for the unknowns

$$y_1 = 4.375$$
$$y_2 = 17,375$$

g_1 and g_3 are satisfied but not g_4.

$$g_4 = 104.1 > 100$$

Therefore this solution is not feasible.

3. Assume g_3 is the only effective constraint. Then

$$L(y_1, y_2, \lambda) = 500y_1 - \frac{y_1^2}{25} + 250y_2 + \lambda(100 - 0.005y_1)$$

The first-order condition is

$$\frac{\partial L}{\partial y_1} = 500 - 0.08y_1 - 0.005\lambda = 0$$

$$\frac{\partial L}{\partial y_2} = 250 \quad\quad\quad\quad = 0$$

$$\frac{\partial L}{\partial \lambda} = 100 - 0.005y_1 \quad\quad = 0$$

The second equation does not hold.

4. Assume g_4 is the only effective constraint. Then

$$L(y_1, y_2, \lambda) = 500y_1 - \frac{y_1^2}{25} + 250y_2 + \lambda(100 - 0.006y_2)$$

The first-order condition is

$$\frac{\partial L}{\partial y_1} = 500 - 0.08 y_1 = 0$$

$$\frac{\partial L}{\partial y_2} = 250 - 0.006\lambda = 0$$

$$\frac{\partial L}{\partial \lambda} = 100 - 0.006 y_2 = 0$$

Solving for the unknowns

$$y_1 = 6,250$$
$$y_2 = 16,666\ 2/3$$

g_1 is satisfied but not g_2.

$$g_2 = 102 > 100$$

5. Assume g_2 and g_4 are the effective constraints. Then

$$L(y_1, y_2, \lambda) = 500 y_1 + \frac{y_1^2}{25} + 250 y_2 + \lambda_2(100 - 0.003 y_1 - 0.005 y_2)$$

$$+ \lambda_4(100 - 0.006 y_2)$$

The first-order condition is

$$\frac{\partial L}{\partial y_1} = 500 - 0.08 y_1 \qquad\qquad - 0.003\lambda_2 \qquad\qquad = 0$$

$$\frac{\partial L}{\partial y_2} = 250 \qquad\qquad - 0.005\lambda_2 - 0.006\lambda_4 = 0$$

$$\frac{\partial L}{\partial \lambda_2} = 100 - 0.003 y_1 - 0.005 y_2 \qquad\qquad = 0$$

$$\frac{\partial L}{\partial \lambda_4} = 100 \qquad\qquad - 0.006 y_2 \qquad\qquad = 0$$

Solving for the unknowns

$$y_1 = 5,555.55$$
$$y_2 = 16,666.66$$

g_1, g_2, g_3, g_4 are all satisfied, g_2 and g_4 with equality.

The marginal-revenue product of commodity 1 is

$$\frac{\partial f}{\partial y_1} = 500 - 0.08 y_1$$

The unit-imputed cost of producing commodity 1 is

$$0.004\lambda_1 + 0.003\lambda_2 + 0.005\lambda_3 = 0.003\lambda_2$$

since $\lambda_1 = \lambda_3 = 0$. Equating these two

$$\lambda_2 = 166{,}666 - 26.6 y_1 = 18{,}889$$

The marginal-revenue product of commodity 2 is

$$\frac{\partial f}{\partial y_2} = 250$$

The unit-imputed cost of producing commodity 2 is

$$0.0025\lambda_1 + 0.005\lambda_2 + 0.006\lambda_4 = 0.005\lambda_2 + 0.006\lambda_4$$

Hence

$$\lambda_4 = 41666.7 - \tfrac{5}{6}(166{,}666 - 26.6 y_1) = 25{,}925$$

MR10   GAME THEORY

The theory of games analyzes the rational behavior when an individual's action depends not only on his but also the other's actions who also face the similar problem. This game-theoretic approach has shown the possibility of other solutions to the past problems in economic theory, for example, in the imperfect competition theory (Part I).

A *two-person, zero-sum game* can be defined in terms of a *payoff matrix*. Assume that there are m strategies open to player P, and n strategies open to player Q, and that a_{ij} is the payoff to P when P selects his i^{th} strategy and Q his j^{th}. The matrix $\mathbf{A} = [a_{ij}]$, $i = 1, 2, \ldots, m$, and $j = 1, 2, \ldots, n$, is the payoff matrix to P; the negative of this matrix is the payoff matrix for Q. Since there are two players, it is called a *two-person* game; since the payoff to P, which is a_{ij}, and the payoff to Q, which is $-a_{ij}$, add up to zero, this is called a *zero-sum* game.

If the payoff matrix has an element a_{ij} which is the minimum of the ith row and the maximum of the jth column, P will select his i^{th} strategy while Q will select his j^{th} at each and every play. Each player is said to adopt a *pure strategy*; and the game is said to be *strictly determined*. This a_{ij} is called the *value* of the game.

Consider the payoff matrix

$$\begin{bmatrix} 1 & 1 & 0 \\ -3 & 2 & -2 \end{bmatrix}$$

If P chooses his strategy first, Q will pick the smallest number of each row, which is 0 and -3 for rows 1 and 2, respectively. P will therefore pick the row having the maximum minimum value, that is, strategy 1, and then Q will choose strategy 3. If, on the other hand, Q is made to choose his strategy first, P will choose the largest number of each column, which is 1, 2, and 0, for columns 1, 2 and 3, respectively. Therefore, Q will pick the column having the minimum maximum value, that is, strategy 3, and then P will choose strategy 1. The game is strictly determined, and the combination of the two optimum strategies has been called the *saddle point*.

If the game is not strictly determined, there is no single optimum strategy for each player. Each player, however, can assure at least a certain amount of payoff by varying his choice from play to play. They are said to adopt *mixed strategies*.

A given mixed strategy for player P is represented by a column vector of probabilities $\mathbf{x} = \text{col.} (x_1, \ldots, x_m)$, where $x_i \geq 0 (i = 1, \ldots, m)$ and $\sum x_i = 1$. In the same way, player Q mixes his strategies according to a column vector of probabilities $\mathbf{y} = (y_1, \ldots, y_n)$, where $y_j \geq 0 (j = 1, \ldots, n)$ and $\sum y_j = 1$. In this case, the *expected value* of the game for P is

$$E(\mathbf{x}, \mathbf{y}) = \sum_i \sum_j a_{ij} x_i y_j = \mathbf{x}'\mathbf{A}\mathbf{y} \tag{1}$$

If vectors $\mathbf{x}^*$ and $\mathbf{y}^*$ can be found so that for any $\mathbf{x}$ and $\mathbf{y}$

$$E(\mathbf{x}, \mathbf{y}^*) \leq E(\mathbf{x}^*, \mathbf{y}^*) \leq E(\mathbf{x}^*, \mathbf{y}) \tag{2}$$

that is,

$$\mathbf{x}'\mathbf{A}\mathbf{y}^* \leq (\mathbf{x}^*)'\mathbf{A}\mathbf{y}^* \leq (\mathbf{x}^*)'\mathbf{A}\mathbf{y} \tag{3}$$

then $(\mathbf{x}^*, \mathbf{y}^*)$ are the *optimum* strategies for players P and Q. The game has a *stable solution* and $E(\mathbf{x}^*, \mathbf{y}^*)$ is the *value* of the game to player P.

If a game has value v, then $\mathbf{x}^*$ and $\mathbf{y}^*$ are optimal strategies if and only if

$$v \leq \sum_i a_{ij} x_i^* \quad j = 1, \ldots, n \tag{4}$$

$$\sum_j a_{ij} y_j^* \leq v \quad i = 1, \ldots, m \tag{5}$$

The first set of relations state that the expected value of the payoff for player P is at least v if player Q employs either of his pure strategies with a probability of one. The second set of relations state that the expected value of the loss for player Q is v or less if player P employs either of his pure strategies with a probability of one.

MATHEMATICAL REVIEW FOR PART II

MR11   LINEAR PROGRAMMING

Linear programming can be taken as a special case of nonlinear programming where $f(\mathbf{x})$ and $g^j(\mathbf{x})$ are all linear functions. It can be stated as follows. Find $\mathbf{x}$ which maximizes

$$\mathbf{c}'\mathbf{x} \tag{1}$$

subject to the constraints

$$\mathbf{Ax} \leq \mathbf{b} \tag{2}$$

$$\mathbf{x} \geq 0 \tag{3}$$

where $\mathbf{c}$ is an n-vector, $\mathbf{x}$ an n-vector, $\mathbf{A}$ an m by n matrix, b an m-vector.

From the discussion of MR10 the Lagrangean expression for this maximization problem is

$$L(\mathbf{x}, \lambda) = \mathbf{c}'\mathbf{x} + \lambda'(\mathbf{b} - \mathbf{Ax}) \tag{4}$$

where λ is an m-vector of Lagrange multipliers. Therefore by the theorems of MR9, the solution to this maximization problem is provided by the saddle point maximizing L with respect to $\mathbf{x}$ and minimizing L with respect to λ.

For every linear programming problem (which we call the *primal*), there exists its *dual*. Consider the negative of (4) which can be written

$$-L(\mathbf{x}, \lambda) = -\mathbf{b}'\lambda + \mathbf{x}'(\mathbf{A}'\lambda - \mathbf{c}) \tag{5}$$

The maximum of L with respect to $\mathbf{x}$ is the minimum of $-L$ with respect to $\mathbf{x}$. Similarly, the minimum of L with respect to λ is equivalent to the maximum of $-L$ with respect to λ. Therefore, the saddle point of L is the same as the saddle point of $-L$, representing the minimum of $-L$ with respect to $\mathbf{x}$ and maximum of $-L$ with respect to λ. The constrained-maximum problem corresponding to (5) is as follows: Maximize

$$-\mathbf{b}'\lambda \tag{6}$$

that is, *minimize*

$$\mathbf{b}'\lambda \tag{6'}$$

subject to

$$\mathbf{A}'\lambda \geq \mathbf{c} \tag{7}$$

$$\lambda \geq 0 \tag{8}$$

This linear programming problem is called the *dual* of the original problem, and λ_i are called the *dual variables*.

To recapitulate, for the linear programming maximum problem, maximize

$$\mathbf{c}'\mathbf{x}$$

subject to

$$\mathbf{A}\mathbf{x} \leq \mathbf{b}$$
$$\mathbf{x} \geq 0$$

there exists a linear programming minimum problem, which is stated as follows: Minimize

$$\mathbf{b}'\lambda$$

subject to

$$\mathbf{A}'\lambda \geq \mathbf{c}$$
$$\lambda \geq 0$$

Note the following relationships between the primal and the dual problems:

1. The coefficient matrix of the constraints of the one problem is the transpose of the other.

2. The coefficients of the objective function of the one are the constants of the constraints of the other.
3. The direction of the constraints' inequality signs of the one is the reverse of that of the other.
4. If the objective function of the one is to be maximized then that of the other is to be minimized.

EQUIVALENCE THEOREM

The analog of the Kuhn-Tucker theorem for linear programming problems (see page 246) is as follows.

Theorem MR11.1 Equivalence Theorem: *A vector* **x*** *is an optimal solution to the primal linear programming problem if and only if there exists a vector* $\boldsymbol{\lambda}^* \geq 0$ *such that* $(\mathbf{x}^*, \boldsymbol{\lambda}^*)$ *is a saddle point of the Lagrangean function*

$$L(\mathbf{x}, \lambda) = \mathbf{c}'\mathbf{x} + \lambda'(\mathbf{b} - \mathbf{A}\mathbf{x})$$

that is, $(\mathbf{x}^*, \boldsymbol{\lambda}^*)$ *satisfies*

$$L(\mathbf{x}, \lambda^*) \leq L(\mathbf{x}^*, \lambda^*) \leq L(\mathbf{x}^*, \lambda)$$

Let **x*** be the solution to the problem (1)–(3), and $\boldsymbol{\lambda}^*$ be the solution to the problem (6)–(8). Since $(\mathbf{x}^*, \boldsymbol{\lambda}^*)$ is the saddle point of the Lagrangean expression (4), *if* $\lambda_j^* > 0$, then

$$\frac{\partial L}{\partial \lambda_j} = 0$$

that is,

$$b_j - \sum_i a_{ji} x_i^* = 0 \tag{9}$$

and *the jth constraint is effective.* Furthermore, *if* $x_i^* > 0$, then

$$\frac{\partial L}{\partial x_i} = 0$$

From (4), the left-hand side of the equation can be written

$$c_i - \sum_j a_{ji} \lambda_j^* = 0 \tag{10}$$

and *the ith constraint of the dual is effective.*
If $\lambda_j^* = 0$, on the other hand, then

$$\frac{\partial L}{\partial \lambda_j} \geq 0 \tag{11}$$

that is,

$$b_j - \sum_i a_{ji} x_i^* \geqq 0$$

$$\sum_i a_{ji} x_i^* \leqq b_j \qquad (12)$$

Furthermore, if $x_i^* = 0$, then

$$\frac{\partial L}{\partial x_i} \leqq 0 \qquad (13)$$

that is,

$$c_i - \sum_j a_{ji} \lambda_j^* \leqq 0$$

$$\sum_j a_{ji} \lambda_j^* \geqq c_i \qquad (14)$$

From (9) and (10)

$$b_j = \sum_i a_{ji} x_i^* \quad \text{for } \lambda_j^* > 0 \quad \text{and} \quad b_j \geqq \sum_i a_{ji} x_i^* \quad \text{for } \lambda_j^* = 0 \quad (15)$$

$$c_i = \sum_j a_{ji} \lambda_j^* \quad \text{for } x_i^* > 0 \quad \text{and} \quad c_i \leqq \sum_j a_{ji} \lambda_j^* \quad \text{for } x_i^* = 0 \quad (16)$$

Therefore

$$\sum_i c_i x_i^* = \sum_i \sum_j a_{ji} \lambda_j^* x_i^* \qquad (17)$$

$$\sum_j b_j \lambda_j^* = \sum_j \sum_i a_{ji} x_i^* \lambda_j^* \qquad (18)$$

that is,

$$\sum_i c_i x_i^* = \sum_j b_j \lambda_j^* \qquad (19)$$

Therefore *the minimum equals the maximum.* Therefore

$$\frac{\partial}{\partial b_j} \sum_i c_i x_i^* = \lambda_j^* \qquad (20)$$

Thus *the Lagrangean multiplier λ_j^* represents the rate of change of the maximand of the original maximization problem with respect to the jth constraint b_j.*

Example 1

Let the primal linear programming problem be to maximize

$$\pi = 3x_1 + 4x_2 \qquad (21)$$

subject to the constraints

$$x_1 + x_2 \leqq 6 \qquad (22)$$

$$2x_1 + 4x_2 \leqq 21$$

$$x_1 \geqq 0, \ x_2 \geqq 0 \qquad (23)$$

The objective function can be shown as in Figure MR11.1.

Figure MR 11.1

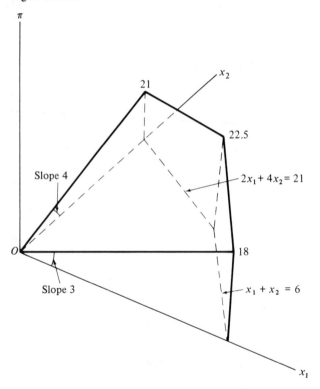

The Lagrangean function for the problem is

$$L(x_1, x_2, \lambda_1, \lambda_2) = 3x_1 + 4x_2 + \lambda_1(6 - x_1 - x_2) \\ + \lambda_2(21 - 2x_1 - 4x_2) \qquad (24)$$

The negative of this Lagrangean function can be written

$$-L(x_1, x_2, \lambda_1, \lambda_2) = -3x_1 - 4x_2 + \lambda_1(x_1 + x_2 - 6) \\ + \lambda_2(2x_1 + 4x_2 - 21) \\ = -6\lambda_1 - 21\lambda_2 + x_1(\lambda_1 + 2\lambda_2 - 3) \\ + x_2(\lambda_1 + 4\lambda_2 - 4) \qquad (25)$$

This is the Lagrangean function for the problem: Maximize

$$- 6\lambda_1 - 21\lambda_2 \tag{26}$$

that is, minimize

$$C = 6\lambda_1 + 21\lambda_2 \tag{26'}$$

subject to

$$\lambda_1 + 2\lambda_2 \geq 3 \tag{27}$$

$$\lambda_1 + 4\lambda_2 \geq 4$$

$$\lambda_1 \geq 0, \lambda_2 \geq 0 \tag{28}$$

This is the dual problem.

The optimum values $x_1^*, x_2^*, \lambda_1^*, \lambda_2^*$ have the following properties: From (MR7.11)

$$\lambda_1^*(6 - x_1^* - x_2^*) = 0 \tag{29}$$

$$\lambda_2^*(21 - 2x_1^* - 4x_2^*) = 0 \tag{30}$$

$$x_1^*(3 - \lambda_1^* - 2\lambda_2^*) = 0 \tag{31}$$

$$x_2^*(4 - \lambda_1^* - 4\lambda_2^*) = 0 \tag{32}$$

Therefore, using (31) and (32)

$$3x_1^* + 4x_2^* = \lambda_1^* x_1^* + 2\lambda_2^* x_1^* + \lambda_1^* x_2^* + 4\lambda_2^* x_2^* \tag{33}$$

and from (29) and (30)

$$6\lambda_1^* + 21\lambda_2^* = x_1^* \lambda_1^* + x_2^* \lambda_1^* + 2x_1^* \lambda_2^* + 4x_2^* \lambda_2^* \tag{34}$$

That is,

$$3x_1^* + 4x_2^* = 6\lambda_1^* + 21\lambda_2^* \tag{35}$$

The value of the minimized objective function of the dual is equal to the value of the maximized objective function of the primal. Therefore if in the first constraint of the primal 6 is changed by 1, then the value of the optimized objective function increases by λ_1^*.

Assume the first constraint is effective but not the second. Then

$$x_1 + x_2 = 6$$

Then the objective function

$$\pi = 3x_1 + 4(6 - x_1) = -x_1 + 24 \tag{36}$$

Therefore, for maximum π,

$$x_1 = 0 \qquad x_2 = 6$$

But this does not satisfy the second constraint. If only the second constraint is effective, then

$$x_1 + 2x_2 = 10.5$$

and the objective function is

$$\pi = 31.5 - 6x_2 + 4x_2 = 31.5 - 2x_2 \tag{37}$$

For maximum π

$$x_1 = 10.5 \qquad x_2 = 0$$

But this does not satisfy the first constraint.
    If both constraints are effective, then

$$x_1 + x_2 = 6 \tag{38}$$

$$2x_1 + 4x_2 = 21 \tag{39}$$

therefore

$$x_1 = 1.5 \qquad x_2 = 4.5 \qquad \pi = 22.5$$

Thus the solution to the primal turns out to be

$$x_1^* = 1.5, \; x_2^* = 4.5, \; \pi = 22.5 \tag{40}$$

Figure MR 11.2

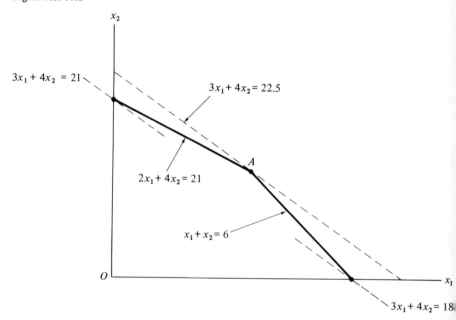

and the solution to the dual

$$\lambda_1^* = 2, \ \lambda_2^* = 0.5, \ C = 22.5 \tag{41}$$

It can be easily verified that these optimum values satisfy (29)–(32).

Graphically the primal problem is to find the point on which the concave objective function assumes the maximum value over the convex feasible region as shown in Figure MR11.2.

Two theorems of importance are stated here. One is *the existence theorem*, which states that there exist optimum solutions for both the primal and dual problem, if and only if there exists feasible solutions for both problems. The other is the *duality theorem*, which states that a feasible solution is optimal if and only if there exists a feasible solution to the dual problem for which the objective functions of both the primal and dual assume the same value.[1]

SIMPLEX METHOD

The simplex method of solving a linear programming problem can be explained as follows. Let the problem be to maximize the revenue

$$f(x_1, x_2) = 3x_1 + 4x_2 \tag{42}$$

subject to the resource constraints

$$x_1 + x_2 \leq 6 \tag{43}$$
$$2x_1 + 4x_2 \leq 21 \tag{44}$$

Let x_3 and x_4 be the unused amounts of the first and second resources, respectively. They are called *slack variables*. Then the problem can be rewritten

$$f = 3x_1 + 4x_2 + 0 \cdot x_3 + 0 \cdot x_4 \tag{42'}$$
$$x_1 + 4x_2 + x_3 = 6 \tag{43'}$$
$$2x_1 + 4x_2 + x_4 = 21 \tag{44'}$$

Note that the inequality constraints have been replaced by equality constraints. Let us use the following activity vectors:

$$P_1 = \begin{pmatrix}1\\2\end{pmatrix}, \ P_2 = \begin{pmatrix}1\\4\end{pmatrix}, \ P_3 = \begin{pmatrix}1\\0\end{pmatrix}, \ P_4 = \begin{pmatrix}0\\1\end{pmatrix}, \ P_0 = \begin{pmatrix}6\\21\end{pmatrix} \tag{45}$$

Each activity vector represents units of the two resources in producing one unit of each output. P_3 and P_4 are *slack activity vectors* and operating P_3 (or P_4) at

[1] *Cf.* Gale (1960), chap. 3.

the unit level leaves one unit of resource 1 (or 2) unused. Then the problem can be rewritten in matrix notation

$$f = (3\ 4\ 0\ 0)\begin{pmatrix} x_1 \\ x_2 \\ x_3 \\ x_4 \end{pmatrix}$$

$$(P_1\ P_2\ P_3\ P_4)\begin{pmatrix} x_1 \\ x_2 \\ x_4 \\ x_4 \end{pmatrix} = P_0$$

Step 1: First Simplex Table

We choose two of the activity vectors to be the basis vectors so that each activity vector can be expressed as a linear combination of the basis vectors. Here the easiest, and therefore logical, initial choice is P_3 and P_4. Since vectors in (45) are all nonnegative, it is clear that each of them can be expressed as a nonnegative linear combination of P_3 and P_4 as follows:

$$P_1 = 1P_3 + 2P_4 \tag{46}$$

$$P_2 = 1P_3 + 4P_4 \tag{47}$$

$$P_3 = 1P_3 + 0P_4 \tag{48}$$

$$P_4 = 0P_3 + 1P_4 \tag{49}$$

$$P_0 = 6P_3 + 21P_4 \tag{50}$$

These can be represented initially in the first simplex table as follows:

First Simplex Table (to be completed)

Basis		3	4	0	0	
		P_1	P_2	P_3	P_4	P_0
0	P_3	1	1	1	0	6
0	P_4	2	4	0	1	21

Zeros to the left of the basis vectors P_3 and P_4 are the same as zeros above P_3 and P_4 at the top of the table.

Step 2: Determining the Activity To Be Introduced

It is clear that operating the first activity P_1 at a unit level contribute 3 to the value of the objective function according to (42). It is also clear from the simplex table that operating P_1 at the unit level uses up the same amounts of the resources as operating P_3 at 1 *and* P_4 at 2 (which gives $0 \times 1 + 0 \times 2 = 0$ for the value of the objective function). Thus introducing P_1 represents a net contribution of 3 to the objective revenue function. This fact is shown by entering $0 \times 1 + 0 \times 2 = 0$ and 3 at the bottom of P_1 column, and similarly for other columns:

First Simplex Table (completed)

		3	4	0	0		
Basis		P_1	P_2	P_3	P_4	P_0	t
0	P_4	1	1	1	0	6	6
0	P_3	2	4	0	1	21	$\dfrac{21}{4}$
		0	0	0	0		
		3	4	0	0		

While one unit of P_1 contributes 3 to the total revenue, P_2 contributes 4. Thus it is desirable to introduce some scalar multiple of P_2 so that one of the present basis vectors will be eliminated.

Step 3: Determining the Process To Be Eliminated

But from (47)

$$tP_2 - tP_3 - 4tP_4 = 0 \tag{51}$$

Therefore

$$P_0 = 0 \cdot P_1 + 0 \cdot P_2 + 6P_3 + 21P_4 + (tP_2 - tP_3 - 4tP_4) \tag{52}$$

that is,

$$P_0 = 0 \cdot P_1 + (0 + t)P_2 + (6 - t)P_3 + (21 - 4t)P_4 \tag{53}$$

We must find the maximum value of t that will not make the scalar coefficients negative. It is 21/4, dividing 6 by 1, 21 by 4, and taking the smaller of the quotients. Setting $t = 21/4$ in (53),

$$\mathbf{P}_0 = 0 \cdot \mathbf{P}_1 + \frac{21}{4} \cdot \mathbf{P}_2 + \frac{3}{4} \cdot \mathbf{P}_3 + 0 \cdot \mathbf{P}_4 \qquad (54)$$

That is, the basis vector $\mathbf{P}_4$ should be replaced by a new basis vector $\mathbf{P}_2$. This is done in the first simplex table by going to the $\mathbf{P}_2$ column, dividing 1 and 4 into 6 and 21 under $\mathbf{P}_0$, respectively, and since 21/4 is smaller than 6, deciding to replace $\mathbf{P}_4$ by $\mathbf{P}_2$ as a basis vector.

Step 4: Second Simplex Table

Now we must express each process vector as a linear combination of the new basis vectors $\mathbf{P}_2$ and $\mathbf{P}_3$. That means solving five sets of simultaneous equations of the form

$$\mathbf{P}_1 \text{ or } \mathbf{P}_2 \text{ or } \mathbf{P}_3 \text{ or } \mathbf{P}_4 \text{ or } \mathbf{P}_0 = a\mathbf{P}_2 + b\mathbf{P}_3 = a\begin{pmatrix}1\\4\end{pmatrix} + b\begin{pmatrix}1\\0\end{pmatrix}$$

This can be accomplished as follows: Write

$$1 \quad 1 \quad 1 \quad 0 \quad 6 \qquad (55)$$

$$2 \quad 4 \quad 0 \quad 1 \quad 21 \qquad (56)$$

Making 4 the pivot element, divide the second row (56) through by 4, thus replacing the pivot element 4 by 1:

$$\frac{1}{2} \quad 1 \quad 0 \quad \frac{1}{4} \quad \frac{21}{4} \qquad (57)$$

Subtract the new row vector (57) from the first row (55)—if the second element of (55) is not 1, say k, we must subtract k times (57) from (55):

$$\frac{1}{2} \quad 0 \quad 1 \quad -\frac{1}{4} \quad \frac{3}{4} \qquad (58)$$

Thus (57) and (58) replace the second and first rows of the first simplex table as follows.

Second Simplex Table

Basis		3 P_1	4 P_2	0 P_3	0 P_4	P_0	t
0	P_3	$\frac{1}{2}$	0	1	$-\frac{1}{4}$	$\frac{3}{4}$	$\frac{3}{2}$
4	P_2	$\frac{1}{2}$	1	0	$\frac{1}{4}$	$\frac{21}{4}$	$\frac{21}{2}$
		2	4	0	1		
		1	0	0	-1		

These elements of the new simplex table mean that

$$P_1 = \frac{1}{2}P_3 + \frac{1}{2}P_2$$

$$P_2 = \qquad P_2$$

$$P_3 = P_3$$

$$P_4 = -\frac{1}{4}P_3 + \frac{1}{4}P_2$$

$$P_0 = \frac{3}{4}P_3 + \frac{21}{4}P_2$$

As before we can determine which process vector should substitute for either of the process vectors, by computing in column P_1

$$0 \times \frac{1}{2} + 4 \times \frac{1}{2} = 2$$

$$3 - 2 = 1$$

and doing the same for other columns. We see P_1 should be introduced as the basis vector; it will make a positive contribution to the objective function. For the same reason as before we divide

$$\frac{1}{2} \text{ into } \frac{3}{4} \quad \text{and} \quad \frac{1}{2} \text{ into } \frac{21}{4}$$

Finding $\frac{3}{2}$ smaller than $\frac{21}{2}$, we decide to remove P_3 as the basis vector.

Step 5: Third Simplex Table

Making $\frac{1}{2}$ the pivot element, divide the first row through by $\frac{1}{2}$ obtaining

$$1 \quad 0 \quad 2 \quad -\frac{1}{2} \quad \frac{3}{2} \tag{59}$$

In order to produce 0 where $\frac{1}{2}$ is in the second row (below the pivot element) of the simplex table, subtract (59) $\times \frac{1}{2}$ from the second row of the same simplex table, thus obtaining

$$0 \quad 1 \quad -1 \quad \frac{1}{2} \quad \frac{9}{2} \tag{60}$$

Thus (59) and (60) replace the first and second rows of the second simplex table, resulting in

Third Simplex Table

		3	4	0	0	
Basis		P_1	P_2	P_3	P_4	P_0
3	P_1	1	0	2	$-\frac{1}{2}$	$\frac{3}{2}$
4	P_2	0	1	-1	$\frac{1}{2}$	$\frac{9}{2}$
		3	4	2	$\frac{1}{2}$	$\frac{45}{2}$
		0	0	-2	$-\frac{1}{2}$	

To find out if it is possible to replace the present basis vectors and increase the revenue function, we compute the numbers below the table, and find it is impossible. Thus

$$P_0 = \frac{3}{2}P_2 + \frac{9}{2}P_1$$

and the value of the objective function is

$$\frac{3}{2} \times 3 + \frac{9}{3} \times 4 = \frac{45}{2}$$

We should produce 1.5 units of commodity 1 and 4.5 units of commodity 2.
It is clear that activities 3 and 4 are operated at zero levels, that is, both inputs are used up.

Example
Maximize

$$2y_1 + 5y_2$$

subject to

$$y_1 \leqq 4$$
$$y_2 \leqq 3$$
$$y_1 + 2y_2 \leqq 8$$

By introducing slack variables y_3, y_4 and y_5,

$$y_1 \qquad + y_3 \qquad\qquad = 4$$
$$y_2 \qquad + y_4 \qquad = 3$$
$$y_1 + 2y_2 \qquad\qquad + y_5 = 8$$

Therefore we obtain the following simplex tables:

		2	5	0	0	0		
	Basis	P_1	P_2	P_3	P_4	P_5	P_0	t
0	P_3	1	0	1	0	0	4	
0	P_4	0	①	0	1	0	3	3 →
0	P_5	1	2	0	0	1	8	4
		0	0	0	0	0		
		2	5	0	0	0		
			↑					

	Basis	2	5	0	0	0		
		P_1	P_2	P_3	P_4	P_5	P_0	t
0	P_3	1	0	1	0	0	4	4
5	P_2	0	1	0	1	0	3	
0	Pe	①	0	0	-2	1	2	2 →
		0	5	0	5	0		
		2	0	0	-5	0		

↑

	Basis	2	5	0	0	0	
		P_1	P_2	P_3	P_4	P_5	P_0
0	P_3	0	0	1	2	-1	2
5	P_2	0	1	0	1	0	3
2	P_1	1	0	0	-2	1	2
		2	5	0	1	2	19
		0	0	0	-1	-2	

The answers are

$$y_1 = 2, y_2 = 3$$

It is clear that activity 3 is operated at 2, and activities 4 and 5 at zero. Hence two units of input 1 remain unused; the first constraint is not effective while the other two constraints are.[2]

---

[2] On linear programming, see Dantzig (1963), Charnes et al. (1953), and Dorfman et al. (1958).

MR12 SOLVING A GAME PROBLEM BY LINEAR PROGRAMMING

A given game has the payoff matrix

$$\mathbf{A} = (a_{ij}) \qquad i = 1, \ldots, m; j = 1, \ldots, n \tag{1}$$

If the maximizing row player adopts a mixed strategy

$$\mathbf{x} = (x_i) \qquad i = 1, \ldots, m \qquad \sum_{i=1}^{m} x_i = 1 \tag{2}$$

his expectation is

$$v = \min_{j} \sum_{i=1}^{m} a_{ij} x_i \tag{3}$$

and he wishes to maximize v. Hence

$$\sum_{i=1}^{m} a_{ij} x_i \geq v \qquad j = 1, \ldots, n \tag{4}$$

Hence in the matrix notation

$$\mathbf{A'x} \geq v\mathbf{\iota} \tag{5}$$

where ι is a *unity column vector* with all elements equal to 1. This expression can be rewritten

$$\mathbf{A'z} \geq \mathbf{\iota} \tag{6}$$

where

$$\mathbf{z} = \frac{\mathbf{x}}{v} \tag{7}$$

v may be negative, depending upon the numerical values of the a_{ij}. But in that case, adding to every element of the original payoff matrix a sufficiently large positive constant can make v positive, so that

$$v > 0 \tag{8}$$

The original constraint was

$$\mathbf{x} \geq 0 \tag{9}$$

so that, from (7),

$$\mathbf{z} \geq 0 \tag{10}$$

Also the original restriction that

$$\sum_{i=1}^{m} x_i = 1 \tag{11}$$

becomes

$$\sum_{i=1}^{m} z_i = \frac{1}{v} \tag{12}$$

When the player maximizes v, he minimizes $1/v$. Hence the optimal strategy is given by z such that

$$\iota' z = \min \tag{13}$$

where ι' is a *unity-row vector* with all elements equal to one, subject to

$$A' z \geq \iota \tag{14}$$

$$z \geq 0 \tag{15}$$

Example 1

Solve the following game problem by the simplex method:

		II's Strategy	
		6	3
I's Strategy	1	2	0
	2	−1	3

Each element of the above payoff matrix represents the gain for I for the corresponding pure strategies of I and II.

To solve this game problem, we first change the payoff matrix by adding 1 to each element.

$$\begin{bmatrix} 3 & 1 \\ 0 & 4 \end{bmatrix}$$

The linear programming problem for I is as follows: Minimize

$$z_1 + z_2$$

subject to

$$3z_1 \geq 1$$
$$z_1 + 4z_2 \geq 1$$

We can solve the above minimization problem directly or solve its dual—a maximization problem. The dual is as follows:

Maximize

$$y_1 + y_2$$

subject to

$$3y_1 + y_2 \leqq 1$$
$$4y_2 \leqq 1$$

The simplex tables are

		1	1	0	0		
		P_1	P_2	P_3	P_4	P_0	t
0	P_3	③	1	1	0	1	$\frac{1}{3}$
0	P_4	0	4	0	1	1	
		0	0	0	0		
		1	1	0	0		

$\uparrow$

		1	1	0	0		
		P_1	P_2	P_3	P_4	P_0	t
1	P_1	1	$\frac{1}{3}$	$\frac{1}{3}$	0	$\frac{1}{3}$	1
0	P_4	0	④	0	1	1	$\frac{1}{4}$
		1	$\frac{1}{3}$	$\frac{1}{3}$	0		
		0	$\frac{2}{3}$	$-\frac{1}{3}$	0		

$\uparrow$

		1	1	0	0	
		P_1	P_2	P_3	P_4	P_0
1	P_1	1	0	$\frac{1}{3}$	$-\frac{1}{12}$	$\frac{1}{4}$
1	P_2	0	1	0	$\frac{1}{4}$	$\frac{1}{4}$
		1	1	$\frac{1}{3}$	$\frac{1}{6}$	
		0	0	$-\frac{1}{3}$	$-\frac{1}{6}$	

So P_1 and P_2 are used, that is, y_1 and y_2 are nonzero. So the constraints 1 and 2 of the primal problem are effective, that is, hold with equality. Therefore,

$$3z_1 = 1$$

$$z_1 + 4z_2 = 1$$

Solving the equations

$$z_1 = \frac{1}{3}$$

$$z_2 = \frac{1}{6}$$

Therefore

$$\frac{z_1}{z_1 + z_2} = \frac{2}{3}$$

$$\frac{z_2}{z_1 + z_2} = \frac{1}{3}$$

are the optimal mixed strategy.

Notice that the negatives of the solution values for z_1 and z_2 appear in the last row of the last simplex table.

Example 2

Given the following payoff matrix,

	1	2	3	4
1	10	1	7	8
2	3	4	5	9
3	6	7	4	2

1. Find the optimum strategy.
2. Find the value of the game.
    This game problem can be converted into a linear programming problem.

Minimize

$$\iota' z$$

subject to

$$A' z \geqq \iota$$

$$z \geqq 0$$

where $z = x/v$ and $\iota' x = 1$. The dual of this problem is as follows:

Maximize

$$\iota' y$$

subject to

$$Ay \leqq \iota$$

Solving the dual problem gives the simplex tables on the following page. Thus

$$y_1 = 0 \qquad y_2 = \frac{15}{207} \qquad y_3 = \frac{24}{207} \qquad y_4 = \frac{3}{207}$$

Normalizing y_i, we obtain the answer,

$$u_1 = 0 \qquad u_2 = \frac{5}{14} \qquad u_3 = \frac{8}{14} \qquad u_4 = \frac{1}{14}$$

			1	1	1	1	0	0	0
		P_0	P_1	P_2	P_3	P_4	P_5	P_6	P_7
0	P_5	1	10	1	7	8	1	1	0
0	P_6	1	3	4	5	9	0	1	0
0	P_7	1	6	7	4	2	0	0	1 →
			0	0	0	0	0	0	0
			1	1	1	1	0	0	0
0	P_5	$\frac{6}{7}$	$\frac{64}{7}$	0	$\frac{45}{7}$	$\frac{54}{7}$	0	0	$-\frac{1}{7}$
0	P_6	$\frac{3}{7}$	$-\frac{3}{7}$	0	$\frac{19}{7}$	$\frac{55}{7}$	0	1	$-\frac{4}{7}$ →
0	P_2	$\frac{1}{7}$	$\frac{6}{7}$	1	$\frac{4}{7}$	$\frac{2}{7}$	0	0	$\frac{1}{7}$
			$\frac{6}{7}$	1	$\frac{4}{7}$	$\frac{2}{7}$	0	0	$\frac{1}{7}$
			$\frac{1}{7}$	0	$\frac{3}{7}$	$\frac{5}{7}$	0	0	$-\frac{1}{7}$
0	P_5	$\frac{24}{55}$	$\frac{526}{55}$	0	$\frac{207}{55}$	0	1	$-\frac{54}{55}$	$\frac{23}{55}$ →
1	P_4	$\frac{3}{55}$	$-\frac{3}{55}$	0	$\frac{19}{55}$	1	0	$\frac{7}{55}$	$-\frac{4}{55}$
1	P_2	$\frac{7}{55}$	$\frac{48}{55}$	1	$\frac{26}{55}$	0	0	$-\frac{2}{55}$	$\frac{9}{55}$
			$\frac{45}{55}$	1	$\frac{45}{55}$	1	0	$\frac{5}{55}$	$\frac{5}{55}$
			$\frac{10}{55}$	0	$\frac{10}{55}$	0	0	$\frac{5}{55}$	$-\frac{5}{55}$
1	P_3	$\frac{24}{207}$	$\frac{526}{207}$	0	1	0	$\frac{55}{207}$	$-\frac{54}{207}$	$\frac{3}{207}$
1	P_4	$\frac{3}{207}$	$-\frac{193}{207}$	0	0	1	$-\frac{19}{207}$	$\frac{45}{207}$	$-\frac{23}{207}$
1	P_2	$\frac{15}{207}$	$-\frac{68}{207}$	1	0	0	$-\frac{26}{207}$	$\frac{18}{207}$	$\frac{23}{207}$
			$\frac{401}{207}$	1	1	1	$\frac{10}{207}$	$\frac{9}{207}$	$\frac{23}{207}$
			$-\frac{194}{207}$	0	0	0	$\frac{10}{207}$	$-\frac{9}{207}$	$-\frac{23}{207}$

Therefore the first constraint is not effective, while the last three constraints are effective. Therefore,

$$z_1 + 4z_2 + 7z_3 = 1$$
$$7z_1 + 5z_2 + 4z_3 = 1$$
$$8z_1 + 9z_2 + 2z_3 = 1$$

Using Cramer's rule,

$$z_1 = \frac{\begin{vmatrix} 1 & 4 & 7 \\ 1 & 5 & 4 \\ 1 & 9 & 2 \end{vmatrix}}{\begin{vmatrix} 1 & 4 & 7 \\ 7 & 5 & 4 \\ 8 & 9 & 2 \end{vmatrix}} = \frac{10}{207}$$

$$z_2 = \frac{9}{207}$$

$$z_3 = \frac{23}{207}$$

These answers can also be obtained from the last row of the last simplex table on the preceding page. Normalizing z, we obtain the answer,

$$x_1 = \frac{10}{42}, x_2 = \frac{9}{42}, x_3 = \frac{23}{42}$$

Since $v = x_i/z_i$, the value of the game is

$$\frac{\dfrac{10}{42}}{\dfrac{10}{207}} = \frac{69}{14}$$

MATHEMATICAL REVIEW FOR PART III

MR13   SETS

A set is any well-defined collection of objects. The objects comprising the set are called *elements* or *members*. The set A of five numbers 1, 2, 3, 4, 5 can be written

$$A = \{1, 2, 3, 4, 5\}$$

Alternatively the set can be written

$$A = \{x \,|\, x \text{ is an integer, } 1 \leqq x \leqq 5\}$$

The fact that 3 belongs to A can be written

$$3 \in A$$

and the fact that 6 does not belong to A can be written

$$6 \notin A$$

Two sets are *equal* if they consist of the same elements. Equality of two sets A and B can be written

$$A = B$$

A set B of elements of the set A is a *subset* of A. This can be written

$$B \subset A$$

If $B \subset A$ and $B \neq A$, then B is said to be a *proper subset* of A.

The *union* of two sets A and B, denoted by

$$A \cup B$$

is the set of all elements which belong to A or B (or both). That is,

$$A \cup B = \{x \mid x \in A \text{ or } x \in B\}$$

The intersection of two sets A and B, denoted by

$$A \cap B$$

is the set of elements which belong to both A and B, that is

$$A \cap B = \{x \mid x \in A \text{ and } x \in B\}$$

We also define an *empty set* as a set containing no elements. When the intersection of two sets A and B is an empty set, we say the two sets are *disjoint*.

Suppose B is a proper subset of A. The set consisting of the elements of A that do not belong to B is called the *complement* of B in A. It is written $A - B$.

Consider two sets A and B. The *Cartesian product* of the two sets A and B, denoted by

$$A \times B$$

is the set of all ordered pairs of the form (a, b). We can write, therefore,

$$A \times B = \{(a, b) \mid a \in A, b \in B\}$$

The concept may be extended to Cartesian products of more than two sets (consisting of triples, quadruples, and n-tuples). The *real plane* may be regarded as the Cartesian product of two real lines. This concept can be extended to three-dimensional, four-dimensional, and n-dimensional space.[1]

MR14   BINARY RELATIONS

A *binary relation* R from a set A to a set B assigns to each pair (a, b) in $A \times B$ exactly one of the following statements:

(a) a is related to b, written $a \mathrel{R} b$
(b) a is not related to b, written $a \mathrel{\not R} b$

---

[1] On the mathematical concepts discussed here, see Yamane (1968), chap. 1; Debreu (1959), chap. 1; McFadden *et al.* (1963); Lancaster (1968), part IV.

Any binary relation R from a set A to a set B uniquely defines a subset R^* of $A \times B$:

$$R^* = \{(a, b) \mid a \text{ R } b\}$$

On the other hand, any subset R^* of $A \times B$ defines a binary relation R from A to B:

$$a \text{ R } b \text{ if and only if } (a, b) \in R^*$$

Hence a binary relation R from A to B is defined as a subset of $A \times B$.

With respect to a binary relation in a set, e.g. from x to x, we define the following two concepts: it is said to be *reflexive* if $x \text{ R } x$, that is, the relation holds with respect to itself; it is said to be *transitive* if $x''' \text{ R } x''$ and $x'' \text{ R } x'$ imply $x''' \text{ R } x'$. When a binary relation is reflexive and transitive, it is called a *preordering*. The binary relation is said to be *complete* when one necessarily has $x'' \text{ R } x'$ or $x' \text{ R } x''$ or both. If not, the relation is called *partial*.

A binary relation R in a set A, that is, a subset R of $A \times A$, is called an *equivalence relation* if and only if it satisfies the following axioms:

Reflexivity: For every $a \in A$, $(a, a) \in R$
Symmetry: If $(a, b) \in R$, then $(b, a) \in R$
Transitivity: If $(a, b) \in R$ and $(b, c) \in R$, then $(a, c) \in R$

If R is an equivalence relation in A, then the *equivalence class* of any element $a \in A$ is the set of elements to which a is related, that is,

$$\{x \mid (a, x) \in R\}$$

MR15   VECTORS IN R^n

The *n-dimensional euclidean space* denoted by R^n is the set of all ordered *n*-tuples

$$\mathbf{x} = (x_1, \ldots, x_n)$$

of real numbers $x_1, \ldots,$ and x_n with associative and commutative *addition* defined by

$$(x_1, \ldots, x_n) + (y_1, \ldots, y_n) = (x_1 + y_1, \ldots, x_n + y_n)$$

and *multiplication by a real number* defined by

$$a(x_1, \ldots, x_n) = (ax_1, \ldots, ax_n)$$

The number n is called the *dimension* of the euclidean space. The vector with all components equal to zero is called the *origin* or the *null vector*.

The *inner product* of two vectors $\mathbf{x}$ and $\mathbf{y}$, written $\mathbf{xy}$ or $\mathbf{x} \cdot \mathbf{y}$, is defined as the scalar $\mathbf{xy} = \mathbf{x} \cdot \mathbf{y} = x_1 y_1 + x_2 y_2 + \cdots + x_n y_n$.

The *sum* of two subsets X and Y of R^n, written $X + Y$, is the set of elements of R^n of the form $\mathbf{x} + \mathbf{y}$ where $\mathbf{x} \in X$ and $\mathbf{y} \in Y$.

The *negative* of set X, written $- X$, is the set of elements of R^n of the form $-\mathbf{x}$ where $\mathbf{x} \in X$.

The *difference* obtained by substracting Y from X, written $X - Y$, is the set $X + (- Y)$.

Consider the sequence $(\mathbf{x}^i)$ in R^n. The sequence is said to *converge* to the point $\bar{\mathbf{x}}$ if

$$\lim_{i \to \infty} d(\mathbf{x}^i, \bar{\mathbf{x}}) = 0$$

where

$$d(\mathbf{x}^i, \bar{\mathbf{x}}) = \sqrt{\sum_k (x_k^i - \bar{x}_k)^2}$$

The convergence of $\mathbf{x}^i$ to $\bar{\mathbf{x}}$ is denoted by

$$\lim_{i \to \infty} \mathbf{x}^i = \bar{\mathbf{x}}$$

A point $\mathbf{x}$ is a *limit point* of a set X if there is a sequence of points of X converging to $\mathbf{x}$.

A subset X of R^n is said to be *closed* if it owns its limit points.

A set is said to be *bounded* if it can be contained in some hypersphere with a finite diameter. The real line is not bounded.

A subset S of R^n is said to be *compact* if it is closed and bounded.

A *convex set* is a set such that the line segment connecting any two points of the set wholly lies within the set.

A *subspace* of R^n is a subset of vectors from R^n which is closed under the operations of addition and scalar multiplication.

MR16   FUNCTIONS, CORRESPONDENCES, AND FIXED-POINT THEOREMS

Let X and Y be two subsets of R^n. A *function* f defines one and only one element $\mathbf{y}$ of Y associated with each element $\mathbf{x}$ of X. It is a binary relation. The function is also called a *mapping* or *transformation*. $\mathbf{y}$ is called the image of $\mathbf{x}$ under f.

Suppose, on the other hand, that with each element $\mathbf{x}$ of set X is associated a nonempty subset $Y(\mathbf{x})$ of Y. Then we have a *set-valued function* or a *correspondence* from X to Y.

UPPER SEMICONTINUITY

In the case of a point-to-point mapping, $\mathbf{y} = f(\mathbf{x})$, *continuity* of $f(\mathbf{x})$ at $\mathbf{a}$ may be defined as follows: $f(\mathbf{x})$ is continuous at $\mathbf{a}$ if $f(\mathbf{x}) \to f(\mathbf{a})$ as $\mathbf{x} \to \mathbf{a}$. That is, the graph of $f(\mathbf{x})$ is connected so that it can be drawn without lifting the pen.

In the case of a point-to-set mapping, $f(\mathbf{x})$ and $f(\mathbf{a})$ are sets rather than points. Therefore, we have the following definitions for continuity of correspondence. The correspondence $f(\mathbf{x})$ is said to be *upper semicontinuous* at $\mathbf{a}$ if *every* sequence in $f(\mathbf{x})$ for which $\mathbf{x} \to \mathbf{a}$ has a limit point which lies in the image set $f(\mathbf{a})$. That is, let S be the set of limit points of all sequences in the graph of $f(\mathbf{x})$. Then $S \subset f(\mathbf{a})$.

That is, consider the correspondence whose image set is a subset of a compact set. Take a sequence $\mathbf{x}^t (t = 1, 2 \ldots)$ that converges to $\mathbf{a}$, and the corresponding sequence $\mathbf{y}^t \in f(\mathbf{x}^t)$. Suppose if $\mathbf{y}^t$ converges to $\mathbf{b}$, then $\mathbf{b} \in f(\mathbf{a})$. Then f is *upper semicontinuous* at $\mathbf{a}$.

If the correspondence is upper semicontinuous at every point of X, then the correspondence f is *upper semicontinuous on X*. Accordingly, if $\mathbf{x} \in X$, $\mathbf{y} \in f(\mathbf{x})$, then the upper semicontinuity of the correspondence is equivalent to the closedness of the set of $(\mathbf{x}, \mathbf{y})$ in the Cartesian product $X \times Y$.

LOWER SEMICONTINUOUS CORRESPONDENCE

The correspondence f is *lower semicontinuous* if every point in the image set $f(\mathbf{a})$ is the limit point of *some* sequence such that each term of the sequence lies in the image set of the associated $\mathbf{x}$. In other words let S be the set of limit points of all sequences in the graph of $f(\mathbf{x})$. Then $f(\mathbf{a}) \subset S$.

That is, consider the correspondence whose image set is a subset of a compact set. Let $\mathbf{x}^t (t = 1, 2, \ldots)$ converge to $\mathbf{a}$, and let $\mathbf{b}$ be a member of the image set $f(\mathbf{a})$ at $\mathbf{a}$. Then there exists a sequence $\mathbf{y}^t$ such that $\mathbf{y}^t$ is a member of the image set of $\mathbf{x}^t$, and that $\mathbf{y}^t$ converges to $\mathbf{b}$.

CONTINUOUS CORRESPONDENCE

The correspondence f is *continuous* at point $\mathbf{a}$ if it is upper and lower semicontinuous at $\mathbf{a}$.

In both (a) and (b) of Figure MR16.1, the image set $f(x)$ at a is the closed interval $[p, q]$. In (a), if

$$x^t \to a \qquad y^t \in f(x^t) \qquad y^t \to b$$

then

$$b \in f(a)$$

Thus f is upper semicontinuous. But in (b), if b is between r and p, or between q and s,

$$b \in f(a)$$

does not hold.

Suppose $x^t \to a$, and $b \in f(a)$. Then there exists a sequence y^t such that

$$y^t \in f(x^t) \text{ and } y^t \to b$$

Then the correspondence f is said to be *lower semicontinuous*. In the second diagram this is true. In the first diagram, however, if b is between p and r or between s and q, there does not exist a sequence that satisfies the above condition.

Figure MR 16.1

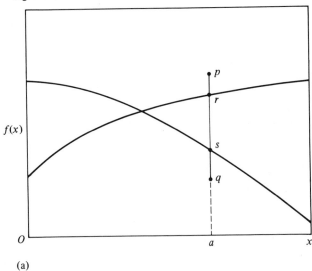

(a)

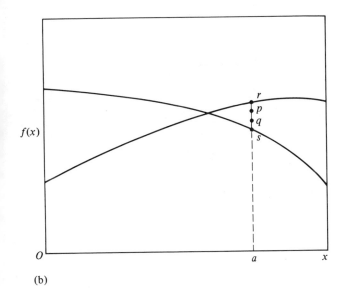

(b)

BROUWER FIXED-POINT THEOREM

If

(a) C is a subset of R^m
(b) C is nonempty
(c) C is compact
(d) C is convex
(e) f is a function from C to C

then f has a fixed point $\mathbf{x^*}$ such that

$$f(\mathbf{x^*}) = \mathbf{x^*}$$

In the one-dimensional case, the theorem asserts that any continuous $f: [0, 1]$ →[0, 1] maps at least one point into itself, as shown in Figure MR16.2.

Figure MR 16.2

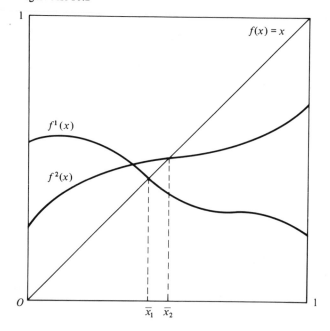

KAKUTANI FIXED-POINT THEOREM

If C is

(a)   a subset of R^m
(b)   nonempty
(c)   compact
(d)   convex

and G is

(e) a correspondence from C to C
(f) upper semicontinuous
(g) such that the image set $G(\mathbf{x})$ is nonempty for all $\mathbf{x}$ in C
(h) such that $G(\mathbf{x})$ is convex for all $\mathbf{x}$ in C

then G has a fixed point, that is, a point $\mathbf{x}^*$ such that

$$G(\mathbf{x}^*) \ni \mathbf{x}^*$$

BIBLIOGRAPHY

BIBLIOGRAPHY

Allen, R. G. D. (1932), "Decreasing Costs: A Mathematical Note," *Economic Journal*, **42**: 323–326.

Allen, R. G. D. (1938), *Mathematical Analysis for Economists*, London: Macmillan.

Allen, R. G. D. (1963), *Mathematical Economics*, 2nd ed., New York: Saint Martin's Press.

American Economic Association (1952), *Readings in Price Theory*, Homewood, Ill.: Irwin.

American Economic Association (1969), *Readings in Welfare Economics*, Homewood, Ill.: Irwin.

American Economic Association and Royal Economic Society (1966), *Surveys of Economic Theory*, vol. 3, *Resource Allocation*, New York: Saint Martin's Press.

Arrow, K. J. (1951), "An Extension of the Basic Theorems of Classical Welfare Economics," in *Proceedings of the Second Berkeley Symposium on Mathematical Statistics and Probability*, Berkeley: University of California Press.

Arrow, K. J. (1951, 1963), *Social Choice and Individual Values*, New York: Wiley.

Arrow, K. J. (1959), "Towards a Theory of Price Adjustment," in M. Abramowitz *et al.*, *The Allocation of Economic Resources*, Stanford: Stanford University Press.

Arrow, K. J., H. D. Block, and L. Hurwicz (1959), "On the Stability of the Competitive Equilibrium, II," *Econometrica*, **27**: 82–109.

Arrow, K. J., H. B. Chenery, B. Minhas, and R. M. Solow (1961), "Capital–Labor Substitution and Economic Efficiency," *Review of Economics and Statistics*, **43**: 225–250.

Arrow, K. J., and G. Debreu (1954), "Existence of an Equilibrium for a Competitive Economy," *Econometrica*, **22**: 625–290.

Arrow, K. J., and A. C. Enthoven (1961), "Quasi-Concave Programming," *Econometrica*, **29**: 779–800.

Arrow, K. J., and L. Hurwicz (1958), "On the Stability of the Competitive Equilibrium, I," *Econometrica*, **26**: 522–552.

Arrow, K. J., and L. Hurwicz (1960), "Decentralization and Computation in Resource Allocation," in R. Pfouts, Ed., *Essays in Economics and Econometrics*, Chapel Hill: University of North Carolina Press.

Arrow, K. J., L. Hurwicz, and H. Uzawa, Ed. (1958), *Studies in Linear and Nonlinear Programming*, Stanford: Stanford University Press.

Arrow, K. J., S. Karlin, and P. Suppes, Eds. (1960), *Mathematical Methods in the Social Sciences 1959, Proceedings of the First Stanford Symposium*, Stanford: Stanford University Press.

Bator, F. (1957), "Simple Analytics of Welfare Maximization," *American Economic Review*, **47**: 22–59.

Bator, F. (1958), "The Anatomy of Market Failure," *Quarterly Journal of Economics*, **72**: 351–392.

Baumol, W. J. (1965a), *Economic Theory and Operations Analysis*, 2nd ed., Englewood Cliffs, N.J.: Prentice-Hall.

Baumol, W. J. (1965b), *Welfare Economics and the Theory of the State*, Cambridge, Mass.: Harvard University Press.

Bergson, A. (1938), "A Reformulation of Certain Aspects of Welfare Economics," *Quarterly Journal of Economics*, **52**: 310–334.

Bergson, A. (1948), "Socialist Economics," in American Economic Association, *A Survey of Contemporary Economics*, vol. 1, Homewood, Illinois: Irwin.

Blau, J. H. (1957), "The Existence of Social Welfare Functions," *Econometrica*, **25**: 302–313.

Boot, J. C. G. (1964), *Quadratic Programming*, Amsterdam: North-Holland.

Bowen, H. R. (1943), "The Interpretation of Voting in the Allocation of Economic Resources," *Quarterly Journal of Economics*, **58**: 27–48.

Bowles, S. (1967), "Efficient Allocation of Resources in Education," *Quarterly Journal of Economics*, **81**: 189–219.

Brown, E. Phelps (1963), *The Framework of the Pricing System*, London: Chapman and Hall.

Buchanan, J. M. (1951), "Knut Wicksell on Marginal Cost Pricing," *Southern Economic Journal* **18**: 173–178.

Buchanan, J. M., and W. C. Stubblebine (1962), "Externality," *Economica*, **29**: 371–384.

Carlson, S. (1956), *A Study on the Theory of Production*, New York: Kelly and Millman.

Carr, C. R., and C. W. Howe (1964), *Quantitative Decision Procedures in Management and Economics*, New York: McGraw-Hill.

Chamberlin, E. H. (1933), *The Theory of Monopolistic Competition*, Cambridge, Mass.: Harvard University Press.

Charnes, A., W. W. Cooper, and A. Henderson (1953), *An Introduction to Linear Programming*, New York: Wiley.

Chenery, H. B., and H. Uzawa (1958), "Nonlinear Programming in Economic Development," in Arrow, Hurwicz, and Uzawa (1958), pp. 203–229.

Chiang, A. (1968), *Fundamental Methods of Mathematical Economics*, New York: McGraw-Hill.

Clark, J. B. (1931), *The Distribution of Wealth*, New York: Macmillan.

Coase, R. H. (1960), "The Problem of Social Costs," *Journal of Law and Economics*, 3: 1–44.

Coleman, J. S. (1966), "The Possibility of a Social Welfare Function," *American Economic Review*, 56: 1105–1122.

Corlett, W. J., and D. C. Hague (1953–1954), "Complementarity and the Excess Burden of Taxation," *Review of Economic Studies*, 21: 21–30.

Cournot, A. (1838), *Researches into the Mathematical Principles of the Theory of Wealth*, New York: Kelley.

Dantzig, G. B. (1963), *Linear Programming and Extensions*, Princeton, N.J.: Princeton University Press.

Davis, O., and A. Whinston (1965), "Welfare Economics and the Theory of Second Best," *Review of Economic Studies*, 32: 1–14.

Debreu, G. (1951), "The Coefficient of Resource Utilization," *Econometrica*, 19: 273–292.

Debreu, G. (1952a), "A Social Equilibrium Existence Theorem," *Proceedings of the National Academy of Sciences of the U.S.A.*, 38: 886–893.

Debreu, G. (1952b), "Definite and Semidefinite Quadratic Forms," *Econometrica*, 20: 295–300.

Debreu, G. (1954), "Valuation Equilibrium and Pareto-Optimum," *Proceedings of the National Academy of Sciences*, 40: 588–592.

Debreu, G. (1959), *Theory of Value*, New York: Wiley.

Debreu, G. (1964), "Continuity Properties of Paretian Utility," *International Economic Review*, 5: 285–293.

Dorfman, R. (1951), *Application of Linear Programming to the Theory of the Firm*, Berkeley and Los Angeles: University of California Press.

Dorfman, R., P. A. Samuelson, and R. M. Solow (1958), *Linear Programming and Economic Analysis*, New York: McGraw-Hill.

Dupuit, J. (1844), "On the Measurement of Utility of Public Works," *International Economic Papers*, 2(1952): 83–110.

Edgeworth, F. Y. (1881), *Mathematical Psychics*, London: Routledge Kegan Paul.

Ellis, H. S., and W. Fellner (1943), "External Economies and Diseconomies," *American Economic Review*, 38: 493–511.

Farrel, M. J. (1958), "In Defense of Public-Utility Price Theory," *Oxford Economic Papers*, **10**: 109–123.

Fellner, W. (1949), *Competition Among the Few*, New York: Knopf.

Fenchell, W. (1953), *Convex Cones, Sets and Functions* (mimeographed), Princeton, N.J.: Princeton University Press.

Fisher, I. (1930), *The Theory of Interest*, New York: Macmillan.

Friedman, M., and L. J. Savage (1954), "The Utility Analysis of Choices Involving Risk," *Journal of Political Economy*, **56**: 279–304.

Gale, D. (1955), "The Law of Supply and Demand," *Mathematica Scandinavia*, **3**: 155–169.

Gale, D. (1960), *The Theory of Linear Economic Models*, New York: McGraw-Hill.

Gorman, W. M. (1957a), "Convex Indifference Curves and Diminishing Marginal Utility," *Journal of Political Economy*, **65**: 40–50.

Gorman, W. M. (1957b), "Intertemporal Choice and the Shape of Indifference Maps," *Metroeconomica*, **9**: 1–22.

Gorman, W. M. (1959), "Are Social Indifference Curves Convex," *Quarterly Journal of Economics*, **73**: 485–496.

Graaff, J. de V. (1957), *Theoretical Welfare Economics*, Cambridge: Cambridge University Press.

Haavelmo, T. (1960), *A Study in the Theory of Investment*, Chicago: University of Chicago Press.

Hawkins, O, and H. Simon (1949), "Some Conditions of Macro-Economic Stability," *Econometrica*, **17**: 245–248.

Heady, E. O., and A. C. Egbert (1964), "Regional Programming of Efficient Agricultural Production Patterns," *Econometrica*, **32**: 374–386.

Henderson J. M., and R. E. Quandt (1958), *Microeconomic Theory*, New York: McGraw-Hill.

Hicks, J. R. (1932), *Theory of Wages*, New York: Macmillan.

Hicks, J. R. (1939, 1946), *Value and Capital*, Oxford: Oxford University Press.

Hicks, J. R. (1940), "The Valuation of Social Income," *Economica*, **7**: 105–124.

Hicks, J. R. (1943), "The Generalized Theory of Consumer's Surplus," *Review of Economic Studies*, **13**: 68–74.

Hicks, J. R. (1956), *A Revision of Demand Theory*, Oxford: Clarendon Press.

Hicks, J. R. (1958), "The Measurement of Real Income," *Oxford Economic Papers*, **10**: 125–162.

Hirschleifer, J. (1958), "On the Theory of Optimal Investment Decision," *Journal of Political Economy*, **66**: 205–228.

Hla Myint, U. (1948), *Theories of Welfare Economics*, London: Longmans.

Hotelling, H. (1932), "Edgeworth's Taxation Paradox and the Nature of Demand and Supply Functions," *Journal of Political Economy*, **40**: 577–616.

Hotelling, H. (1938), "The General Welfare in Relation to Problems of Taxation and of Railway and Utility Rates," *Econometrica*, **6**: 242–269.

Houtthakker, H. S. (1952), "Compensated Changes in Quantities and Qualities Consumed," *Review of Economic Studies*, **19**: 155–164.

Houtthakker, H. S. (1961), "The Present State of Consumption Theory," *Econometrica*, **29**: 704–740.

Hutchinson, T. H. (1953), *A Review of Economic Doctrines*, Oxford: Clarendon Press.

Johansen, L. (1965), *Public Economics*, Chicago: Rand McNally.

Kahn, R. F. (1935), "Some Notes on Ideal Output," *Economic Journal*, **65**: 1–35.

Kaldor, N. (1939), "Welfare Propositions in Economics," *Economic Journal*, **49**: 549–552.

Karlin, S. (1959), *Mathematical Methods and Theory in Games, Programming and Economics*, Vols. 1 and 2, Reading, Mass., Addison-Wesley.

Kemeny, J. G., O. Morgenstern, and G. Thompson (1956), "A Generalization of the von Neumann Model of an Expanding Economy," *Econometrica*, **24**: 115–135.

Kuenne, R. E. (1963), *The Theory of General Economic Equilibrium*, Princeton, N.J.: Princeton University Press.

Keynes, J. M. (1936), *The General Theory of Employment, Interest and Money*, New York: Harcourt Brace Jovanovich.

Klein, L. R. (1962), *An Introduction to Econometrics*, Englewood Cliffs, N.J.: Prentice-Hall.

Kogiku, K. C. (1967a), "A Model of the Raw Materials Market," *International Economic Review*, **8**: 116–120.

Kogiku, K. C. (1967b), "An Alternative Econometric Growth Model of Developing Countries," *Economic Studies Quarterly*, **18**: 17–24.

Koopmans, T. C., Ed. (1951), *Activity Analysis of Production and Allocation*, New York: Wiley.

Koopmans, T. C. (1957a), *Three Essays on the State of Economic Science*, New York: McGraw-Hill.

Koopmans, T. C. (1957b), "Allocation of Resources and the Price System," pp. 1–126 in T. C. Koopmans (1957a).

Koopmans, T. C., and A. F. Bausch (1959), "Selected Topics in Economics Involving Mathematical Reasoning," *SIAM Review*, **1**: 79–148.

Kuhn, H. W. (1946), "On a Theorem of Wald," chap. 16 in Kuhn and Tucker, Eds., *Linear Inequalities and Related Systems*, in *Annals of Mathematics Studies*, **38**: 265–273.

Lancaster, K. (1968), *Mathematical Economics*, New York: Macmillan.

Lange, O. (1936–1937), "On the Economic Theory of Socialism," *Review of Economic Studies*, **4**: 123–144.

Lange, O. (1942a), "Say's Law: A Restatement and Criticism," pp. 49–68 in Lange *et al.*, Eds., *Studies in Mathematical Economics and Econometrics*, Chicago: University of Chicago Press.

Lange, O. (1942b), "The Foundations of Welfare Economics," *Econometrica*, **10**: 215–228.

Lange, O. (1949), "The Practice of Economic Planning and the Optimal Allocation of Resources," *Supplement to Econometrica*, **17**: 166–171.

Lange, O., and F. M. Taylor (1938), *On the Economic Theory of Socialism*, Minneapolis: University of Minnesota Press

Leontief, W. W. (1936), "Composite Commodities and the Problem of Index Numbers," *Econometrica*, **4**: 39–59.

Leontief, W. W. (1941, 1951), *The Structure of American Economy*, New York: Oxford University Press.

Leontief, W. W. (1953), "The Input–Output Approach in Economic Analysis," in Netherlands Economic Institute, *Input–Output Relations*, Leiden: H. E. Stenfert Krosse.

Leontief, W. W., *et al.* (1965), "The Economic Impact—Industrial and Regional—of an Arms Cut," *Review of Economics and Statistics*," **47**: 217–241.

Lerner, A. P. (1934), "Economic Theory and Socialist Economy," *Review of Economic Studies*, **2**: 57–61.

Lerner, A. P. (1938–1939), "Theory and Practice in Socialist Economics," *Review of Economic Studies*, **6**: 71–75.

Lerner, A. P. (1946), *Economics of Control*, New York: Macmillan.

Lipsey, R. G., and R. K. Lancaster (1956), "The General Theory of Second Best," *Review of Economic Studies*, **24**: 11–32.

Little, I. M. D. (1951), "Direct versus Indirect Taxes," *Economic Journal*, **61**: 577–584.

Luce, R. D., and H. Raiffa (1957), *Games and Decisions*, New York: Wiley.

McFadden, M., J. W. Moore, and W. I. Smith (1963), *Sets, Functions, and Relations*, New York: McGraw-Hill.

McKenzie, L. W. (1954), "On Equilibrium in Graham's Model of World Trade and Other Competitive Systems," *Econometrica*, **22**: 147–161.

McKenzie, L. W. (1956–1957), "Demand Theory Without a Utility Index," *Review of Economic Studies*, **24**: 185–189.

McKenzie, L. W. (1960), "Stability of Equilibrium and the Value of Positive Excess Demand," *Econometrica*, **28**: 606–617.

Makower, H., and W. J. Baumol (1950), "The Analogy between Producer and Consumer Equilibrium Analysis," *Economica*, **17**: 63–80.

Malinvaud, E. (1953), "Capital Accumulation and Efficient Allocation of Resources," *Econometrica*, **21**: 233–268.

Markowitz, H. (1952), "Portfolio Selection," *Journal of Finance*, **7**: 77–91.

Marshall, A. (1920), *Principles of Economics*, 8th ed., London: Macmillan.

Meade, J. E. (1952), "External Economies and Diseconomies in Competitive Situations," *Economic Journal*, **62**: 54–67.

Metzler, L. (1945), "Stability of Multiple Markets: The Hicks Conditions," *Econometrica*, **13**: 277–292.

Mishan, E. J. (1960), "A Survey of Welfare Economics, 1939–1959," *Economic Journal*, **70**: 197–265.

Mishan, E. J. (1962), "Second Thoughts on the Second Best," *Oxford Economic Papers*, **14**: 205–217.

Mishan, E. J. (1965), "Reflections on Present Developments in the Concept of External Effects," *Canadian Journal of Economics and Political Science*, **31**: 3–34.

Morishima, M. (1961), "Proof of a Turnpike Theorem: the 'No Joint Production Case,'" *Review of Economic Studies*, **28**: 89–97.

Morishima, M. (1964), *Equilibrium, Stability, and Growth*, Oxford: Clarendon Press.

Morrison, C. C. (1968), "Generalizations on the Methodology of Second Best," *Western Economic Journal*, **6**: 112–120.

Negishi, T. (1958), "A Note on the Stability of an Economy Where All Goods Are Gross Substitutes," *Econometrica*, **26**: 445–447.

Negishi, T. (1962), "Stability of a Competitive Economy: A Survey Article," *Econometrica*, **30**: 653–659.

Nelson, J. R. (1964), *Marginal Cost Pricing in Practice*, Englewood Cliffs, N.J.: Prentice-Hall.

Nikaido, H. (1956), "On the Classical Multilateral Exchange Problem," *Metroeconomica*, **8**: 135–145.

Pigou, A. C. (1920), *The Economics of Welfare*, London: Macmillan.

Prest, A. R., and R. Turvey (1965), "Cost-Benefit Analysis: A Survey," *Economic Journal*, **75**: 683–735.

Quirk, J., and R. Saposnik (1967), *Introduction to General Equilibrium Theory and Welfare Economics*, New York: McGraw-Hill.

Reder, M. (1947), *Studies in the Theory of Welfare Economics*, New York: Columbia University Press.

Robbins, L. (1930), "On the Elasticity of Demand for Income in Terms of Effort," *Economica*, **9–10**: 123–136.

Robinson, J. (1933), *The Economics of Imperfect Competition*, London: Macmillan.

Rothenberg, J. (1961), *The Measurement of Social Welfare*, Englewood Cliffs, N.J.: Prentice-Hall.

Ruggles, N. (1949–1950), "Recent Developments in the Theory of Marginal Cost Pricing," *Review of Economic Studies*, **17**: 107–126.

Ruggles, N. (1949–1950), "The Welfare Basis of the Marginal Cost Pricing Principle," *Review of Economic Studies*, **17**: 29–46.

Samuelson, P. A. (1938), "A Note on the Pure Theory of Consumer's Behavior," *Economica*, **5**: 353–354.

Samuelson, P. A. (1947), *Foundations of Economic Analysis*, Cambridge, Mass.: Harvard University Press.

Samuelson, P. A. (1948), "Consumption Theory in Terms of Revealed Preference," *Economica*, **15**: 243–254.

Samuelson, P. A. (1953–1954), "Prices of Factors and Goods in General Equilibrium," *Review of Economic Studies*, **21**: 17–20.

Samuelson, P.A. (1954a), "The Pure Theory of Public Expenditures," *Review of Economics and Statistics*, **36**: 387–389.

Samuelson, P. A., Ed., (1954b), "Mathematics in Economics: Discussion of Mr. Novick's Article," *Review of Economics and Statistics*, **36**: 359–386.

Samuelson, P. A. (1955), "Diagrammatic Exposition of A Theory of Public Expenditure," *Review of Economics and Statistics*, **37**: 350–356.

Samuelson, P. A. (1956), "Social Indifference Curves," *Quarterly Journal of Economics*, **70**: 1–22.

Samuelson, P. A. (1958), "Aspects of Public Expenditure Theories," *Review of Economics and Statistics*, **40**: 332–338.

Samuelson, P. A. (1961), "A New Theorem on Nonsubstitution," in H. Hegeland, Ed. *Money, Growth and Methodology, and Other Essays in Honor of Johan Akerman*, Lund: C. W. K. Gleerup.

Scitovsky, T. (1951), *Welfare and Competition*, Homewood, Ill.: Irwin.

Scitovsky, T. (1954), "Two Concepts of External Economies," *Journal of Political Economy*, **62**: 143–151.

Shephard, R. (1953), *Cost and Production Functions*, Princeton, N.J.: Princeton University Press.

Slutsky, E. E. (1915), "On the Theory of the Budget of the Consumer," reprinted in the American Economic Association (1952).

Smith, V. (1961), *Investment and Production*, Cambridge, Mass.: Harvard University Press.

Stackelberg, H. von (1934), *Marketform und Gleichgewicht*, Vienna & Berlin: Julius Springer.

Steiner, P. O. (1959), "Choosing Among Alternative Public Investments in the Water Resource Field," *American Economic Review*, **49**: 893–916.

Stigler, G. (1941), *Production and Distribution Theories*, New York: Macmillan.

Turvey, R. (1963), "On Divergences Between Social Cost and Private Cost," *Economica*, **30**: 309–313.

Uzawa, H. (1958) "The Kuhn-Tucker Theorem in Concave Programming," in Arrow, Hurwicz, and Uzawa (1958).

Uzawa, H. (1960a), "Market Mechanisms and Mathematical Programming," *Econometrica*, **28**: 872–881.

Uzawa, H. (1960b), "Preference and Rational Choice in the Theory of Consumption," in Arrow, Karlin, and Suppes, Eds. (1960).

von Neumann, J. (1945), "A Model of General Equilibrium," *Review of Economic Studies*, **13**: 1–9.

von Neumann, J., and O. Morgenstern (1947), *Theory of Games and Economic Behavior*, Princeton, N.J.: Princeton University Press.

Viner, J. (1931), "Cost Curves and Supply Curves," *Zeitschrift für Nationalöconomie*, **3**: 23–46, reprinted in *American Economic Association* (1952).

Wald, A. (1951), "On Some Systems of Equations of Mathematical Economics," *Econometrica*, **19**: 368–403.

Walras, L. (1926), *Elements of Pure Economics*, translated by W. Jaffe (1954), Homewood, Ill.: Irwin.

Yamane, T. (1968), *Mathematical Analysis for Economists*, 2nd ed., Englewood Cliffs, N.J.: Prentice-Hall.

INDEXES

INDEX OF SYMBOLS

$\mathbf{a}, \mathbf{A}$	vector or matrix, 222
$\mathbf{A'}$	transpose of matrix $\mathbf{A}$, 222
$\mathbf{A}^{-1}$	inverse of matrix $\mathbf{A}$, 222
$\mathbf{I}$	identity matrix, 222
A	determinant of matrix $\mathbf{A}$, 222
$\mathbf{0}$	zero vector, origin, 222
$\mathbf{a} = \mathbf{0}$	$a_i = 0$ for all i, 225
$\mathbf{a} \geqq \mathbf{0}$	$a_i \geqq 0$ for all i, 225
$\mathbf{a} \geq \mathbf{0}$	$\mathbf{a} \geqq \mathbf{0}$ and $\mathbf{a} \neq \mathbf{0}$; that is, $a_i \geqq 0$ for all i, and $a_i > 0$ for at least one i, 225
$f'(x)$	derivative, 229
$f''(x)$	second derivative, 230
$f_i(\mathbf{x})$	partial derivative with respect to the ith argument, 231
$f_{ij}(\mathbf{x})$	second-order partial derivative, 232
dy	differential of y, 232
d^2y	second-order differential of y, 233
$a \in A$	a is an element of A, 282
$A \subset B$	A is a subset of B, 283
$\cup$	union, 283
$\cap$	intersection, 283

$X + Y$	sum of two sets X and Y, 285
$X \times Y$	cartesian product of two sets X and Y, 283
R^n	n-dimensional euclidean space, 284
R^n_+	nonnegative orthant of R^n, 195
R^n_-	nonpositive orthant of R^n, 197
$\mathbf{xy}, \mathbf{x} \cdot \mathbf{y}, \mathbf{x'y}$	inner product of two vectors $\mathbf{x}$ and $\mathbf{y}$, 284
R	binary relation, 284; weak preference relation, 9, 192
P	strong preference relation, 193
I	indifference relation, 11, 193
$\min(x, y)$	smaller of x and y, 152

SUBJECT INDEX

Allen, R. G. D., 51, 67, 225, 230, 238, 293
American Economic Association, 101, 293
Arrow, K. J., 67, 94, 208, 213, 293, 294
Average-cost pricing, 114

Bator, F., 101, 111, 293
Baumol, W. J., 294, 297
Bausch, A. F., 297
Bergson, A., 101, 103, 114, 294
Bilateral monopoly, 139–142
Binary relation, 283–284
Blau, J. H., 294
Block, H. D., 293
Boot, J. C. G., 294
Boundary optimum, 19, 57–58, 62, 243–244
Bounded set, 285

Bowen, H. R., 294
Bowles, S., 294
Brown, E. Phelps, 90, 294
Buchanan, J. M., 111, 294
Budget equation, 15

Capital, 147
Carlson, S., 294
Carr, C. R., 249, 295
Cartesian product, 283
Cassel, G., 151
Chamberlin, E. H., 135, 295
Charnes, A., 274, 295
Chenery, H. B., 294, 295
Chiang, A., 295
Clark, J. B., 295
Closed set, 285
Coase, R. H., 295
Cobweb theorem, 82–84
Cofactor, 223